D0970093

Untapped
Potential

Untapped Potential

Turning Ordinary People into Extraordinary Performers

Jack Lannom

THOMAS NELSON PUBLISHERS
Nashville

Copyright © 1998 by Jack Lannom

All rights reserved. Written permission must be secured from the publisher to use or reproduce any part of this book, except for brief quotations in critical reviews or articles.

Published in Nashville, Tennessee, by Thomas Nelson, Inc.

Unless otherwise noted the Bible version used in this publication is THE NEW KING JAMES VERSION of the Bible. Copyright © 1979, 1980, 1982, Thomas Nelson, Inc., Publishers.

Scripture quotations marked (NLT) are taken from the *Holy Bible*, New Living Translation, copyright © 1996. Used by permission of Tyndale House Publishers, Inc., Wheaton, Illinois 60189. All rights reserved.

Library of Congress Cataloging-in-Publication Data
Lannom, Jack.
     Untapped potential / Jack Lannom.
        p.   cm.
     ISBN 0-7852-7455-3 (pbk.)
     1. Success—Religious aspects—Christianity. I. Title.
   BV4598.3.L37   1998
   158—dc21

                                                                98-14654
                                                                CIP

Printed in the United States of America

1 2 3 4 5 6 7 DHC 04 03 02 01 00 99 98

Dedication

I dedicate this book to the most influential woman in my life. She is the reason I was able to write this book, because I learned these principles from her as a child. If you were to ask me what this book looks like in action, I would point you to my mother, Mrs. Joyce M. Lannom Reasons. My mother is a Proverbs 31 woman. She is a virtuous wife and a godly mother.

> She opens her mouth with wisdom, And on her tongue is the law of kindness. She watches over the ways of her household, And does not eat the bread of idleness. Her children rise up and call her blessed; Her husband also, and he praises her: "Many daughters have done well, But you excel them all." Charm is deceitful and beauty is passing, But a woman who fears the LORD, she shall be praised. Give her of the fruit of her hands, And let her own works praise her in the gates. (Prov. 31:26–31)

I love you, Mother, and I rise up and call you blessed. Thank you for leading me to the Lord and His matchless Word. I owe everything to you, my beloved mother.

Contents

Acknowledgments

I BELIEVE WE NEED LEADERS who see more than just the seed in the apple. They must see the apple in the seed. Ron Land is just that kind of leader. I am deeply indebted to Ron Land of Thomas Nelson Publishers for seeing the apple in the seed of *Untapped Potential*. Without Ron Land's belief in me this book would have never been a reality. Ron assembled an incredible team of believers that got behind this book to turn it into a first-class project. I want to thank Ted Squires, Gary McCauley, and Sharon Gilbert for being part of that professional team at Thomas Nelson that brought this book to life.

I must give thanks for another surprise blessing. One of the greatest assets to an author is to have an editor who is wise, patient, and flexible. I have been blessed with editors who have all these qualities and much more. I want to thank my editors, Curtis Lundgren and Cindy Blades, for all of their gracious help.

I especially want to thank Dan Philips for all his literary skills in taking my thoughts and making them come across so eloquently. Dan Philips has been helping me teach these principles to topflight companies in America for several years. When I send Dan into a company to teach for me, I know they will love Dan Philips, because Dan is a living model of the principles in this book. Without Dan's contribution I would not have been able to bring this book out of my mind and onto the printed page. Thank you, Dan, for the months and months of hard work you have put into this book.

I want to thank my best friend for thirty years, Bobby Cassell, for his self-sacrificial time in helping me flesh out and develop the chapters on values and choices. Bobby took time off from a very busy schedule and time away from his family to pour himself into making this book the most transformational book any person could ever own. Bobby is my spiritual mentor, and that is why I called upon his wisdom in helping me make the chapters on values and choices the best they could possibly be.

The next person I want to thank is Victor Dingus for his contribution on the vision chapter. Victor is one of the best transformational consultants in this world today. Victor knows all about transformation through the visioning process.

I also want to thank Rudy Trevino for his insights into the chapter on meaning. Rudy has been a wonderful friend and spiritual confidant for the past fifteen years.

I would also like to thank Dr. Mark Cosgrove for being my mentor in the essence of human nature.

My special thanks to Terry Lynn Betor for her excellent help on the physical chapter. I thank you, Terry, for your labor of love.

I am also deeply grateful to Denise M. Caligiuri for helping me meet two important deadlines. If she had not dropped everything she was doing to help me give the publishers the proposal for the book, I would have been waiting another year for the book to have been released.

Finally, I want to thank my wife, Debbie, for being patient during this very stressful time of being with me while I was at the computer for all those days and nights, giving birth to this manuscript. I thank you, Debbie, for being my editorial director and for your superlative literary nuggets that improved the book immensely.

I also must tell my children, Christy, Lori, and Joe, that I love you with all of my heart. I love you so deeply, I can't find the words that will properly express it. I thank you for giving your dad time away from you so I could finish this book. I have really missed you. I hope this book will break the chain in our family, and that we will, now and forever, turn our backs on building loot and passing on lunacy. Let us, together, build lives and pass on a legacy!

I am a wealthy man to have friends and family like you. God bless all of you in your labor of love in bringing this book to life for our wonderful Lord.

Introduction:
Searching for the Essence of Motivation

As a teacher, trainer, writer, and motivational speaker, I have dedicated the past twenty-five years of my life to extracting excellence from people at all levels—mental, physical, spiritual, social, financial, and emotional. And that is what I want to help you do—to tap your full potential. I have an acronym that fully expresses the intent of my life's passion and the goal of this book: T.H.A.T.—Totally Human and Alive Totally.

But what is the key that can unlock the potential in human beings so they can be Totally Human and Alive Totally? I have always believed that for people who feel a real sense of *significance,* who truly believe that they make a difference, the sky is the limit in terms of personal satisfaction and professional performance. The question for me was, How could I impart that sense of significance to the large groups of people I was working with? How could I truly empower people to rise to their highest and to be their best?

Never in my life have I aspired to be an entertainer. I have no desire to stand up on a stage or before a television camera and "give the people a good show." I want my audiences to leave my seminars with information and skills they can *use,* ideas that they can take home and share with their wives, their children, and their coworkers.

So I read, researched, and studied thousands of volumes about learning, behavior, and leadership, determined to find the one concept that would bring the message home to people. I carefully pored over the works of the men and women who are widely acknowledged to be the best in the field of human performance.

The "Experts" Weren't So Expert!

Would you believe that I spent thousands of hours in relentless study and years of practical, professional experience applying the teachings of these individuals, and all I knew at the end of that time was that I *still* didn't have the answer? Something was missing. Even the best advice that the "experts" had to offer produced only temporary results, at best. The true potential for greatness, which I am convinced lies within the reach of every one of us, remained untapped and undefined. *What is missing?* I asked myself. *What have all these teachers failed to learn?* Yes, these men and women have a great many *good* ideas, but the *good* is the enemy of the *best!* I didn't want to labor with all my energy merely to produce *good* results.

Then in 1977 I met a professor who would dramatically change my life, my very concept of mankind. His name is Dr. Mark Cosgrove. Dr. Cosgrove is a scientist, psychologist, and the author of *The Amazing Body Human* and *The Essence of Human Nature*. It was through this second book, along with his personal friendship and guidance, that Mark Cosgrove taught me the absolute essence of human motivation, an essence so basic and fundamental that all the acknowledged experts in the field of human performance had missed it! Now I am going to share that information with you.

When I digested what I had learned, and took *Untapped Potential* into the companies I was working with, the results were dramatic. Today I consult with Fortune 500 companies, I am invited regularly to appear on television and radio, and I conduct seminars all around the United States. These truths about the foundation of motivation are what has made my company so successful, and they will make *you* massively successful, in both your personal *and* professional life!

Personhood: The Foundation of Motivation

Before you go up you must go down. In other words, before you build a great superstructure you must first build a great substructure. The great substructure of this book is built on the meaning of the word *personhood.* If you are going to develop a program for human transformation it must begin with a definition of what it means to be a *person.* This book will be an unpackaging of what it means to be a person. How can I motivate you if I can't define who you are?

It may seem strange that I would base an entire book on the definition of personhood; however, in all my studies of the secular mainstream books on human betterment, I never found one that began with a definition of who human beings really are. And a diminished view of personhood equals a diminished view of potential. My threefold purpose in writing this book is to redefine *personhood,* revisit *potential,* and rekindle *passion.*

Looking Under the Hood of Personhood

The book is titled *Untapped Potential: Turning Ordinary People into Extraordinary Performers.* This book contains truths about the personhood of human beings. When you behold these twelve truths and examine the marvel within your own personhood, you will know you were designed for greatness. These twelve attributes represent the truth about who you *really* are and form the foundation of human excellence, from which we learn to value, honor, esteem, and respect human worth and dignity. These truths give us our unity as human beings, as well as our diversity as individuals. They represent the tremendous potential that lies within each of us and are designed to move us toward fulfillment and completeness.

A Bold, New Vision

The information I am about to share with you in this book will dramatically alter your vision of yourself. It will give you a new identity and a newfound sense of freedom. No longer will you or your family need to compare, compete, impress, or prove yourselves to anyone! You'll no longer be working *for* self-worth. You'll be working *from* a secure platform of self-worth.

Each chapter will showcase a single truth of your personhood, and from that grand showcasing you will be encouraged to now live in harmony with who you were intended and designed to be. I will give you specific how-to techniques for the outliving of your inliving potential. You will never see yourself or anyone else the same way again. You will regain your "wowness" for every human being and bring out the best in yourself and everyone around you. You will be a more effective worker, a better parent, a truer friend, a more devoted and faithful spouse than you had ever thought possible! The twelve truths wield equal power in the boardroom or the living room.

Please don't think that what you'll discover in these pages is merely an attitude. This is an *action*-oriented book. I am going to provide you with specific, practical applications for the recognition and the celebration of the human spirit that will extricate us from being mere "performance puppets" and elicit discretionary effort. It's simply a matter of recognizing and accessing our natural, God-given assets.

I hope you'll sit down and share this book with *all* of your family, your spouse and your children. This will be a tremendous resource for knitting your family unit closer together and for helping your children grow straight, strong, and true. Take *Untapped*

Potential to work and utilize these tools with your staff and peers. The results will be nothing short of sensational!

This book was written and designed to stretch your mind, broaden your belief, increase your effectiveness, and enrich your spirit. This information will sharpen your will to win and allow you to bring out the best in the people around you, as well. You will notice an immediate and profound impact on the quality of your interpersonal relationships. I intend to reawaken and reinvigorate a whole new passion in you to connect with other human beings and to bring out your personal best. You can take *Untapped Potential* and sit down with anybody—your spouse, your children, a coworker— and say to them, "Here is a model, a blueprint, that will help you become a more *productive, responsible,* and *caring* human being."

I want to state a disclaimer at the outset of this book. I have not arrived, and I don't expect to arrive in this life. However, I have learned and I am still learning many valuable truths about human transformation. My intent is not to come across as the guru of human motivation. My heart's desire is to share with you timeless, transcendent truths that have changed me, and millions like me, forever. If you believe these same truths, they will also change your life forever.

A Walk Through the Vault

Long ago, I remember reading a story that related the tale of an old Navajo Indian who had spent his entire life eking out a meager existence raising sheep on a ramshackle farm outside of a small town in New Mexico. One day, in the process of trying to dig a new well to water the sheep, the old Navajo discovered the Black Gold—oil! Overnight, he went from being dirt poor to being filthy rich. He could have lived anywhere in the world, but old habits die hard, and the old man chose to continue working his farm as he always had. It was the only life he had ever known.

The old Navajo could now make regular visits to town to buy supplies and draw money from his new savings account. The banker in town was often struck by the old man's face. In spite of his newfound wealth, the Navajo's eyes were usually downcast, and his countenance was dour. Finally, curiosity got the best of the banker.

"Sir," he asked the Navajo, "what's the matter? You look so unhappy."

"The well has gone dry," the old man responded morosely. "The grass is brown. The sheep are all sick."

"I see," the banker replied. "Would you please come with me for a moment?" The banker took the old man by the arm and led him back into the bank's vault. Once inside, the banker sat the old man down on a folding chair and started to lug several large sacks of money over to the Navajo and laid them by his feet. "All this is yours," the banker informed him. "This is what you possess. You own it all. Sit here for a while. Take your time. Count it all up."

The old man sat for hours, counting the greenbacks and certificates of deposit, letting the gold coins sift through his fingers. When he emerged from the vault, he was a changed man. His bearing was confident, his eyes bright. Striding toward the door, he beamed at the banker. "The well is all full! The grass is all green! The sheep are all well!" The old Navajo had started to *reflect* his assets.

It is my desire that this book will allow *you* to count your assets and to help you to allow others to do the same. I want to make you a leader in your home and workplace, reflecting your titanic worth and divine value. So, let's swing back the door to the vault and begin to count the incredible wealth that lies within!

I T WAS TEN YEARS AGO, but I remember it as if it were yester-day. My family and I, along with millions of other Americans, sat tensely in front of the television, watching the dramatic live broadcasts of the attempts to rescue little Jessica McClure, who had fallen down an abandoned well in Midland, Texas. I remember watching with fascination and mounting anxiety as the hours slipped away, the little toddler still trapped alone in the darkness, wedged into a narrow, suffocating tunnel, with no food or water. I marveled at all the action and equipment and energy that went into the rescue attempts: men and women worked around the clock; trucks and tractors and all kinds of heavy equipment were utilized; specialists drove for hours to lend their assistance. A huge crowd of onlookers gathered at the site, along with a national TV audience, waiting, hoping, watching, and praying. Finally, the crowd erupted in cheers as one of the rescuers emerged with the toddler—alive! I wept without shame, and my family, grouped around the television set, was crying also.

I like to reflect on all the incredibly brave and sacrificial efforts and expense that went into that wonderful rescue. Thousands of dollars and hours were expended, all for a tiny child, not yet two years old.

This was not the president of the United States who was in danger, or some superstar of the athletic world, or the CEO of a major corporation, but a little girl—and the value and worth that was placed on her by her rescuers and a watching nation was monumental!

Divine Viewpoint:
Humans Possess Dignity and Worth

Jessica McClure is just an example of the value we should place on every human being. Think about this: every person possesses exalted worth and exalted dignity. Look at the words *exalted worth* and *exalted dignity.* The word *exalted* is used to express the truth that humans are the apex, the zenith, of God's creation. To be a person means you are God's image. God created every human being in His image after His likeness. We are the only creatures that bear the likeness of the living God. Consequently, this is the only foundation for human worth, human dignity, and human rights. The effectiveness of every interpersonal encounter is ultimately predicated by an accurate view of the dignity and incalculable worth of man's personhood.

Human Life Is Spiritual and Sacred

You may say at this time that this book sounds like a spiritual book, and you are correct—it is spiritual. Anytime you discuss human nature you must recognize that it is spiritual and sacred, from conception to the grave. The essence of who we are as persons is preeminently and profoundly spiritual and sacred. It is that we come from the Father and Creator of the universe, and not from Mother Earth, that gives us sacred and eternal worth. The value of human worth is not found in the condition of human life but in the sanctity of human life. That is why we are to look upon the person who is born without any arms or legs, or is considered by society to be a vegetable, to have the same exalted worth and exalted dignity as any other human being.

In the Netherlands, people are being involuntarily euthanized. The elderly are afraid to go to the hospitals in that country, because they know the doctors can kill them without their consent.[1] It is no different from a dog going to the pound to be put to sleep. The doctors in the Netherlands have adopted a man-centered economic formula to determine if a person has enough worth to be allowed to live. They are playing God with immortal souls.

God's economic formula is different from man's economic formula: God values human life in all of its forms; the spiritually fallen man does not. In America we are moving in the same direction as the Netherlands because we have moved away from a God-centered position on human worth and embraced a man-centered view of human worth.

Success:
A Faithful Response to God's Truth

This book is God-centered and not man-centered. The goal of this book is for God's glory and our good. This chapter is seeking God's truth about who we are and God's truth about human performance. Consequently, I am contending for the highest possible view of man in order to appeal to every person on the noblest foundation to be what God designed, equipped, and intended for us to be.

The only way that this can happen is to learn the definition of success early in your life's journey. True long-term, sustainable success is simply a faithful response to God's truth. This response to God's truth is summed up in two twin concepts. We must be dependent on God and responsible to God.

The root cause of all evil in this world comes from rebelling against these two divine absolutes. This definition of success is the foundation that makes it possible for people to be their best and do their best. These outcomes of human excellence are called BEST EVERS. With the help of these truths you can learn to create a transformational environment that constantly empowers every person to produce "best evers."

The Four Kingdoms

A man-centered view of human worth is not new. Ever since we were children, we have been taught that there are three kingdoms: animal, vegetable, and mineral. Ptolemy dominated the intellectual world for more than a thousand years until Copernicus came along and refuted the notion that the earth was the center of the universe.[2] Likewise, this teaching of the three kingdoms had dominated intellectual thought for hundreds of years, and it is time for that teaching to rest on the ash heap of history, as well! This limited view of life is a *defining down* of life. It suffers from the *error of reductionism.*

There is a fourth kingdom, which is the kingdom of *humankind.* We in the United States and throughout much of the industrialized West have forgotten what it means to be human! *This* is the reason why families are splitting apart at such an alarming rate and why so many of our children seem apathetic, at best, and become violent killers, at worst. *This* is why a young girl can go to her prom, slip into the bathroom and deliver a baby, stuff the child in a trash can, and then coolly go back to the dance and request another song. *This* is the reason why companies don't do as well as they should, why so many of our corporations are struggling in the arena of global competition. All of the education and all of the quality management programs in the world will never work if we treat people as if they were members of the animal kingdom! If we tell children and adults that they are part of the animal kingdom, guess what: they are going to begin to *act* as if they were animals! We are told that our sexual desires are no different from those of animals in heat, and so every kind of sexual perversion and immorality takes hold of our land today, and, in many cases, is even glorified in our popular culture.

I work with multibillion-dollar companies every year. They have various quality management programs in place and expensive business systems up and running. Their leadership assures me, "It'll take us about five to seven years to get where we want to be on our quality program." Time after time, I've watched companies embark on these projects, but they rarely seem to work because the *people* who are the vitally important cogs in the machinery are *dehumanized*. All too often I meet CEOs and CFOs who are far more impressed with themselves than they are with the human beings who are responsible for making their programs work! They'll take me on a tour of the facility, pointing out all kinds of expensive equipment, and never once introduce me to the human beings who keep the equipment running! Then when I visit the production areas alone and talk to the folks who have to work under this kind of "leadership," the workers tell me, point-blank: "No one treats me like a *person* here. I'm devalued."

If people are treated as human *doings* instead of human *beings*, they will never perform to their highest and their best. Within these huge companies, workers are doing little more than what it takes to get by, relationships are strained and splintered, and production moves ahead in fits and starts. This is because *the incorporation of sound furnishings does not make up for an unsound foundation!*

The vitally important foundation that is missing in all these programs is the definition of *personhood*. I challenge you to remember the last time you walked into a classroom or seminar and were asked: "Tell me, what is a person?" When was the last time you were given a working definition of what it means to be *human?* The best questions determine the best approach, and the best approach will yield the best results. What I am proposing is that most of us have never been taught what the right *questions* are! Think about it for a minute. How can you or I motivate others to their highest and their best, how can we work in harmony with other human beings, if we don't really know who they are? How can the renowned teachers of human performance write books about how to motivate me if they are unable to explain *who I am?* I promise you this: if they have defined me as a member of the animal kingdom, they have *not* defined me—or you.

The Error of Reductionism

For centuries, it was generally recognized that we human beings have a *soul,* a spiritual aspect of our nature, that separates us from the beasts of the field. Then empiricism, which claimed that we can know only what we have experienced, that we can only examine and understand what the physical world has revealed to us, came creeping up on us in the early 1800s. Empiricism reduced humankind to the observable and the physical. In 1859 Darwin's *Origin of Species* reduced us to the animal. The disastrous effects of these twin hammer blows to humanity are still reverberating throughout our society and our world today.[3]

The denial of the spiritual self strips us of our dignity and worth as human beings. This fundamental denial of who we *really* are robs us of the grandest pursuits for which we were designed by our Creator to achieve! We are intended, equipped, and designed to live a life that models excellence in all six dimensions of human development: mental, physical, spiritual, social, emotional, and financial. However, when one is defined down to membership in the *third* kingdom—the animal kingdom—there is absolutely no incentive to aspire to excellence other than the naked acquisition of power! If you define away the spiritual aspect of our lives, you define away *self-sacrifice,* the noblest and grandest pursuit of all.

As a result, we live lives that are substandard. "For what profit is it to a man," God asks us, "if he gains the whole world, and loses his own soul?" (Matt. 16:26). We are reduced to spiritual beggars, sifting through the dumpster of New Age religion, hoping to find some scraps that will sustain us. We have been prohibited from aspiring to the highest pinnacle of life, which is the spiritual! We don't honor human beings, we dishonor their dignity and worth. We strip away *personhood*. We strip man of a regal human garment, one that is rightfully his to wear with thanksgiving and pride and passion. Instead, we clothe man in animal skins. We treat human beings as if they were animals or machines. This is an animalistic, mechanistic approach to human nature. We deny the very essence of humanity by disowning, discrediting, disallowing, and devaluing *who we are!*

Darwinism, behaviorism, and empiricism all throw the kill switch on the human spirit! So many of us are walking around with clipped wings, our spirit locked in a cage of unbelief. We're supposed to fly, but we're crawling on all fours. Ours is a *learned helplessness*. God never intended for us to live by the law of the jungle—killing, clawing, and stealing for survival. Think of the tragedy that crushes the lives of the many men and women whose society taught them to climb the ladder of success. They pushed and shoved and climbed the ladder to the very top, only to discover that it was leaning against the *wrong wall*. The bottom line for success should be, "Am I all that I was designed and intended to be, both internally and externally?" Let us determine up front who we were designed and intended to be, and then develop life skills to live in harmony with that knowledge!

The Queen Who Lived Like a Dog

I once heard a story told about a powerful queen who used to go out on campaigns of conquest with her ships. One day, while her ship was in port for supplies, the queen was separated from her entourage and became lost. The captain of her ship scoured the port looking for her and finally found the great queen dressed in rags, living in a filthy hovel, and working as a prostitute. She had become ill and was suffering from amnesia. She no longer had any idea who she was!

The captain saw her and stammered, "Your Majesty!" The queen looked back at the captain blankly, disinterestedly. The captain spoke to her clearly and firmly: *"You* are the Queen!" Hearing those words, the true definition of who she was, the queen's eyes cleared, and she stood up. With great dignity, despite her foul surroundings, she stretched out her arm for him to take, and said, "Let us go, Captain."

The captain had appealed to her *according to who she really was.* That brought her back to her true identity. She regained her regal posture and walked away from the degradation she had been subjected to.

Clarity, meaning, insight, and understanding begin with one word: *definition.* Definition demands distinction; if a word means everything, it means *nothing.* So to properly define something, we must not only understand what it is, but also what it isn't: i.e., a human being is not an animal. When you know what something isn't you can draw a line of demarcation. In this way, we create *clarity.*

When I describe man as an animal, I have *blurred* the distinction between man and animal. If man is defined as an animal, I have *robbed* man of the dignity of his personhood! If I don't know who I am, there's a great possibility that I may incorporate what I'm *not* into who I *am.* What do I have then? I have become a *distortion* of a human being.

If you take totally pure water, with no mineral content at all, and then you add a drop of mud—or poison—you have then *adulterated* the purity of that water. You've tampered with the purity of the water by adding another substance to it. The *distinction* of water has been blurred. Throughout this book, I want to stress and contend for the precious uniqueness of humanity. I want to celebrate the apex of God's creation.

The noted physicist Dr. Bohm said, "Only *meaning* arouses energy." The more meaning we can drive into the word *person,* the more the value of personhood appreciates. This is the only thing that will extricate human beings from mediocrity and propel them into magnificence! But we have been taught just the opposite: evolution, empiricism, and behaviorism have reduced personhood to a formula—a stimulus-response mechanism. We've poisoned the water!

A Society Reflects Its Citizens' Worldview

The societal implications of reductionist thinking are staggering. Every nation is the outworking of the definition of what it means to be human. In 1981, Francis Schaeffer estimated that only about 25 of the 150 nations then in existence enjoyed any real freedom.[4] These twenty-five free nations held their citizens in the highest regard; they valued the personhood of their citizens. After all, a culture is nothing more than a group of people outliving their inliving beliefs about God and man. Every government document ever written is a presuppositional model of that society's view of mankind. How we *live* comes from a presupposition of *who* we are. The reason that many countries suffer under Marxist or totalitarian regimes is because these governments have stripped man of his dignity, potential, and worth. The citizens groan under this kind of repression; they have suppressed the human spirit. Every fiber of their being strains against the stifling effects of the tyranny that inevitably springs from this behavioristic, evolutionary mind-set. *The depersonalization of people extracts mediocrity!* A perfect recent example is the contrast between East and West Germany during the Cold War. West Germany valued its citizens, and the nation boomed. East Germany denied the humanity of its citizens, fenced them in with guns and barbed wire, crushed their spirits with repression and terror, and the prosperity and quality of living there languished.

This is the inexorable, inevitable outcome of a society that views its citizens as merely the product of random, impersonal chance. If we are, as the theory of evolution proclaims, merely a cosmic accident, how can you possibly ascribe any value or worth to anyone we meet or anything we do? We have no *identity*. We have no foundation to build upon. We are working *for* an identity, rather *than from* one.

Values come from one of three sources: self, society, or a sovereign God. If our values are created by self or society, then the rules for living are made simply by the person or group who wields the most power. Once you have defined humanity down to the level of animals, you have created the perfect environment for an Adolf Hitler or a Joseph Stalin. Suddenly blacks, Jews, Christians, or unborn children become subhuman and are worthy of only slavery or death. One nineteenth-century evolutionist, John Fiske, believed that man in his physiological form was barely distinguishable from primates. And once you see no difference between man and animal, you must inevitably arrive at the same conclusion as humanist Kurt Baier:

> Evolution . . . is a ceaseless battle among members of different species, one species being gobbled up by another, only the fittest surviving. Far from being the gentlest and most highly moral, man is simply the creature best fitted to survive, the most efficient if not the most rapacious and insatiable killer.[5]

What a horrifying view of life! If Mr. Baier is correct, then the atrocities of barbarians like Hitler or Idi Amin are normal, natural, and logical! These monsters are merely fulfilling their evolutionary destiny! Those who share the unfortunate worldview of Mr. Baier must accept with equanimity the deaths of the tens of millions of victims of communism during the twentieth century as the natural order of things. As I said earlier, if you keep telling a society that they are no better than animals, they will begin to act like animals!

The American Experiment

What makes the United States so unique? How is it that America has enjoyed such tremendous prosperity over the last two hundred years? Why has a country like France gone through several series of governments, while our republican model of government is still intact? It is because of the Founders' view of God, the world, and man. Our Declaration of Independence explains, "We hold these truths to be self-evident, that all men are created equal. That they are endowed by their Creator with certain inalienable Rights, that among these are Life, Liberty, and the pursuit of Happiness. That to secure these rights, Governments are instituted among Men, deriving their just powers from the consent of the governed."

Daniel Webster warned, "If God and His Word are not known and received, the devil and his works will gain the ascendancy; if the evangelical volume does not reach every hamlet, the pages of a corrupt and licentious literature will; if the power of the Gospel is not felt throughout the length and breadth of the land, anarchy and misrule, degradation and misery, corruption and darkness will reign without mitigation or end."[6]

George Washington, the father of our country, said in his Farewell Address on September 19, 1796, "Of all the dispositions and habits which lead to political prosperity, Religion and morality are indispensable supports. In vain would that man claim the tribute of Patriotism who should labor to subvert these great Pillars of human happiness—these firmest props of the duties of Man and Citizens. . . . Let us with caution indulge the supposition that morality can be maintained without religion . . . reason and experience both forbid us to expect that national morality can prevail in exclusion of religious principle."[7] In other words, the "great pillars of human happiness" were a God-centered worldview. Those who worked to knock down these pillars were no friends of the United States. For without the idea that God has endowed man with dignity and worth, national prosperity and morality would not prevail, just as they did not in countries like Russia and East Germany.

Our Founders had a *theistic* orientation—they believed that God exists and created man with "inalienable" dignity and worth. Which commandments did Jesus say were most important? Essentially, love God and love people (Mark 12:28–30). This was the basis on which our laws were written. The United States is slipping away from that orientation, and even a cursory glance at today's newspaper will reveal the national calamities that have befallen us as a result. Robert Winthrop, a descendant of the first governor of the Massachusetts Bay Colony, declared: "Men, in a word, must necessarily be controlled either by a power within them, or a power without them; either by the word of God, or by the strong arm of man; either by the Bible or by the bayonet."[8] When we take our focus off God, we inevitably place our trust in "the strong arm of man," and the resulting oppression is *always* destructive of the health and productivity of nations, businesses, and homes.

If people are not viewed and treated as *people,* they will never perform at their highest and their best, but inevitably at their lowest and their least. When a society defines away personhood for a certain class of individuals, there are these inexorable, tragic consequences: oppression, violence, death. Once the dignity and worth of mankind have been removed, life becomes cheap, just as it did in Cambodia following the takeover of the Khmer Rouge, when well over a million people were slaughtered.[9] B. F. Skinner, one of the most influential of the behaviorists, was quite forthright about the outliving of his worldview. He titled one of his books *Beyond Freedom and Dignity*! There is no freedom, no dignity, and no value in human life that is relegated to the status of the animal world.

Man Is the Image of God

Sink this truth deep within your soul: you possess exalted worth and exalted dignity because you are made in God's image. Your sense of identity, significance, and meaning as a person is unalterably linked to this truth. Self-esteem is really God-esteem. In order to have theistic self-esteem we must esteem what God has made. In other words, we esteem God's image in us and thank Him for that image. Our goal in life is to reflect His image to the world, as the purpose of a mirror is to reflect a reality other than itself. Humanism tells us that we must *work for* self-worth in order to become somebody. God-centered theism tells us that we *work from* self-worth because we are somebody. This is the key to personal and professional transformation and the only basis for profound change. When you grasp this truth you are free from the need to compare, compete, or prove to anyone that you are somebody. It sets you free to love others because you no longer need them for self-validation.

The Human Race Is the Superior Race

We are living in an age that exalts diversity at the expense of unity. We must put the *unity* back in *community*. There are only two ways in which human beings can relate to one another: either we can focus on what makes us different (e.g., race, religion, sex, culture) or we can focus on what we have in common. And what we have in common is that we are all human, made in God's image, possessing exalted worth and exalted dignity. We all belong to a superior race, the *human race.*

The notion that one race is more important than any other race is a foreign concept to God. In the Bible God says, "And He has made from one blood every nation of men to dwell on all the face of the earth" (Acts 17:26). In this one verse God is striking a death-blow to all racial prejudice by saying that we are all one blood, one race: the human race. We must become color-blind and "person-sighted." Right this minute God has five billion images of Himself on this planet, and He doesn't have a black image, a white image, a red image, or a yellow image. God has a human image. Red, yellow, black and white—they are all precious in His sight.

Seeing God in the Face of Humanity

Mother Teresa, when asked what the secret was to the success of her ministry, said, "I simply see the face of God in every person"[10] When she looked into the eyes of every person, she didn't see a particular race; she saw the image of God. If we can consider an encounter with someone as an encounter with God's image, then we can know the truth that we both have the same exalted worth and exalted dignity.

The Holy Bible tells us in the book of Genesis that "God created man in His own image; in the image of God He created him; male and female He created them" (Gen. 1:27). God "breathed into [the man's] nostrils the breath of life; and man became a living being" (Gen. 2:7). When you or I encounter another human being, we are *not* bumping into an animal that is more highly evolved than a dog or a cow or a monkey. We are meeting a walking marvel, a miracle, and a mystery that has been created in the very image of the Creator of the universe!

Think of your spouse, who wakes up in the morning a little quiet and surly until he or she has had a dose of morning coffee—that human being is made in the image of God! Your child, whom you just shouted at for careening noisily through the living room—that child is made in the very image of God! Your boss, who gave you a chewing out, and whom you called a "jerk" under your breath as he walked away—that man is created in the image of the Maker of the universe! The homeless man you saw digging through the dumpster downtown—that man, too, was created in the image of almighty God!

Take a moment to give this idea your full consideration. Once you have understood that a man or a woman is a unique and special creature, made in the likeness of God, you will never again look at people as you have in the past. Would you say to God, "Man, your face is a *wreck* this morning"? If God wanted to play in your living room for a little while, would you suddenly turn in your chair and scream at Him to "Shut up!"? If God told you, "I'm unhappy with the way you're performing at work," would you call God a "jerk" when His back was turned? If God had no place to live (Jesus once told a religious leader, "Foxes have holes and birds of the air have nests, but the Son of Man has nowhere to lay His head" [Matt. 8:20]), would you mutter to yourself "Why doesn't God just go get a job," or would you stop and help Him? James, the brother of Jesus Christ, admonished Christians who "curse men, who have been made in the similitude of God" (James 3:9).

Once we truly strive to see the face of God Himself in the face of everyone we meet, can we thoughtlessly demean those individuals? Truly, our whole disposition changes when we see each other in this new and divine light! When we view a human being as made in the *image of God,* we instantly realize that each and every human being has *exalted* dignity and *exalted* worth. How, then, can I do anything else but to *honor, esteem, respect,* and *value* every individual with whom I come into contact? I can't help but see relationships in an entirely different way. I understand that the quality of relationships means everything—whether I am operating in the personal or professional arena.

I want to emphasize that this is not a consulting *technique* that I am describing to you here. This is *truth*. This is not the *right* way to interact with others. It is *the* way, the only way to treat another human being.

This truth has transformed my whole life. The way I interact with others is on an exalted level. I have learned how to honor, esteem, value, and respect all human beings regardless of the color of their skin or the mental and physical condition of their person. No longer are my interactions with others close encounters of the impersonal kind. Now I can't wait to open doors for people, serve others, love others, find out who they are, and encourage them on their life's journey. I have watched people transform before my very eyes when I treat them like royalty.

People Respond to Truth!

When I walk into a room and start telling people that, yes, they *do* make a difference, I can see and sense the response immediately! I see their eyes light up, and I feel their human spirit resonate to the truth they are hearing! All the discoveries that have been made by scientists and behaviorists in the field of human performance technology have been infinitely eclipsed by this! Quite simply, this is because people *react* to a theory, but they *respond* to the Truth! They will reorder their lives around Truth. When their lives are given the energy that Dr. Baum said *only* comes with meaning, they can live and work with passion and with excellence. They regain their sense of awe and wonder for others, they see other human beings as a precious resource, a treasure, and then they set out to polish those gems and make them shine!

We can't *wait* to meet other people! We can't *wait* to be engaging. Mind-set always precedes skill-set, belief precedes behavior, theory precedes practice, knowledge precedes application, and philosophy precedes performance. I cannot have the proper action, the proper energy, without belief. This knowledge that must precede my behavior is that you are the apex, the zenith of creation! God made men and women "just a little lower than the angels, and . . . crowned [them] with glory and honor" (Ps. 8:4). Then, from this philosophy, comes my performance, my action: I honor, respect, esteem, and *value* you.

The transformation that will take place in your home and your company when you begin to apply this knowledge is electric. Imagine a society in which every individual is taught that we are God's image-bearers and representatives. Parents would sit at the dinner table and tell their children, "Honey, you are somebody *very* important, not because of your beauty, your brains, your brawn, or your bucks, but because God loved you enough to make you in His image!"

I have been writing and speaking on this theme for the last twenty years, and every single time I do, people come back and tell me that adopting this philosophy has dramatically altered the quality of every relationship, whether they are interacting with their loved ones at home, operating in a professional environment, or even experiencing those encounters with strangers on the street or in a store. These men and women have responded to the truth, and the truth has, indeed, set them free!

The Seven Powers of Personhood

Now for some very practical techniques to put this first truth to work. I want to introduce you to "The Seven Powers of Personhood." These Seven Powers of Personhood are seven conditions that you can create with God's strength to help other people to believe they possess exalted worth and exalted dignity. They're called "powers" because they are abilities all human beings have, although few of us ever exercise them. My right-hand man, Dan Philips, came up with a brilliant acronym for the Seven Powers of Personhood: S.T.A.B.L.E.R. STABLER makes up the first seven letters of the Seven Powers of Personhood: Servanthood, Trust, Authenticity, Belief, Love, Encouragement, and Respect.

The word *stabler* means "firm, steadfast," and "not easily moved." It also carries with it the idea of being stable in character and purpose. STABLER perfectly communicates the outcome of your life once you put these Seven Powers of Personhood to work. You will become STABLER in character, purpose, and resolution. Please join me at the front line of upholding human worth and human dignity.

1. The Power of Servanthood

This is the first power of personhood, because it is the logical outliving of the belief that every person possesses exalted worth and exalted dignity. The logical question should be, Since every person possesses exalted worth and exalted dignity, how then should I live? The answer is that royalty should serve royalty. Because we are all royal members of the human race, made in God's royal image, we should honor each other by serving one another. We should all think when we meet each other, because we are in the presence of royalty, *How may I serve you?* You may think for a moment that this makes you appear to be inferior. When we think of servants waiting on us, we think of them as being people who have a lower status in life. However, that isn't the proper context for this word. Let me give you a different context, and it will completely change the meaning of the word. Think of the president of the United States of America, whose office is looked upon as one of the most esteemed elected positions in our country. However, the preeminent purpose behind this lofty position is to be the greatest servant of the people of the United States of America. That is why the president is called a public servant.

We should look upon the position of servanthood as the highest calling in life. The servant is a giver and not a taker. He sows the seeds of self-sacrifice in order to reap a great harvest of good for others. The attitude of the servant isn't one of self-interest, self-centeredness, self-serving, self-seeking, or self-occupation. Servanthood is the exemplary model of personhood.

Only in being occupied with other people's interests do we find true freedom from the slavery of selfism. God hasn't designed us so that the grand pursuit of our lives is self-interest. He designed us to be servants, to serve Him. And we are serving Him when we serve the needs of others.

I encourage you to use this first power of personhood to serve others for the glory of God. We ascend to greatness by descending into servanthood.

2. The Power of Trust

The second power of personhood flows naturally from the first power of servanthood. When a person sees in you a desire to serve them they will begin to trust you. Through servanthood you are telling them, "I mean you no harm; I care about you and desire to serve you." Trust is the foundation for all relationships.

In my consulting business, this phrase is repeated over and over again: "I don't trust my boss." If you are a business owner, ask your associates if they trust you. If they don't trust you, you should ask them how their trust in you has been broken. Trust is a faithful response to truth. If there is any duplicity in our behavior, then we can't be trusted because we aren't truthful. If trust has been lost with your associates, you need to seek their help in restoring their trust in you.

When people trust each other there is nothing they can't accomplish. However, when people don't trust one another there isn't any discretionary effort put forth and the simplest tasks take forever to accomplish. In contrast to this, mutual trust is the essence of true synergy, and *synergy* is the maximization of collective potential.

God tells us to trust in Him because He is trustworthy. In Proverbs 3:5–6 God says, "Trust in the LORD with all your heart, / And lean not on your own understanding; / In all your ways acknowledge Him, / And He shall direct your paths." Only by your trusting in God can you become trustworthy, because by trusting in God you will grow in His truth.

Grow in this power of trust by asking yourself, "How can I become more trustworthy in all my relationships, personal and professional?"

3. The Power of Authenticity

The power of authenticity tells everyone you are real, genuine, aren't playing a role, and that you have no hidden agendas. Openness, transparency, disclosure, and vulnerability are all part of the power of authenticity. These characteristics tell others that you are human. People follow vulnerability, not perfection. People love it when you are you. They will, however reject you when you are artificial. When you believe everything about yourself, that you are God's image with exalted worth and exalted dignity, then you are set free from the temptation to be artificial. You no longer have to prove to anyone that you are somebody. You don't have to compare, compete with, or impress anyone. You can rest in the truth that you are somebody as a gift from God. This truth will wean you from the need of pretentiousness.

The more you grow in this truth, the more authentic you will become. The more authentic you become, the more influence you will have on people's lives. Authenticity is the transparency of your being. The clearer your being, the greater the impact you will have on the world. Genuineness is ultimate personal power, because the genuine person possesses the power of credibility.

I encourage you to celebrate the uniqueness of your personhood and humbly grow in the power of authenticity.

4. The Power of Belief

Mind-set precedes "skill-set," philosophy precedes performance, theory precedes practice, knowledge precedes application, and belief precedes behavior. Before you *do* something, you must first of all *believe* something. This power of personhood calls on you to believe something, to embrace it with your whole being. What we are to believe is what God says about each and every human being: that we are the image of God. If you get up tomorrow believing this truth about your spiritual identity and treat every human you meet that day on the basis of this truth claim, you will have one of the best days of your life. This belief will transform you and everyone around you.

Dear Reader, belief is the center and circumference of all human accomplishment. When you exercise this power, this is your first step to becoming intensely personal with yourself and with everyone you encounter. It is the only true basis for human identity.

When I give my seminars, I always pick out certain people and tell them that they make a difference. I take them by the hand and look into their eyes and say, "You are so special," "You count," "You have infinite worth." Almost every time I do this, it has such an overwhelming impact that they begin to cry.

Remember you can't impart what you don't possess. First of all you must believe this truth about yourself before you can impart it to anyone else. Please believe that you count, you make a difference, and you are very special.

Believing is seeing. I hope you will operate on this truism for the rest of your life. You must turn your thinking around from "seeing is believing" to "believing is seeing."

When Mrs. Sullivan, who was Helen Keller's teacher, saw Helen Keller, she didn't see a child who was blind, deaf, and mute. Mrs. Sullivan looked beyond these finite physical limitations and, with the eyes of faith, saw a human spirit with unlimited potential.[11] If Mrs. Sullivan had operated on the "seeing is believing" system of thinking, Helen Keller would have never become one of the greatest inspirational stories of all human history.

We need to look beyond the seed in the apple and learn to see the apple in the seed. That is the "believing is seeing" philosophy.

You *become* what you *believe!* Mrs. Sullivan looked beyond what she saw and believed great things for Helen Keller; therefore, Helen believed what Mrs. Sullivan believed, and Helen became the world-renowned transformation of Mrs. Sullivan's belief. Mrs. Sullivan was an Achiever's Believer. Helen was the Achiever, but she needed a Believer. We all need an Achiever's Believer.

Everyone you know knows what you believe about them. The way you act around them tells them exactly what you believe about them. I challenge you to ask this question to everyone you know: "How do you feel about yourself when you are around me?" The answer is very telling. Some people may give an encouraging answer: "I like myself the most when I am around you." (That is because they feel special around you.) Others may give an eye-opening answer, "I dislike myself the most when I am around you." (This is because you don't believe they are special, and they are painfully aware of your belief about them.) *Our unbelief in human beings throws the kill switch in their human spirit.*

If you are serious about transformation in your family, where all transformation must begin, then constantly tell your loved ones what you believe about them. Don't let them guess or wonder. Take the initiative, and lovingly tell them that they are very special to you and why they are special. If you become their Achiever's Believer, you will witness one of the greatest transformations in human experience. Get into the habit of making value deposits in, and not withdrawals from, your loved ones' human spirit. Never make them feel inferior. Inferiority can become a multigenerational disease.

How would you feel if you were around a person who delighted in building you up? Someone who was right there to congratulate your progress every time you did something right? Wouldn't you feel like you could accomplish anything? Wouldn't you want to be around them because they always brought the best out in you? You may not have anyone in your life right now to do that; however, the good news is that you can become that very person right now for someone else, through this power of belief. Now you are armed with the fourth great power of personhood, the power of belief, and I encourage you to put this power to work in your life today and turn frustration into celebration.

5. The Power of Love

I believe this power of personhood, beyond all the other six powers, enables you to become the most personable that you can possibly be. I know I have learned that the secret to lasting success is to love God and to love people. When you make the central focus of your life to love God and to love people you will have embraced the true purpose of your life. And you will also live with a constant sense of fulfillment and contentment of soul. One of the additional by-products of loving God and loving people is mental health. If you want to experience sanity at its highest, start loving God and loving the ones He has made in His image. When we aren't loving, we are denying the greatest aspect of our human-ness, and we are being antihuman.

Hate destroys the hater, but love edifies the lover and the beloved. We are made in God's image, and God is the greatest Lover in the universe. When we hate other people made in God's image it is like pouring sand in our spiritual gas tanks. We just don't func-tion properly. We are designed to run on love, not hate. I know a lot of people I don't like, but I love them apart from the things I don't like about them. I encourage you to let go of any bitterness you have toward anyone right now and give it to God, confess your bitterness, and ask Him to enable you to forgive them and love them. We must do this, because no one wins in hate and bitterness; it is a lose-lose proposition.

True godlike love is unconditional love. It doesn't ask for any-thing in return; it gives freely, without obligation or manipulation. Love is a mental attitude of commitment, not an unstable, whimsi-cal feeling. Therefore, love isn't a feeling to be felt but a commitment to be consecrated. Unconditional love is based on the sustained, responsible commitment of the lover, not on the changing nature of the beloved.

When we love as God loves we don't *need* for others to respond to or appreciate our love, because the source and impetus of our love isn't in them but in our obedient response to God's command to love them.

We need to love in word and deed. We need both to *tell* and to *show* people we love them. It is so important to love your employees and love your customers. Have you ever told your employees or your customers that you love them? To whom in your life do you make it a practice to say "I love you"?

I love to look at total strangers and smile and think to myself, *You are the image of God, and I love you.* Someone might say, "How can you love them, when you don't even know them?" But you don't understand; I know all I need to know about them to love them deeply and truly: they are God's image, and they can have my love on that basis only, without having to do anything to earn or solicit it. When we carry this truth to its deepest purpose and motive, we are really loving God when we love human beings made in His image.

Therefore, quit looking for excuses not to love people, and begin loving them unconditionally, as God loves. This is the greatest power of personhood for human transformation. Use this power of love, and your life will be worth modeling and you will have found a faith fit to live by, a self fit to live with, and a purpose fit to live for.

6. The Power of Encouragement

Emerson said, "Our chief want in life is somebody who shall make us do what we can."[12] I believe Emerson meant that we are all looking for someone who will encourage us to be what we know we can be! When you embrace the truth that we are all made in God's image, which means our spirits are infinitely upgradable, then you will see the importance of practicing the power of encouragement. *Cor* is the Latin root for *courage,* and it means "heart." Therefore, when you give someone encouragement, you give them "heart." We are designed by God to live with heart. Without heart we have no confidence to achieve greatness. And everything about our personhood screams that we are engineered for greatness.

It is criminal and antihuman not to encourage people. How would you like to have been the person who encouraged Thomas Edison, Albert Einstein, or Michelangelo? Dear Reader, the Edisons, Einsteins, and Michelangelos are all around us just waiting for us to encourage them to be what they know they could be. I heard a story about a man who asked Michelangelo how he was able to sculpt a beautiful angel out of stone. Michelangelo is said to have confidently replied, "I see the angel in the stone, and I take my hammer and chisel and set it free." We need to follow his example and take the hammer and chisel of our words and use them to set people free to be all they can be.

Are you known as an encouraging person? Do you encourage people with constant inspiration? This, like no other power I have ever witnessed, truly leverages the human spirit. Find out what people want to accomplish in their lives and lovingly give them the encouragement they need to fulfill their dreams. Have you ever watched a little child walk for the first time and observed the parents' enthusiasm, encouragement, and belief in their child? The parents say to the child, "Come on, honey, you can walk! Walk to Mommy and Daddy!" The parents give their child heart power so that their child can achieve foot power. We are all still little children desperately looking for someone to encourage us to walk where we have never walked before.

Is the power of encouragement active in your family, in your company, and in your church? It is tragic that we are so wrapped up in ourselves that we don't notice that everyone around us is dying for encouragement.

I love being around encouraging people. I feel so alive, because they touch my spirit with words of confidence, hope, and inspiration. They make value deposits in my soul and not withdrawals. They delight in watching me grow, and they are always there to celebrate all my accomplishments. They always pull me up to my highest and best and not down to my lowest and least.

Dear Reader, I want to plead with you to be moved by what you just read and find someone you can encourage; see the angel in the stone and set it free.

7. The Power of Respect

This is the last of the Seven Powers of Personhood, and it is an indispensable power for honoring human beings. Where does respect begin? Secular humanism would say it begins with ourselves. I could not disagree more, because spiritually fallen man isn't a source for anything. That is why I disagree with the popular concept of the "inside out" approach to life. I believe in the "outside-inside out" approach to life. Let me explain what I mean by this philosophy. When we start from inside of ourselves as the source of power, then we are saying "I don't need God's power," which comes to us from the outside. God is the only beginning point for human respect, and we get this truth exclusively from God and not from man. What we learn from history is how to kill each other, not respect each other.

While the true cost of the denial of God's existence may never be known, knowledgeable sources have estimated that communism, in China and the former Soviet Union *alone,* is responsible for the deaths of as many as 142 *million* people![13]

Why did the communists murder tens of millions of people made in God's image? Because they didn't respect God. In the Bible, God makes a statement that tells us exactly why the communists have slaughtered millions: "For whoever finds me finds life, / And obtains favor from the LORD; / But he who sins against me wrongs his own soul; / All those who hate me love death" (Prov. 8:35–36).

The power of respect begins with respecting God's Being and God's Word. Apart from respecting God there is no basis for respecting any person: "The fear of the LORD is the beginning of knowledge, / But fools despise wisdom and instruction" (Prov. 1:7). The Hebrew word for *fear* means "a great and awesome respect for God's Being." We are to respect His holiness, righteousness, justice, and His hatred for evil. When we start from this basis we have established the foundation for all human rights. God is the only One who can give rights; man has no rights to give.

When we try to rule over people, we strip them of respect and dishonor them. That is why Franklin D. Roosevelt said with such conviction, "There never has been, there isn't now and there never will be, any race of people on the earth fit to serve as masters over their fellow men!"[14] That is why I strongly resent any employer referring to his associates as "my people." When we say things like that, we are disrespecting the image of God. We don't own anyone, we don't even own ourselves—God owns everything.

Now with this truth in mind, go out today and honor, esteem, value, and respect everyone—whether they deserve it or not. We need to operate from our power and not from their weakness. Look for opportunities to honor people. Here are a few things we can do to show others we believe they are made in God's image: open the doors for strangers, let people go ahead of you, stand when someone enters the room and leaves the room, let other people express different opinions, and don't interrupt others when they are talking. Maintain a constant willingness to treat people with deference. This power of courteous respect is one of the most winsome characteristics of personhood.

We are to do this not because others will appreciate our kind consideration or it will make us feel good, but solely because it is the right thing to do. If you haven't been honoring people as you should, then begin today, because it is never too late to do what is right. This truth has changed my whole life, because I know when I honor someone I am honoring God's image, and when I am honoring God's image I am honoring God.

Loved, Laughed, and Left a Legacy

Our goal in life should be to build a life and pass on a legacy, not to build loot and pass on lunacy! When all is said and done, which of these two epitaphs would be your first choice: "Hurried, Worried, and Buried" or "Loved, Laughed, and Left a Legacy"?

Dear Reader, you have come to the end of the first secret to tapping into your potential, and I commend you for reading this truth. Now I want to exhort you to put this truth to practice in your life. Remember, you can't impart what you don't possess, so own this truth by believing it. God bless you in your pursuit of His Truth.

Passion Produces Excellence

2

THE GOD WHO MADE YOU in His image is a passionate God. The Bible is replete with references to the strongly passionate nature of God. The beauty in creation speaks of God's personal passion. Walk outside tonight and look at the sunset, or watch the sun rise tomorrow morning. Go to the beach and enjoy the sunlight glittering on the ocean. Drink in the majesty of a mountain range. Can't you just feel the passion of the Creator?

When you visit a museum of art and view great masterpiece paintings or sculptures, you often say, "Wow, the artist really poured himself into that sculpture!" or "She really painted that from her heart!" All great artists work with passion. Can you listen to the great works of music from composers like Bach or Beethoven and not hear passion in that music? The same is true of the great inventors, like Edison, who was famous for being consumed by his work.

Any created thing you see, whether it is a painting, an automobile, or a book, is evidence of self-reflective thought. When an artist adds a brush stroke here, or a splash of color there, she is engaging in self-conscious conversation, such as "Let's see, this would look good here," or "No, I don't like that." Animals don't engage in self-reflective thought. You would never hire an ape as an architect. Animals have no self-consciousness to put into a rendering or a blueprint. All art reflects the self-consciousness and passion of the artist. True art is not just splashes of paint arbitrarily thrown onto a canvas in a "ho-hum" kind of way. There's no passion in that!

Someone might glance at a Swiss watch, and exclaim, "Why would they put all those jewels in there?" The answer is that the Swiss watchmaker is not just an artisan, he is also an *artist*. He poured himself into creating intricate machinery of the finest quality that is humanly possible.

Any of you who have ever been involved in creating something, whether it be music, writing, building, or art, know what it means to "get in the flow," to "get on a roll," etc. These phrases indicate the emergence of *passion* in creation, when you lose track of time, forget about hunger or fatigue, and become consumed by the flow of creativity and productivity that is pouring out of you.

Whether it is an entire ecosystem or just a tiny tropical fish or a butterfly, all creation reflects God's passion. There is such incredible intricacy of design, such unparalleled excellence of craftsmanship, that it's really quite impossible to believe that this creation is the result of random, mindless chance.

When you see that Swiss watch, do you imagine that there was no watchmaker? Do you suppose the watch is an accident, a product of random chance? Do you suppose for even a second that if you took all the incredibly tiny springs and gears nestled within that watch, placed them in a box, and shook that box for hundreds or thousands or millions of years, that you might one day reach into that box and pull out the perfection that is a Swiss watch? Of course not! Such an idea is patently absurd. Yet isn't this precisely what we have been told regarding the origins of the earth?

If you were walking down a deserted beach, and you found a large heart drawn in the sand, big enough for twenty people to stand in, with the words "JACK *REALLY* LOVES DEBBIE!"

neatly centered inside the giant heart, would you really wonder if the wind and waves and rain had gradually formed this? Nonsense! You'd grin a little, and think, *The guy who drew that in the sand is really in love! Look at the size of that heart! He was really passionate about what he was doing.* When you hold an infant in your hands, and those warm, trusting, humorous eyes look deep into yours, and as you tug on tiny, yet perfectly formed fingers and toes, do you wonder to yourself, "Gosh, millions of years ago this little creature was a monkey?" I say, "Nonsense!" You are looking at the handiwork of the Grand Master, Himself, who told mankind, "Can a woman forget her nursing child, and have no compassion on the son of her womb? Even these may forget, But I will not forget you. Behold, I have inscribed you on the palms of my hands" (Isa. 49:15–16). Dear Reader, God is passionate about you!

Teaching with Passion

You'd think that after twenty-five years of teaching and giving motivational speeches all over the country it might be hard to remember the most fun I ever had working with a group of people. Hardly! The day is a shining, crystal-clear memory. Perhaps it's so memorable because of the way it started.

I was invited to conduct three eight-hour training sessions for a company of over one hundred employees. Each day, a different group would come in. At the end of the second day, the general manager informed me, "Jack, you're doing a great job, but you're going to have a tough time tomorrow. In fact, it will probably be the worst eight hours you have ever spent in your life!" The manager went on to explain that tomorrow's group had given another corporate trainer a hard time last year. This bunch didn't like consultants or trainers, he told me.

"There's one guy, Jim, who will try to intimidate you," the manager warned. "And there's another man who will probably keep interrupting you, to disrupt your train of thought. If somebody gets up and walks out in the middle of your presentation," he finished glumly, "don't be surprised. They'll show you absolutely no respect."

I sat with the manager and asked him some questions about this third group. I learned their names and what their hobbies were. When we were finished, I told him matter-of-factly, "This is going to be one of the best classes ever. I'm willing to bet this will be the *best* eight hours I've ever spent in my life!"

The next morning, my group came filing quietly into the training room. Immediately, I started talking to the intimidator, Jim. "Jim, tell me what your favorite hobby is."

He looked surprised. "I like to collect guns," he told me.

"All right, I love guns too," I responded truthfully. "What's your favorite gun?"

"I like to shoot a .357 Magnum," he told me.

"I like to shoot a Magnum too!" I enthused. I was excited about his gun collection!

Then I addressed the man I had been told would keep interrupting me. "Bob, what's your favorite hobby?" It turned out that this man liked to work with wood. As he talked about his hobby, his eyes began to shine with remembered pleasure. I went around the room, asking what everyone's favorite activity was. I asked about what brought them joy. One man enjoyed boating with his family; another one had fun teaching Sunday school. Within fifteen minutes, the room was starting to crackle with energy and excitement!

Just before lunch, I called the manager on my cellular phone. "Listen to this," I told him, and held up the phone toward the meeting room. They were laughing, cheering, high-fiving—having the time of their lives! The manager didn't believe it. "You told them to do that," he insisted.

He hadn't planned on visiting with this group at all, but this was something he wanted to see! A little before 5:00 P.M., he dropped by the classroom. The group was pumped up! We were celebrating each other, clapping, whistling, and cheering. The manager couldn't conceal his astonishment! The group told him that this was the best training they'd ever attended, but it was also *my* best class ever. Why? I got personal and passionate with that group, and they responded. I tapped into *their* passion.

Sometimes people ask me why I get so excited when I'm speaking, and I tell them the truth from my heart: I am passionate because I am in love with a passionate God. I take my cues from God, who poured His passion into His creation. Can I do anything less with my work? Everything God created is a total reflection of His being. You need to look no farther than your own body. Look at the incredible intricacy of the bone structure in your hands; feel the power in your thighs; meditate on the remarkable ability of your eyes, which have a built in speedometer and range finder. Your body loudly proclaims God's passionate creative skill!

When we unleash that kind of passion in our lives, we unleash excellence. When you walk into companies where the leadership has released the passion in the staff, you sense the difference from the moment you're greeted at the front desk. There's something extra in the way people speak and in the sparkle in their eyes. Unfortunately, I visit too many companies where there is no passion or excitement. People look listless, lethargic. Yet you'll see those same people absolutely transformed when they're working on their personal hobbies. The perfect example is Jim, "the intimidator," who suddenly transformed when discussing his gun collection. Jim tried to railroad other trainers because they had never tried to tap into his passion!

We've got to allow people to display passion in the workplace! I remember the CFO at one company who acted like a particularly cold fish. He felt his position dictated that he be sober and serious. After all, the finances of the corporation were his ultimate responsibility. So he showed no emotion at work; he was totally *dis*passionate. Then, one day, he led a pep rally for a company function. Suddenly this man, who had seemed so devoid of warmth, was a different person! He was out of his role. He was funny, engaging, and warm. People all throughout the room were laughing in surprise and delight. He was *real!*

Later I asked him, "Why can't we behave like this in the board meetings?"

"Well, Jack, I just didn't think it would be proper," he replied with some surprise.

"Did you see the way people responded to you today?" I countered. "They were energized. They were *cheering* for you. They were totally on your team. Isn't that what you want every day?"

He agreed to give it a try, and the company was transformed from a stiff, sterile environment to a culture of recognition and celebration. The staff affectionately called it being "Lannomized."

Too many people are trapped in another kind of culture at work. Many companies have a stifling environment, as if there were signs posted on the wall reading, "NO SMILING," or "NO FUN." Everywhere I go, I ask people if they have enough fun at work, and they invariably tell me, "No."

Hardball and Softball Management

Many organizations adopt one of two management styles: "hardball" or "softball" management. Both are a *reactionary* management style. Hardball managers are high-command, high-control types. They rule by the power of their position or the power of their personality. They are rigid and inflexible.

Softball managers have allowed the pendulum to swing to the other extreme. Softball management is laissez-faire. There are no consequences for poor performance, no accountability or responsibility. Workers have total freedom to "do their own thing." Neither of these management styles is even slightly proactive. The hardball manager is reacting to the chaos that befalls companies that are run by softball managers. At the other end of the spectrum, the softball managers have usually come out of a high-control, power management structure, and they are determined not to subject their staff to the bitterness and malicious obedience that hardball management invariably produces. Whichever way the pendulum has swung, these two styles don't elicit the best from people. People never bring their best to work, because their best is not encouraged in either situation.

What I am contending for is to return the pendulum to the center point. At this point you're no longer playing hardball or softball, but Incredi-ball, Unstoppa-ball, Unconquera-ball! This is not power management or passive management, but *passion* management. The leadership is creating the kind of culture that makes it possible for people to *be* their best and to *do* their best. Companies that practice Incredi-ball management leverage the human spirit to its fullest potential. People look forward to coming to work and to putting forth discretionary effort in this kind of an environment.

Turning the Workplace into a Fun Place

Let me share five secrets that keep the management pendulum resting comfortably at the center point. These are principles I have taught and seen used effectively at companies all over the country. I've put them together in an acronym you can easily remember: *LAUGH.*

> L eadership
> A ttitude
> U nleash potential
> G ive of yourself
> H igh challenge, low threat

Leadership

When I think of superior leadership, two men come immediately to mind. One of them is Bob Kramm, president of Pro Player

Stadium, home to the Miami Dolphins and Florida Marlins. My relationship with Bob goes back several years, to when Bob was vice president of marketing for the Marlins. When Bob was promoted to the top position at the stadium, he invited Dan Philips, the director of training for my consulting company, and me to conduct a six-month, in-depth training program with his key leadership personnel. When the bulk of the training was completed, Bob invited me to attend what he called a "working breakfast/celebration" to review the progress that had been made through our program.

When I walked into the conference room, I could hardly believe my eyes! The room was decorated like a New Year's Eve party. Balloons and crepe paper were everywhere. Brightly colored signs, made especially for the occasion and lettered with oft-repeated themes from the training such as "Recognize and Celebrate" and "Suspend Judgment and Emotion," were displayed prominently around the room. Bob's staff was busily engaged in pelting each other with silly string and confetti. Bob conducted several workshops that were designed to review the key points of the training, and participants were tossed prizes, such as T-shirts, coffee mugs, golf balls, and so on. One man won a weekend cruise for himself and his wife. Trophies were awarded to those whom the staff had voted "Most Valuable Players" of the training, people who had best modeled the principles for unleashing untapped potential. The meeting began promptly at 8:00 A.M., but not one person looked the least bit sleepy. Instead, the room was filled with laughter and applause. It was an incredibly exhilarating experience, but it was also a busy morning. The group engaged in lateral thinking exercises (see Chapter 5) that were designed to put their training to long-lasting effect within the stadium structure. Two groups developed core process maps for different procedures they had performed, demonstrating the validity and benefits of such maps. Plenty of work was accomplished, but the morning literally flew by in a sea of shining eyes and joyful sound.

The high point of the morning came when the trophies were awarded. The staff had voted the largest trophy to . . . Bob Kramm! When the award was given, the room erupted with cheers and applause. The entire group, about seventy people, rose to their feet as one to proclaim their appreciation for this outstanding leader who had tapped into their passion.

The results of the training were resounding and far-reaching. One of the security supervisors told Dan that staffers all over the stadium had commented on changes they had seen in the leadership personnel. One of the announcers commented that he had seen a real quantum leap in creative and cooperative thinking.

A fan in one of the luxury suites mentioned to a food server about how much he liked the embroidered shirt she was wearing, which bore his favorite team logo. "Where can I buy one of those?" he asked.

"I'm sorry, sir," she responded politely. "These shirts aren't for sale. They're used to identify stadium personnel." The customer indicated his disappointment, and then promptly forgot about the matter. As the game neared its conclusion, the food server unexpectedly reappeared in the suite. She had brought not one, but *four* shirts for the man and his guests. He was delighted!

Another fan saw an usher holding an official big-league baseball. He asked the usher where he could purchase one of the balls. The usher explained that it was a game ball, the first one he had ever caught in all his years of working professional events. The fan's face fell. He explained he had been trying for years to get a game ball for his young son, who was seated next to him. The usher didn't hesitate. "Here you go, young man," he said, holding the ball out to the boy. "I've got plenty of chances to pick up another one." The boy's eyes filled with joy at the unexpected prize.

There is no pay plan in the world that buys this kind of commitment to exceeding the expectations of customers. It all begins with the passion of the *leadership*, in this case the dynamic leadership of

Bob Kramm, who is totally committed to modeling excellence in every aspect of his life.

Every day, superior leadership models a relaxed mental attitude, openness, and humanity. It is this transparency and authenticity that sets people free to be passionate about their work. When people are actually excited about coming to work every day, nobody can hire them away from you!

Superior leadership is solidly connected to core values. The purpose that directs us springs from our core values. What kind of core values will cause a family or a workforce to rally around its leaders? Superior leaders have chosen not to rally around *profits*. Instead, they have elected to rally around *people*. They truly believe in their hearts that *people* are the most important asset that any corporation can possess. They do not see people as spare parts, to be used and tossed aside when they begin to burn out. Rather they see people as unique and precious, made in the image of God and bursting with unlimited potential, like a priceless diamond with multiple facets to be polished and developed. It is the connection of the leadership to the purpose of unleashing untapped potential that broadens the belief, enriches the spirit, and releases the will to win of the entire staff of an organization. Believe me, an investment in people will result in an infusion of profits. Just ask Bob Kramm.

Attitude

In Chapter 3, I'm going to tell you about the vibrant power of encouraging words. The attitude of any successful family or organization should be to create a culture that catches people doing something right, instead of consistently looking for what has gone wrong. This creates a *trust*-based environment. People become champions of change, willing to step out and take a risk when in the pursuit of excellence because they know their initiative will be recognized and rewarded, even when the results are less than sparkling. Unleashing untapped potential means giving people permission to fail when they reach for previously unscaled plateaus.

In the *fear*-based environment (hardball all the way), you find victims of circumstance, people who have had all personal power and resourcefulness stripped away. Their only desire is to keep their heads down and stay out of the line of fire. Rather than focusing on accomplishment, the hardball managers have concentrated their attention on accusation, pointing the finger to attach blame and shame to whatever goes awry.

Either attitude is highly contagious and will rapidly spread throughout the entire organization. An attitude that is liberating will make "empowerment" a shining reality for a staff that strives for constant, continual improvement. An attitude that is confining and controlling, on the other hand, stifles the human spirit and fosters indifference at best, animosity at worst.

I recently talked to a staffer at an organization that tends to bring a hardball attitude to its leadership style. This unhappy woman told me, "There is no *spirit* here, no feeling of caring and giving. If we could just agree to be focused on caring about our customers *and* each other, we'd be so much better off!" Attitude begins at the top and permeates an entire organization. At the same time, each of us has the opportunity, indeed, we have the *responsibility*, to bring an attitude of celebration and contribution to our homes and schools and businesses. Even if our leaders aren't modeling excellence, we, ourselves, *can!* We must! It is up to each individual to develop a *passion* for catching people doing something right, and letting them know how much we appreciate it.

Unleash Potential

This whole book is about developing a passion for growth: our own personal ripening and the nourishment of others. I've already introduced you to one outstanding leader. Now meet Dennis Collins, general manager for Jefferson Pilot Communications' three radio stations in the Miami market. Dennis may be the smoothest incorporation of personality traits of anyone I know. He brings competitiveness and intensity, coupled with careful deliberation, all wrapped up in the delightfully charismatic qualities of a real "people person." Frankly, however, I've met other executives who fit that description. It's the fourth aspect of Dennis Collins's personality that I want to hold up to the light, and that is his desire to contribute to everyone with whom he comes in contact.

Dennis's team is truly a learning organization. Dennis is a teacher and a trainer. He told me that the greatest pleasure he receives from his job is helping people grow and advance. Some managers seek to acquire and hold power, much like an army occupying the high ground and defending it against the enemy. Dennis Collins has absorbed the truth that true power is the art of making other people powerful. Dennis buys books, reads them, and passes the best ones on to his managers. He has surrounded himself with an aggressive, young staff, and he constantly invests in them. He hired my company to come in and work with his entire full-time staff on a long-term basis. He sees the *mind*-set is there among the people he works with, he fuels their passion for excellence, and he continually works to increase their *skill*-sets, as well.

Every time Dennis introduces a new training program or video series to the staff, every time he hands someone a book or a cassette tape, he is communicating to them that he values them and is committed to their personal and professional growth. He is constantly looking for ways to stretch their minds and contribute to their learning.

The flip side of Dennis Collins's learning organization is that Dennis, himself, is constantly listening to and learning from his staff. Dennis wants to hear, and consistently encourages, feedback. When Dennis was introduced to the same Lateral Thinking skills you will soon be learning yourself, he embraced the concept wholeheartedly. He purchased books on the subject and began to utilize

Lateral Thinking with his management team. He held staff meetings and took copious notes as the staff applied Lateral Thinking skills to various concepts.

Great leaders encourage feedback, good *and* bad. They provide encouragement and training to the people they work with, and they promote and prod for feedback *from* the people they work with. These upper-echelon environments enjoy the best possible flow of vertical and horizontal communication because leaders like Dennis Collins develop a reciprocity of feedback within the organization.

I have said for years that every human being walks around with four letters stamped plainly on their foreheads: MMFI, which stands for "Make Me Feel Important!" Dr. Paul Tournier, the noted Swiss psychologist, once said, "It cannot be overemphasized the immense need human beings have to be really listened to, to be understood, and to be taken seriously." Dennis Collins's passion is *people.* He makes them feel important by developing and listening to them. The result is an environment that literally explodes with energy and enthusiasm. Dennis's group is breaking sales records right and left, and the turnover among the on-air personnel is among the lowest in the industry.

When you walk into the offices of Jefferson Pilot Communications–Miami or Pro Player Stadium, you instantly realize you've stepped into something special. From the initial greeting from the receptionists to the warm and personal attention you receive, you see men and women who radiate excitement. The excitement begins with two men, Dennis Collins and Bob Kramm, who bring a passion for excellence and a passion for people to work with them every single day.

Give of Yourself

If true power is the art of making other people powerful, then unleashing untapped potential involves teaching people how to be *givers.* The family or organization that gives reflects caring and contribution. This mirrors the Spirit of God, which prompted the apostle Paul to urge, "Let nothing be done through selfish ambition or conceit, but in lowliness of mind let each esteem others better than himself. Let each of you look out not only for his own interests, but also for the interests of others" (Phil. 2:3–4).

This servant's spirit must be modeled by the top leadership. No training course can provide this spirit of contribution to a leader or to anyone else. It is an attitude of the heart, a philosophy that one lives. One of Dennis Collins's many fine staffers, Sheila McCray, said it perfectly: "I just try as best I can to add something to everyone's day. If there is something I can do to make their job easier or more enjoyable, I'll go out of my way to do that. It makes *them* feel better, it makes *me* feel better, and the whole work environment becomes that much more pleasant." Beautiful! When a philosophy like this pervades an organization, you don't have a corporation, but a community. People are not looking for what they can *take*, but what they can *give*. The customers aren't shortchanged, and the staff isn't demeaned or exploited. You don't have a firm, you have a family.

Customers walk away from such an organization, saying, "Wow! Did you see how they treat each other? Did you see how they love each other? What a wonderful place to do business!" When customers leave your company feeling a warmth like that, you can significantly reduce your advertising budget because your customers will advertise for you!

High Challenge, Low Threat

Avoid the hardball style of "high threat, low challenge." This doesn't mean we shouldn't expect and encourage excellence. Bob Kramm preaches "standards" to his staff consistently. He creates an atmosphere of high expectations. He demands excellence because he knows he has surrounded himself with excellent human beings, and he invests himself in their personal and professional growth.

The leader who turns the workplace into a fun place, for example, is able to elicit such excellence because there is a vital and visible link between challenge and celebration. People who dare to make a dramatic difference in the organization, who share their leaders' passion for people and commitment to excellence, know that their accomplishments will be rewarded in a way that is sincere, specific, immediate, and personal. They *welcome* the high level of challenge because they know that there is an equally high level of recognition and reward for their effort and attitude, as well as for their successes.

Instead of hardball management, leaders should *play* hard. Instead of high *command* and high *control,* the truly transformational leader brings high *intensity* to the workplace. This leadership style of passion-based management will unleash, rather than stifle, the true potential that lies within all the members of the culture.

We have a choice. Do we want to spend our lives "hurried, worried, and buried"? Or do we choose to live with *passion,* with fire, with a level of commitment and excitement that galvanizes everyone around us with a desire to live their personal and professional lives at the pinnacle of excellence? Wouldn't we rather "laugh, love, and leave a legacy"?

We've just infused the word *laugh* with an entirely new meaning: Leadership, Attitude, Unleash Potential, Give of Yourself, and High Challenge— Low Threat. We love the people around us, we stand in awe of remarkable human beings made in God's image. We build lives and pass on a legacy of excellence, instead of building languor and passing on only loot.

Once again, this is the very mind-set, the very essence of God Himself: "Whatever you do," Colossians 3:23 instructs, "do it heartily, as to the Lord and not to men." Whatever you do, do it *passionately!* Let your excellence reflect the excellence of your Creator.

My hope is that what you have just read will inspire you to reach for the untapped potential that exists within you and all the people with whom you live and work. You may be thinking, "Yes, Jack, I want to do that, but *how?* You haven't yet shown me how!" Believe me, I'm well aware that exhortation without explanation leads to frustration! I'm not going to tell you what it looks like without teaching you how to accomplish it. By introducing you to men like Dennis Collins and Bob Kramm, I wanted to show you living, breathing leaders—people I've met and worked with—who model passion and excellence in everything they do. In the chapters that follow, I'll set forth the skills and tools that will allow you, too, to become a master of human performance technology.

Good Words
Build Great People

Y EARS BEFORE JESSICA McCLURE'S parents had been born, another little girl was trapped in a prison of silent darkness. Like Jessica, this child was trapped in inky blackness. She cried out her fear, but heard no response. She struck at the walls that imprisoned her, to no avail. She wept there, alone in the blackness. Would no one come to rescue her?

Unlike Jessica, this little girl's nightmare lasted four years! Eventually, however, she was rescued from her prison, a prison made not of concrete, but of human frailty and misunderstanding. Her name was Helen Keller. At nineteen months of age, Helen was struck with a near-fatal fever that left her deaf and blind. She was unable to speak normally. Frustrated at her inability to see and communicate, Helen's early childhood was marked by increasingly violent temper tantrums. Some people mistook Helen's disabilities for mental retardation and suggested that she be institutionalized.

Fortunately, Helen's parents ignored this "advice."[1] When Helen was six years old, her parents finally found the proper training for Helen (which was far less common than it is today), and in 1904 Helen Keller graduated with honors from the prestigious Radcliffe

College in Massachusetts. Helen went on to publish several books, and even conducted lectures, with Anne Sullivan speaking for her.[2]

Helen Keller's remarkable story highlights the power of the third secret for unlocking untapped potential: the power of words. Anne Sullivan, Helen's teacher, wrote in incredibly moving terms of how the simple act of learning the names of various objects transformed an angry, unruly child into a radiantly beautiful little girl. Anne Sullivan said that every time Helen learned a new word, she grew as a person.[3] While most of us may not respond in such dramatic fashion, words are essential to our emotional development, because we all communicate with ourselves and with each other in words. We reason and relate in words. We respond to the word pictures that a good communicator can paint.

Uniquely Created to Speak

This aspect of our human nature is one of the clearest reflections of the image of our Creator. God is a word Being. Psalm 29:4 tells us, "The voice of the LORD is powerful . . . [and] full of majesty." God spoke the universe into being! "Then God said, 'Let there be light'; and there was light" (Gen. 1:3). The entire creation account describes God's speaking. "By the word of the LORD the heavens were made" (Ps. 33:6).

In creating us in His image, God gave us a speech center in our brains. Our mouth, throat, lips, tongue, and teeth are designed to *speak.* We are specifically designed for personal communication. No other creatures are designed for the manufacturing and manipulation of words. Everything about us, mentally *and* physically, is hardwired for the transmission and reception of words. The mouths of animals are not designed for speech. If it were scientifically possible to transplant the brain of a human being into the body of an animal, that creature would *still* not speak as we do, because their mouths and throats are incapable of forming speech![4]

Words are an inseparable part of our growth. They play a crucial role in giving us our sense of identity and self-consciousness. Children who have grown up alone in the wild, removed from any contact with other human beings, truly lack the attributes that we would call *personhood*. As much as anything, it is through words that we learn who and what we are supposed to be.

Since we are created and designed to send and receive messages with words, in order to live up to our maximum potential, we should use words the same way our Creator does. God is a builder. God *spoke* life into being. Our words, then, should be used to build up and to create, not to destroy. Our words should be crafted and designed to bring out the best in ourselves and in others. The things we say should encourage life and harmony and love.

The Bible is filled with references to the power of the spoken word:

"The tongue of the wise promotes health." (Prov. 12:18b)

"Anxiety in the heart of a man causes depression,
But a good word makes it glad." (Prov. 12:25)

"Pleasant words are like a honeycomb,
Sweetness to the soul and health to the bones." (Prov. 16:24)

Scripture is equally clear in admonishing us that a thoughtless word can wound others:

"There is one who speaks like the piercings of a sword."
(Prov. 12:18a)

"Look also at ships: although they are so large and are driven by fierce winds, they are turned by a very small rudder wherever the pilot desires. Even so the tongue is a little member and boasts great things. See how great a forest a little fire kindles! And the tongue is a fire, a world of iniquity. . . . It is an unruly evil, full of deadly poison." (James 3:4–6a, 8b)

"He who covers a transgression seeks love,
But he who repeats a matter separates the best of friends."
(Prov. 17:9)

Our speech can be used to deceive, to gossip, and to wound. When we first started our Quantum Quality Management training at one company, the CEO there said, "I would like managers to gain a greater realization of the *shattering* effect of some of the things we say and do. A single word can be devastating!" The apostle Paul would have heartily approved of this man's observation. "Don't use foul or abusive language," Paul urged the Ephesians. "Let everything you say be good and helpful, so that your words will be an encouragement to those who hear them" (Eph. 4:29 NLT).

Positive people are able to inspire others to scale previously unimagined heights. The four most important words anyone can hear are "You make a difference." A healthy self-consciousness believes, "Yes! I am somebody. I do make a difference!" From this platform of mental health and strength, we can reach out and touch others with a positive sense of self. This in turn enables others to move forward with a renewed sense of self-worth and contribution. I have introduced thousands of men and women to the "Pyramid of People Power" of words that can be used to build and contribute. These are words that turn on the human spirit, rather than hitting the kill switch.

Pyramid of People Power

Yes!
Thank you!
I need you!
I believe in you!
I am proud of you!

These are words that create a culture of competency in our homes and businesses. People you meet who are confident and engaging have absorbed encouraging words. Conversely, people will have little or no belief in self if no one believes in them. Our personhood flourishes in a culture that is rich in encouraging words. *So we should create environments of celebration, not condemnation!* We can use our words to turn frustration to celebration. It is physically impossible for me to reach out and touch your human spirit with my hands, but I *can* hug your spirit with my words!

Let me challenge you to ask the most important people in your life what may be the toughest question you'll ever ask: "How do you feel about yourself when you're around me?" Go to your spouse and to your children. If you're a manager, ask the people who work for you. If you're not married or if you're not a manager, ask your closest friends. What you *hope* you'll hear is, "I like myself most when I'm with you." But imagine how you'll feel if someone is brutally honest with you and says, "I dislike myself most when I'm with you."

We have that kind of power in our spoken words. I recently interviewed a young woman at a company that hired us to come in and help them improve their customer service skills. This organization invests hundreds of thousands of dollars in advertising, encouraging people to trust them. Yet this woman, intelligent, attractive, and articulate, who holds a prestigious, high-paying job in the company, said this about the investment that was made in her: "Nobody talks to each other. There is no respect and no support. We're treated like so many little pieces of garbage. They treat us like complete idiots. They slap us and beat us, but they never support us. They've broken my spirit here. It's a punitive situation."

No one should have to endure a single day like this. Yet there are homes and schools and workplaces all over America that operate in the harsh environment this woman described. She didn't mean that she was being *physically* slapped and beaten, but the pain was no less real. We have the power to build—or to destroy—with our words.

The Power of Encouraging Words in the Workplace

My company has conducted thousands of hours of interviews and training with a broad spectrum of companies throughout the United States. One of the most common comments that our associates will hear sounds like this:

> I've really enjoyed your program. You've helped me grow in both the personal and professional areas, and I've noticed a real difference in the way our company is operating. But there is one problem. There's this person in my department who just *doesn't get it*. He doesn't seem to have any desire to improve or to cooperate with anyone who wants to implement positive change. How do I get that person on board?

This is a familiar lament for many of us. All too often, we seem only to elicit *malicious obedience* from the people we work with. They seem to perform at a level just slightly above minimum standards. To a large extent, *discretionary effort,* which is people doing whatever it takes to get the job done right the first time, no matter what effort is required, is not part of these individuals' workdays.

We have all practiced malicious obedience. Children are particularly adept at this. "Johnny," roars an exasperated father, "if you don't get your toys picked up RIGHT NOW, you're going to be sorry!" If little Johnny believes that Dad really means business, he'll get to work on his toys, but it is clear that his heart is not in it. Where do you think the phrase "foot-dragging obedience" came from? The child's actions speak plainly: "I'm doing this, Dad, but only because you yelled, not because I want to." The father's words inspired *fear*, not desire.

We really don't change that much when we're older! We've just learned to mask our emotions with greater sophistication. If I were your supervisor, and during a meeting I suddenly thundered at you to "SHUT UP AND SIT DOWN!" some of you might walk out, but most of you would probably submit to my authority and sink slowly back into your seat—*but in your minds, you'd* still *be standing!* You wouldn't hear anything else I said throughout that meeting, because your mind would be filled with anger and resentment. I might have gotten you to do what I wanted, but not because you wanted to! I have relegated you to the role of Performance Puppet. In the future, I will always see you doing whatever you think I want to see, but internally, you are assuring yourself, *"He'll never get my best efforts. Never!"* And it doesn't take such an extreme event to create malicious obedience. Studies and surveys consistently reveal that many of us do not put forth our best efforts with any kind of consistency.

I have met many well-intentioned men and women who believe they are facing an uphill battle when it comes to motivation. They are not ogres or tyrants. In fact, many of these managers are often the hardest workers in the organization. They sacrifice their bodies, and too often their families, to achieve organizational goals. Unfortunately, they employ an archaic management style. They have learned, often by observing *their* manager, to use a "my way or the highway" approach. They wield words like a club. "I don't have *time* to pussyfoot around with people," they say. "I need people around me who can take the ball and run with it. For goodness' sake, I'm not a baby-sitter!"

I agree with that sentiment only to a slight degree. Unquestionably, the goal of all the best leaders is to unlock passionate performance from everyone within their sphere of influence. The dynamic leader seeks to encourage everyone around him to exercise the true empowerment that comes from freedom and shared vision and values. But this excellence will not happen merely by saying it should! The role of the effective parent, teacher, or manager is to model and mentor that which he or she seeks to instill in others. This excellence comes only through careful nurturing and attention.

The manager who understands the secrets of untapped potential is focused on the long-term life and vitality of the people *and* the company. Fear will only motivate temporarily, if at all. "Do this or be fired" usually produces immediate, short-term results. But we must look beyond the immediate future. We want *long-term* existence coupled with high productivity and job satisfaction. Anyone who has worked in a fear-based environment will tell you that the short-term results gained by fear carry a long-term price tag: resentment.

Love and Leadership

Here is the bottom line of all successful motivation: *Whatever a company wants its customers to feel, the people must feel first!* You cannot impart what you do not possess. If I, as a leader, do not affirm you, my purpose partner within the organization, how can I possibly expect you to affirm your coworkers or your customers?

The very best customer service professionals operate from the mental model of love. I have heard several top sales trainers summarize this philosophy perfectly: people don't care how much you know, until they know how much you care. True masters of human performance technology don't throw their arms around customers and bawl, "I love you, man!" They don't need to. Their every action and effort speak for themselves. They demonstrate their love by truly listening to their customers' needs, by seeking to understand before they are understood, and by treating customers as they themselves would like to be treated.

The culture that releases untapped potential is one in which the leadership always models love to the organization, and *the words they use reflect that love!* If leadership truly loves the people who work with them, if the leadership honors, values, and esteems the incredible worth and dignity of every magnificent individual, then those individuals will know what love looks like! They will know what love sounds like! Then they can model it for customers, because it has been modeled for them. Their service will be infinitely superior to their competitors', and profits, quite naturally, will follow. Your company will consistently display high energy, and you will maintain a high retention level of employees *and* customers.

I was scheduled to give a Breakthrough and Beyond presentation in Jacksonville, Florida, when I discovered that one button was missing from my shirt. I went to a clothing store and told the salesperson that I needed a new shirt. She asked me what kind of shirt I was looking for, and I explained that I was merely looking to replace the shirt with the missing button.

"Oh, you don't need to buy a new shirt just for that," the woman assured me. "I'll sew a new button on for you." I was nonplussed! "You don't have to buy a shirt from us just to get a new button," she repeated. "It'll only take a minute for me to fix it." And she did! I left that store with my shirt repaired . . . and with three new ones, as well. I had intended to buy only one shirt when I walked in. But I couldn't help but respond to this woman who was so rich in spirit. She gave first, and I wanted to give in return.

As leaders, we should *want* to discover, recognize, and celebrate the men and women within our organization who maintain a loving attitude toward our customers. This loving and giving comes from people who have been affirmed. It flows from them naturally. Words of affirmation should flow from *us* naturally!

For the rest of this chapter, I intend to discuss specific motivational strategies that parents, teachers, and managers can employ to develop "champions of change." But I cannot stress this often enough: all the techniques and all the skills are *meaningless* if we do not believe with every fiber of our being the central truth of the immeasurable greatness of humanity!

One person looks at the Empire State Building and marvels, "What a structure!" But the more perceptive leader looks at that same building and muses admiringly, "What a foundation!" In other words, the magnificence of the edifice lies in the greatness of the foundation. Our foundation must rest squarely on the personal nature of God, Himself. "Beloved, let us love one another, for love is of God; and everyone who loves is born of God and knows God. He who does not love does not know God, for God is love" (1 John 4:7–8).

The ABCs of Motivation
(Antecedents, Behaviors, and Consequences)

Once we are grounded on this vitally important foundation of the dignity and worth of mankind, we can begin to use some simple behavioral tools to encourage and motivate others. I am indebted to Victor Dingus of Eastman Kodak for his help in developing this information. I'm delighted to incorporate some of his principles in this book. Victor gave me tremendous insight into the ways that antecedents and consequences affect behavior.

Antecedents precede behavior, and often cause the behavior to take place. I look at my watch and realize that I am late for an appointment. Suddenly anxious, I snap off my computer and dash out the door. The antecedent for my quick departure is the time. Or perhaps my department manager walks into my office and asks me to schedule a meeting with an important client. I dutifully pick up the phone and make the call. The antecedent to my behavior was my manager's request.

The *consequences* of my behavior are the results that follow my action. On a sticky August day, I come into the house after mowing the lawn. I am dripping with sweat and covered with dust and blades of freshly cut grass. I immediately peel off my clothes and step into the shower. The consequence of that behavior is that I emerge feeling clean and refreshed. Later, I arrive at school to pick up my six-year-old son. As soon as I see him, my face breaks into a big smile, and I drop to one knee and spread my arms wide. The consequence to my behavior is that he breaks into a run and hurls himself into my arms.

Consequences fall into one of three categories: (1) positive or negative; (2) immediate or future; and (3) certain or uncertain. In both scenarios I just described, the consequences for my behavior were positive, immediate, and certain. I knew with certainty before I acted exactly what the results would be, I obtained the results immediately, and I felt positive about them.

Let's look at some other behaviors and consequences. I arrive at the local high school to pick up my *sixteen*-year-old son. I repeat the same greeting I gave my little one: big smile, down on one knee, arms open wide. But the reaction from this boy is dramatically different. Instead of rushing to return my affection, he glances around furtively, hoping that none of his friends are looking. Then he fixes his gaze at a point on the horizon and hurries past me. I rise awkwardly to my feet and follow his rapidly retreating form. I finally catch him in the parking lot, and he turns to confront me, red-faced with anger and embarrassment. "What's the *matter* with you, Dad?" he hisses at me. "You made me look like a *baby*!" These consequences were negative, immediate, and should have been fairly certain to me. If I were to greet the older boy in the very same way, tomorrow, the consequences are *quite* certain!

Imagine an automobile salesman who obtains a list of customers who purchased cars at his dealership three years ago. He plans to call everyone on that list, knowing that a certain percentage of car buyers trade cars every three years. If he makes enough calls, he will enjoy the positive consequences of making some contacts that he can convert into sales. Statistical evidence asserts that he will.

Unfortunately, these contacts may take weeks, months, perhaps years to develop. The extent of the positive consequences is uncertain and will occur sometime in the future.

However, our enterprising salesman will likely receive a great many negative, immediate consequences as well. Some of the customers he will call may be very unhappy with their purchase and will tell him about it in no uncertain terms. Others may have had bad experiences in the dealership's service department, an area that is totally out of the salesman's control, and these customers will angrily inform him that they will *never* buy a car at that dealership again. Still other customers who dislike being contacted by telemarketers will hang up or speak rudely to him. After a few hours of this process, our salesman will become discouraged, decide "I don't like this cold-calling!" and give up, *in spite of the fact that his manager has assured him that these calls will boost his sales!* In the salesman's mind, the immediate, negative consequences of the phone calls outweigh the uncertain future benefits.

Antecedents work only temporarily. The dealership's manager can provide the sales staff with statistical evidence extolling the positive benefits of calling customers; and the manager may wheedle, or even threaten the sales staff; but if that staff does not perceive enough positive consequences (immediate or future), and if they believe the immediate negatives are too unpleasant, their performance on the phones will be halfhearted, at best. They'll probably look for any and every opportunity to be busy elsewhere when they are supposed to be on the phones. If the consequences do not match the antecedents, the desired behavior will not continue with any consistency at all.

Four Types of Consequences

Leaders can provide four types of consequences that reinforce behavior. These are: (1) positive reinforcement, (2) negative reinforcement, (3) extinction, and (4) correction. Positive and negative reinforcement encourage behaviors to increase, while extinction and correction cause behaviors to cease.

Positive reinforcement occurs when I receive something that I like. The feeling of refreshment after a shower, the unaffected love of a six-year-old, these are positive reinforcers for certain behaviors I exhibited. In a business setting, there are any number of positive reinforcers, such as pride in a job well done; praise and appreciation from a boss, coworker, or customer; promotions; letters of commendation; bonuses, etc.

Negative reinforcement is the threat of some unpleasant consequence or punishment; we perform an action because we wish to avoid some undesirable consequence: we drive on the expressway at or near the speed limit to avoid speeding tickets. If I work until midnight because I know my manager will yell at me in the morning if all the work isn't finished, that is negative reinforcement.

Let me establish a critically important distinction between positive and negative reinforcement. If the positive reinforcement is pleasant enough, I will strive to behave in ways that cause that reinforcement to reoccur. However, if I am merely seeking to avoid negative consequences, I will generally do just enough to avoid that unhappiness, and little more. Positive reinforcement elicits discretionary effort; negative reinforcement produces only malicious obedience.

Extinction, quite simply, provides *no* consequence. Extinction ignores the behavior. If I work on that project until midnight because I want to go the extra mile, and my discretionary effort is ignored by my managers, I may well question the need for extra effort in the future. If I go "above and beyond the call of duty" on a few more occasions, and my dedication remains unacknowledged, I will likely decide that an eight-hour day is quite sufficient.

Correction is specific action that is taken to cause an individual to stop a certain activity. Calling an employee into the office for a formal counseling session or an informal "chewing out," a warning letter in the personal file, demotion, suspension, and termination are all various forms of correction.

Please remember this truth that too many managers ignore: *positive reinforcement produces positive results!* Positive reinforcement is not only the right way to treat another human being—*it works!*

Timing and Progress

Once you're ready to implement positive reinforcement, don't forget that *how* you use it can make all the difference. Here are two vitally important principles.

1. Timing

Delayed reinforcement is diluted at best, meaningless at worst. Positive reinforcement must be delivered as soon as possible. We should provide positive feedback on the very same day as the behavior we wish to encourage, and certainly no later than within three days of the event. If we are geographically separated from the individual we wish to reinforce, as might be the case with national sales reps, we should waste no time in picking up the telephone to offer recognition and celebration. *Reinforcement delivered weeks or months after the desired activity carries little or no impact.* This is one reason why some profit-sharing plans do not deliver the desired motivational effect. The positive reinforcement (a profit-sharing check) may arrive months after the work that earned it was performed, so there is only a tenuous connection between the two events in the recipient's mind.

2. Reinforcing Progress

If we wait to deliver positive reinforcement until someone has improved his attitude or performance to the ultimate level we have set for him, we may be in for a long, cold wait. We should reinforce progress, the effort that is being made to reach those new performance levels. Positive feedback for positive behavior encourages more positive behavior.

Celebrate the behavior that leads to success, not just the success itself. I recently worked with a fine, growing organization that markets extended warranties for cars and boats. A sizable portion of their business is generated through telephone solicitation. One of the group leaders in the phone room decided to employ what some might consider an unusual motivational strategy: "Everywhere I've ever worked, the recognition and awards have gone to the top producers—the salesperson of the month or salesperson of the quarter," she explained. "I wanted to let my group know I appreciated their efforts, as well as their results. So I started to award trophies for the sales rep who demonstrated the biggest improvement each month. You should see the change in attitude!"

Earlier, I cited a complaint I hear from managers who do not properly understand the use of encouraging words in motivation: "I need people around me who can take the ball and run with it. For goodness' sake, I'm not a baby-sitter!" It is important to respond to this, because the answer lies in one of the important characteristics of reinforcing behavior. As time passes, and the positive performance has become a habit, we can reduce the *frequency* of the positive reinforcement. We should never eliminate it, because a culture that elicits extraordinary performance thrives on positive reinforcement. But we do not need to provide later on the steady diet of reinforcement that we have to apply in the early stages of shaping behavior. As time passes, and we see that a particular individual is consistently exhibiting the kind of behavior we desire, we can moderate the frequency of reinforcement.

There is another reason why top leaders always remember to reinforce the positive performance of all team members on an intermittent basis: *The less reinforcement that an environment provides, the more the people who live or work in that environment will compete with each other to get it.* This tenet follows the basic economic principle of scarcity. The more scarce something is, the more valuable it becomes. If four men have been wandering in a desert for days without water, and they suddenly discover a small cup of cold water, they may well fight and claw to get to it first. I have seen this kind of behavior take place in expensive, air-conditioned office buildings, as well. If the leader doles out only a limited amount of praise and attention, staffers often engage in politics and backbiting, hoping to acquire some of this precious commodity. Rather than compete with the external competition, these thirsty staffers do battle with each other. Innovative ideas are sabotaged or kept under wraps for fear that someone else might discover it and get the glory. Teamwork becomes a stretch goal, rather than the integral component of success that it should be.

SSIP: A Good Scorecard

The acronym SSIP—Sincere, Specific, Immediate, Personal—is an easy and effective reminder for parents and leaders who wish to check the effectiveness of their reinforcement.

Sincere

Our recognition and celebration must be genuine! The only thing worse than a manager who gives no reinforcement is the motivational wanna-be who breezes through the workplace, airily informing anyone and everyone that they're doing a "great job, great job. Keep up the good work." Such empty talk is meaningless and demotivating.

Many staffers who hear such false acclaim think, *If you were paying any attention, you'd know that I'm not doing a "great job." In fact, I've really been struggling!* Staffers may quite rightly surmise that the manager doesn't care enough about them or their job to actually look and see *how* they are doing! They soon tune out this idle chatter, and the manager's credibility is diminished.

There is another pitfall to the misguided use of "blind reinforcement." If a staffer who *is* putting forth discretionary effort sees a manager praising a slacker, the hard worker actually feels a sense of *punishment* for her extra efforts. The lazy nonproducer is praised, and she is treated no better, or perhaps even ignored. How much of this "reinforcement" do you think it takes to eliminate discretionary effort?

Specific

Many well-meaning managers reinforce the right people but fail to specify the behavior he or she wishes to encourage. Never forget the two reasons why we recognize and celebrate the accomplishments of others:

It's the right thing to do. The mission of leaders who wish to turn ordinary people into extraordinary performers is to build lives and to pass on a legacy of passion and long-term vitality. The use of encouraging words is not a technique we employ, it is the *essence* of the way we want to live and work! We don't put this personality on like a lab coat in the morning, and hang it back up again on a rack in the office when we leave. It is not a five-day philosophy we employ at work but abandon at home. This is a *moment-by-moment* philosophy. Unleashing untapped potential is a *life skill* that we can, through consistent desire and practice, elevate to an art form. We constantly look for ways to reinforce and celebrate our spouse, our children, our neighbor, and our minister. We might use our encouraging words to build an extraordinary human at a toll booth, or in the checkout line at the market. I am not describing *a* way of life—it is *the* way to live. We positively reinforce other human beings because it is consistent with the very essence of our humanity—using words to build something beautiful.

Reinforcement causes behavior to increase. Each and every one of us has some traits that need to be strengthened and reinforced and others that should be reduced or eliminated. Reinforcement increases, extinction and punishment eliminate. If we seek to build others' lives, then we need to recognize and reinforce the strengths of those with whom we live and work. So we should always be specific about those positive traits that we see.

For example, which reinforcement do you believe would be more effective?

- "Ozzie, you really did a fine job with that sales presentation!"

- "Ozzie, that was a great job! You were animated without being overbearing. You asked probing questions that identified the customer's needs. Then you tailored your presentation to show how our product meets those needs. You sold benefits, not features. And you remembered to ask for the order. That's the road that will lead you to a ton of sales!"

Both managers reinforced. But only one shaped the positive performance that she wished to see continue.

Immediate

Immediacy is the third element of effective positive reinforcement. We have already discussed the importance of timing. Timing puts a responsibility on leaders to create a culture of catching people doing something right. Too often we allow good work to pass unremarked, while we immediately jump on mistakes and bad behavior. We are quick to address the *negatives,* not the positives.

Managers have been trained to spot what's gone *wrong* and take immediate steps to correct it. Dear Reader, understand me: I am not saying that an effective manager will never discuss problems.

We all want our leaders to tell us what displeases them, so that we can correct it. At the same time, it is vitally important for *every* spouse, *every* parent, and *every* manager to continually be on the lookout for what's gone *right* and to promptly recognize and celebrate the contributions of others.

Personal

If we wish to generate positive efforts, then it is impermissible for us to take the easy street and say, "The accounting department did a great job this month!" Did they really? Or did some members carry the load, while others idled? Make the extra effort to investigate who shouldered which responsibilities and mention their individual contributions.

Types of Reinforcement

There are three types of positive reinforcement: *natural, social, and tangible.*

Natural

Natural reinforcement occurs without any delivery efforts from another human being. Natural reinforcement is derived from the behavior or accomplishments themselves. That cool, refreshed feeling after a good shower is a natural reinforcer. Pride in a job well done is natural reinforcement. An individual who works in some form of manufacturing often will take pride in seeing neat stacks of a completed product crowding his area. If I take the time to reorganize my cluttered desk, I experience the personal satisfaction of a clean, neat workstation.

An astute leader will look to accentuate the effects of natural reinforcement. One great way to do this is through *diagrammatical visual representation* (e.g., graphs, charts, etc.). What better way to accentuate the natural pride workers take in an increase in production than to post a large, boldly colored graph that depicts that improvement? The graph itself should be as dramatic as possible, with steep lines (I recommend the color green, for "go") clearly showing significant improvement. Be sure to keep these graphs current. Nothing could be more *de*motivating than sweating out July's production schedule and looking up at a large graph that depicts April's output. Can you say "extinction"?

Social

This type of positive reinforcement consists of what you say to people. This reinforcement is primary and essential for people to receive. Remember, we all need to know that who we are and what we do has meaning and significance. However, it is not enough for me to merely know this intellectually. I need to *believe* it. Yes, it involves a leader's time and attention to transmit this sense of belief. But this is what *everyone* in the organization needs to see and hear! Get everyone on the team involved in creating a culture that catches people doing something right, instead of one that nails people doing something wrong! It is not that difficult to create a climate that takes the use of encouraging words seriously. Team reinforcement exponentially multiplies the reinforcement received by all.

Tangible

Tangible reinforcement requires out-of-pocket money. There are two categories here: pay plans and facilitators of social reinforcement.

Money as a motivator. Naturally, every good employer will strive to offer competitive compensation to workers. Companies that are serious about recruiting and retaining the best quality employees put a great deal of effort into creating the most attractive combination of pay and benefits. However, it is my emphatic contention that money is the second most overrated motivator in the manager's toolbox, surpassed only by fear.

A paycheck does not provide much of a consequence for behavior. With the obvious exception of the salesperson who operates on a commission basis, the paycheck comes regardless of our behavior. Sure, some of us receive overtime pay, but that is largely a reflection of *hours worked,* not a result of any particular discretionary effort. Dear Reader, we all work for money, and I'm not saying that companies should discontinue giving raises and overtime compensation. But over and over, I hear managers say, "I give them a good paycheck. What more do they need from me?" The answer is, a *lot* more.

Monetary reward has little or no "salvage value." It provides only short-term reinforcement. Where social reinforcement is primary and necessary, tangible reinforcement is secondary and optional. It is nice if you can provide it, *but it is not essential.* Consider this comment we received during an interview we conducted with the warranty company I mentioned earlier: "I've been offered higher paying jobs with other companies. I don't stay here for the money. I stay because I believe in this company, and they believe in me."

Financial rewards, however pleasing they may be, do not penetrate to our essence. Money does not celebrate my humanity. If we only operate at the financial level, we are operating at the base level. We don't strive to reach the higher plateaus of our personhood. The men and women we work with need a physical paycheck, and we should make every effort to supply workers with competitive wages. Equally important, however, is their need for *psychological paychecks*—positive, encouraging words.

One of the most poignant comments I have ever heard came from a man who had become disillusioned with the trends he saw in his company. He recalled the strong sense of belonging, "family" as he called it, that used to exist in his company and that he felt had eroded over the years. He believed that the family feeling had been displaced by a hardball management style. He concluded by saying sadly, "I used to like working here, but now that this has become just a job, the pay isn't all that good." Since there were no psychological paychecks coming in, his whole focus was now on the *physical* paycheck, and that alone was insufficient.

Tangible reinforcement as an aid to social reinforcement. A second use of tangible reinforcement is to facilitate social reinforcement. These would include plaques, T-shirts, trophies, letters of appreciation, small bonuses, etc. These types of reinforcement are *cognitive*—what they represent is important, not what they actually are.

A perfect example is the phone room supervisor I mentioned earlier who gave small trophies to the most improved salesperson of the month. She bought these trophies with her own money. The cost of the trophies was unimportant. They were merely a symbol of the primary, social reinforcement that the supervisor wanted to provide. The trophies provided a visual reminder of the supervisor's effort to catch people doing something right.

Our Attitudes Shape Our Actions

So far in this book we have discussed the idea of a worthy model of man. We are discussing reality—the truth of human dignity. We need to honor that human dignity—from the elderly to the embryo, and certainly in the arena of employee relations. It is a fact that individuals and organizations cannot rise any farther than their philosophical foundations. The philosophy of the leadership of any organization will shape the *culture* of that organization. The culture consists of the beliefs, attitudes, and the interrelationships of the firm; it is the heartbeat of the company. From that culture come both the *antecedents* and the *consequences* that are provided by the organization to the people who work there. The culture we create is the foundation for the success of any home or business.

Therefore, if we begin with a *great* foundation (and what foundation could possibly be more great and true than the dignity and worth of all humanity, created in God's image?), we will rise to unprecedented heights of passionate performance and prosperity! And we will begin this meteoric journey only when we acknowledge, respect, and value these aspects that are so intrinsic to our human nature! Our words are some of the most powerful tools we possess to demonstrate our belief in the value of people.

Encouraging words *do* build extraordinary human beings. We can use our words as our Creator did—to bring life and health and hope to the people around us. As we make value deposits in others, we are also making value deposits in ourselves. It is my prayer that you will personally experience this joy, as I have. Don't miss the opportunity!

Quality Relationships Undergird Success

4

GOD IS A SOCIAL BEING. "The LORD God said, 'It is not good that man should be alone'" (Gen. 2:18). God created family. God is the grounding for all relationships. He said it was not good for us to operate in isolation, but rather in community. The highest freedom I have is the freedom to love others. King David, the man after God's heart, wrote, "Behold, how good and how pleasant it is / For brethren to dwell together in unity!" (Ps. 133:1).

In order to faithfully respond to the truth of our social nature, it is important to absorb the principles of unity and diversity. One way of expressing this idea is through the age-old concept of "the One and the Many." The human body is the perfect living example. Your body is the One, the sum total of its many parts and partnerships. Each of us has one body. The One gives us our unity, our sameness. Within each of our bodies are 206 bones[1] of assorted shapes, sizes, and strength, ranging all the way from the large and incredibly strong femur bone in our leg to the tiny, delicate bones of the inner ear. These 206 bones of the body are the Many. The Many equals diversity, the widely varied members of one unified system. Each member is vitally important and makes its own unique, indispensable contribution. God, Himself, is the ultimate example of this principle. He is the One, God. But He is also the Many: God the Father, God the Son, and God the Holy Spirit.

All of thought, indeed, all of life, is a reflection of the eternal truth of the One and the Many. In expressing ideas and concepts, there is no such thing as a fact (the Many) that is unrelated to a principle (the One), and no principle is unrelated to facts. It is meaningless to express brute factuality unless those facts are united by an overarching principle. The environmentalists of the 1970s did us an enormous service by demonstrating the unity and diversity of the ecosystems that exist on earth. All of the members of an ecosystem, from the tiniest microscopic forms of life to the most massive, are vitally interrelated and completely dependent on each other for survival. No one member enjoys superiority over the other.

Unity and diversity enjoy *equal ultimacy*—one is not reducible by the other. The East has said that truth (ultimacy) lies with unity—the team, the society (the One). The West has placed ultimacy on diversity—the individual, the entrepreneur (the Many). Both of these approaches reflect a lack of balance. If you take the East's focus on the One to its extreme, you arrive at despotism, authoritarianism, and communism. On the other hand, if you follow the West's emphasis on the Many to its logical outcome, you tumble into anarchy and rebellion. We must not sacrifice unity on the altar of diversity, and the reverse is true as well. It is vitally important to have *balance!*

Marriage is another example. The married couple are the One; the man and the woman are the Many. If one partner is consistently elevated in importance over the other, if that one partner is given unequal ultimacy, then there *is* no unity, and the One, the marriage partnership suffers. *Connectedness* is the substructure of all reality.

Our Unity and Diversity as Individuals

Dear Reader, the twelve truths of our humanity that we share give us our *unity* as human beings. One of the best ways we can build community is to concentrate on what we have in common with others. We should celebrate that unity, that oneness that we enjoy as human beings. Our unity is our strength, our identity. At the same time, it is absolutely essential that we recognize and celebrate our diversity. Every individual represents a unique combination of strengths, talents, and brilliance. Each of us has different weaknesses and areas for improvement, as well. Where one is strong, another is weak. This diversity, rather than being a source of comparison and competition, should be a source of wonder and admiration.

Our strength lies not in our independence but in our *interdependence,* our interconnection. This is where we strike the critically important balance between unity and diversity. When we acknowledge the importance of each individual's diverse contribution to the dynamically effective whole, we will then achieve our maximum effectiveness.

Only when we recognize our unity and diversity as individuals can we achieve the good communication and quality relationships that are the foundation to success. One way to do this is to examine the tendencies of our personalities. Some of us share certain personality traits with others. At other times, our personalities may be so widely disparate that, unless we build a bridge of awareness regarding our differences, meaningful communication becomes virtually impossible.

Let's look at our own inclinations, with the goal of learning to appreciate the strengths of other personality styles that differ dramatically from our own, and ultimately developing strategies that enable us to encourage *style synergies* within our personal spheres of influence. *Synergy* means, literally, "together energy." In the context of this discussion, I define *synergy* as "the maximization of our collective potential." I want to discuss how to act in *community,* in *concert* with each other. In learning the marvelously diverse ways in which we interact, you will broaden your response range to dispositions that differ from your own.

What Are Your Tendencies?

Please work quickly through the following twenty questions, selecting the answer that *most nearly* describes your response to people or situations. I understand that the responses provided won't always describe you exactly, or cover the myriad emotions and reactions that are generated within each of us. When you read each question, ask yourself, "In general, which of these answers *usually* would apply to me?" Move through the questions rapidly, trusting in your intuitive response, which is usually the most accurate.

1. I like to help people
   1) understand the proper facts.
   2) enjoy themselves.
   3) accomplish a task.
   4) feel better.

2. I rarely hear myself say,
   1) "I'll do it immediately."
   2) "I'll give this careful thought and study."
   3) "I'll do whatever you say."
   4) "You're wrong."

3. I most desire to
   1) understand.
   2) have fun.
   3) conquer challenge.
   4) forge closer relationships.

4. I would describe myself as
   1) thoughtful and deliberate.
   2) friendly and energetic.
   3) goal-oriented and driven.
   4) loyal and committed.

5. I have the most difficulty with

    1) operating at a rapid pace for extended periods.

    2) following up every little detail.

    3) being patient with others' procrastination and weaknesses.

    4) asserting myself.

6. I enjoy giving people

    1) correct information.

    2) a laugh.

    3) a challenge.

    4) a helping hand.

7. I could easily put together a long list of

    1) facts about a given subject.

    2) my friends.

    3) my goals.

    4) my values.

8. I most dislike

    1) being rushed.

    2) being alone.

    3) losing.

    4) attacking someone.

9. I am motivated by

    1) a desire to learn and the satisfaction of a job well done.

    2) excitement and variety.

    3) challenge and crisis.

    4) building relationships with others.

10. My decisions are usually

    1) careful and reasoned.

    2) emotional and impulsive.

3) quick and decisive.

4) based on others' feelings, as well as my own.

11. My friends would most likely say that I am

1) careful and knowledgeable.

2) friendly and fun to be with.

3) strong and fearless.

4) loyal and patient.

12. I most fear

1) chaos and crisis.

2) being disliked.

3) losing control.

4) confrontation.

13. I dislike people who are

1) making me hurry.

2) boring.

3) weak.

4) insensitive.

14. I am confident that

1) I can learn a lot about almost anything.

2) I can overcome most obstacles by the power of my personality.

3) I can meet and master any challenge.

4) I will always treasure my friends and family over financial success.

15. When I have an important decision to make, I would be most likely to

1) gather all the relevant information, consider it thoroughly, and then arrive at a carefully reasoned decision.

2) make a snap decision based on my feelings at the time, and I might change my mind later.

3) quickly arrive at the best possible decision, and I expect others to go along.

4) ask others how they would be affected by the consequences of my actions, and I would try to consider their best interests, not just my own.

16. If I could select only one word to describe myself, it would be
1) intelligent.
2) friendly.
3) strong.
4) faithful.

17. I enjoy
1) learning.
2) talking.
3) winning.
4) giving.

18. I prefer to do things
1) the correct way. I like things to be done accurately.
2) the fun way. I enjoy variety and excitement.
3) my way. I like to be in charge.
4) the nonconfrontational way. I'd rather not conflict with the desires of others.

19. I like people who are
1) logical and patient.
2) spontaneous and energetic.
3) capable and cooperative.
4) friendly and kind.

20. I like to think that I am
   1) correct.
   2) cheerful.
   3) in control.
   4) compassionate.

And the Survey Says . . .

Add up the number of questions you answered with Response #1, with Response #2, and so on. Write your totals below:

_____ 1 (Thinker)   _____ 3 (Achiever)

_____ 2 (Energizer)   _____ 4 (Mediator)

If you answered the most questions with Response #1, your preferred personality style is that of a Thinker. If you answered the most questions with Response #2, you are primarily an Energizer. A preponderance of Response #3s indicates that you are mainly an Achiever, and if the majority of your answers were Response #4, you are predominantly a Mediator.

Within each of us, there is a blend of all four of the personality quadrants, but most of us employ what I call a preferred style and a backup style. Our preferred style is our "autopilot" style, the one we access without effort or thought, especially when we are excited or stressed. Most of us also draw heavily from at least one of the other four temperaments.

A few of you have an almost equal balance of answers. You have come close to five answers from all four categories, or to six or seven answers from three of the categories. While this is more rare than the primary-and-backup-style pattern I have just described, you should be pleased that your personality is more fully rounded than many of us. Our goal should be to access the strengths of all four of these personality styles, so the closer you are to doing that naturally, the better!

THINKER

Description	Strengths	Weaknesses	Desires	Dislikes
Learner	Logical	Inflexible	Knowledge	Risk
Analytical	Reasoning	Critical	Competence	Hurry
Competent	Thorough	Perfectionistic	Systems	Hype
Intelligent	Planner	Impatient	Details	Disorder
Methodical	Organized	Indecisive	Security	Surprise

Affirmations	Developmental Needs	Likely Attributes	Likely "T"s
Precision	Patience	Intelligent	Sherlock Holmes
Respect	Interpersonal skills	Imaginative	Albert Einstein
Completion	Enthusiasm	Self-determined	Ted Koppel
Competence	Stress management	Purposeful	George Bush
Consultation	Time management	Self-conscious	Janet Reno

ENERGIZER

Description	Strengths	Weaknesses	Desires	Dislikes
Stimulating	Communication	Taking criticism	Excitement	Routine
Enthusiastic	Motivation	Impulsiveness	Challenge	Dry data
Gregarious	Relationships	Planning	Recognition	Isolation
Impulsive	Creativity	Execution	Goals	Indecision
Emotional	Humor	Ego	Actualization	Rigidity

Affirmations	Developmental Needs	Likely Attributes	Likely "E"s
Listening	Planning	Verbal	Rush Limbaugh
Conversation	Calm	Emotional	Bob Euker
Openness	Time management	Imaginative	Rosie O'Donnell
Enthusiasm	Focus	Social	Bill Clinton
Celebration	Teamwork	Physical	Robin Williams

ACHIEVER

Description	Strengths	Weaknesses	Desires	Dislikes
Bold	Decision making	Insensitive	Results	Weaknesss
Confident	Crisis management	Impatient	Efficiency	Sentiment
Competitive	Perseverance	Domineering	Compliance	Losing
Creative	Leadership	Poor listener	Competition	Compromise
Forceful	Risk taking	Quick to anger	Challenge	Boredom

Affirmations	Developmental Needs	Likely Attributes	Likely "A"s
Financial success	Interpersonal skills	Self-sufficient	Chuck Yeager
Respect	Stress management	Self-determined	Norman Schwarzkopf
Professional success	Listening skills	Purposeful	Jimmy Johnson
Accomplishment	Patience	Visionary	Hillary Rodham Clinton
Innovation	Warmth	Imaginative	George Steinbrenner

MEDIATOR

Description	Strengths	Weaknesses	Desires	Dislikes
Loyal	Service	Overcompliant	Security	Change
Patient	Dedication	Indecisive	Tradition	Discourtesy
Reliable	Listening	Cautious	Relationships	Conflict
Trustworthy	Team playing	Passive	Kindness	Aggression
Peacekeeping	Interpersonal skills	Slow to change	Belonging	Insincerity

Affirmations	Developmental Needs	Likely Attributes	Likely "M"s
Support	Decision-making skills	Social	"Ashley Wilkes"
Explanation	Conflict-resolution skills	Purposeful	Joan Lunden
Appreciation	Assertiveness	Principled	Barbara Bush
Reassurance	Accepting challenge	Verbal	Bob Dole
Encouragement	Accepting change	Spiritual	Gen. Omar Bradley

The Four Faces of Personhood

Before I jump into this fascinating study of people and personalities, I wish to present one word of caution. Please bear in mind that these four quadrants of personality are designed to describe general *tendencies* only! There are absolutely no hard-and-fast rules when it comes to human nature. As you read these descriptions of the strengths, attributes, and desires that characterize the four personality styles, remember that no one fits these parameters exactly. For example, it's just my guess, based on my observations, that the famous people I've mentioned in the preceding chart fall into these categories. If I knew them intimately, I might well find that they are totally, delightfully different from the personalities I perceive. That is why I say that each and every human being is a walking marvel, miracle, and mystery, because God created every human being to be magnificently unique! We are so tremendously complex, we'll never completely come to know ourselves, so how could we possibly hope to thoroughly know someone else? The answer is, of course, that we can't. But these patterns of behavior described on the following pages will help you appreciate and relate to others. You will gain greater enjoyment for people who behave and react differently from you and acquire a clearer vision of where their strengths lie.

Learn to love the differences in people around you! Jesus Christ said the two greatest commandments were to love God and to love people. Loving people is not just the right thing to do, it is the only way to live. When we have learned how to build quality relationships, we will model *partnership* and *interdependency*. We will recognize and celebrate the talents, strengths, and abilities of the people with whom we live and work, and we will offer to lend our strengths in the areas where our partners are struggling. We will delight in the differences of others, because we understand that God created us in spectacular diversity. It was never God's plan for us to fit into some identical, cookie-cutter mold. In our remarkable diversity, we represent the incredible complexity of the mind and the nature of God!

True growth will never occur in isolation. Growth occurs in *community*. We help others to grow stronger by partnering with them and encouraging them to flex the muscles of their personality. We offer to lend our own unique blend of the four personality quadrants to help them become more totally human and alive totally. When we do those things, we are modeling recognition and celebration of the human spirit. Notice that I've designed the four personality quadrants—Thinker, Energizer, Achiever, and Mediator—to form one acronym: TEAM. Don't read only about the quadrant you fall into. Learn about each personality style so you can know how to draw on the strength of others and deal with them effectively to form one efficient, harmonious TEAM.

The Thinker

Thorough, organized, and deliberate, Thinkers are essential to every team. When we need information about a particular subject, we immediately turn to the Thinker, who either remembers the facts we need or knows exactly where to find them. When we are about to make an emotional snap decision, the Thinker reminds us of the "cold realities." Although the more impulsive members of the team may become impatient with their cautious, logical approach, we ignore their counsel at our peril, because it is always well reasoned. When a work group begins a project of problem solving or process improvement, it is essential to include at least one strong Thinker on the team.

Thinkers are logical and painstaking. They possess strong planning and organizational skills. They enjoy learning and therefore are not easily intimidated or bored by reams of information, technical manuals, or computer data that might discourage others. Thinkers are tremendous administrators.

As conversation swirls around them, Thinkers listen, consider, and formulate ideas. If we ask them for their opinion, they may actually hesitate for a noticeable moment before responding, while they organize their thoughts in logical order. A Thinker would never dream of buying a new car on impulse and would be somewhat disdainful of anyone who did. He would visit several dealerships, collect brochures, sift through all the information, check the weekend classified ads for all the best advertised prices, and so on. Thinkers will not be rushed to a decision and are suspicious of anyone who tries to force them to hurry their decision-making process.

This instinctive caution can be a weakness for some Thinkers. While most successful entrepreneurs are risk takers by nature, the Thinker may be so averse to risk that he becomes paralyzed by indecision. There is never quite enough information available to allow them to take the plunge. Furthermore, Thinkers want to be respected for their thought processes and may become resentful if their carefully reasoned cautions are ignored, while a bolder leader moves ahead on a plan with which the Thinker disagrees.

In dealing with others, Thinkers have to guard against coming across as dour or dry. Their need for information and for the time to study and verify it can strike some as fussy or prissy. Sometimes their studious attention to the minutiae can manifest itself in a personality that seems aloof, bland, or emotionless. Thinkers may be perceived as lacking warmth, and they must constantly remind themselves to strive to make the *emotional connection* with others, particularly with the Energizer and the Mediator. Indeed, being naturally cautious, Thinkers are usually the least outgoing of the four groups, and an innate shyness coupled with above average intelligence can easily be mistaken for arrogance by others. Indeed, Thinkers often are the slowest of the four groups to form deep friendships. But when they do, they can be as good and loyal a friend as one could possibly hope to have. The old phrase "Still water runs deep" accurately describes the Thinker.

Thinkers must also guard against a tendency to be too wordy. They quite naturally wish to share and explain their carefully reasoned analyses in detail, which may exasperate the results-oriented Achiever and bore the Energizer. The Thinker wants to build a clock, the Achiever just wants to know what time it is! The fun-loving Energizer is far more likely to jump from concept to concept, quite content to focus on "the big picture," and does not share the Thinker's desire to explore a subject in detail. When a proposal is made to Thinkers, their analytical minds immediately begin to explore the pros and cons of the idea, and since some of their more emotional counterparts may be extolling the virtues of a new idea, Thinkers may often feel compelled to play the devil's advocate and come up with a formidable list of negatives. Their crisp, precise language may drive the Mediator, who dislikes confrontation, into retreat, and may aggravate the Achiever, who will perceive the Thinker's caution as resistance.

Thinkers need to guard against impatience. They can easily become cutting or sarcastic with those who react emotionally to situations rather than applying logic. Thinkers are irritated by incompetence, and many are not good teachers. *They* have taken the time to learn and master a particular skill or discipline, and they believe others should not take shortcuts. Furthermore, they are loathe to repeat themselves if they feel they are restating that which is glaringly obvious (to them), though others may have not yet caught up with their train of thought.

Thinkers despise rush and chaos (something that Energizers thrive on). The Thinker student begins work on a reading or research project several weeks before it is actually due. In business situations, however, they often need to be monitored to ensure that they are not falling behind on a project. Thinkers may frequently run afoul of time constraints; in fact, they often resist them, since there is *always* more data to be gathered and processed. Business leaders must be careful not to apply too much pressure. Unlike the typical Energizer or Achiever, Thinkers do *not* respond well to tension or pressure and may begin to slow down under stress, in order to make doubly sure not to make a crucial mistake.

Being somewhat critical by nature, Thinkers have a strong tendency to internalize criticism and allow it to fester within themselves. The high-powered personalities of the Achiever and Energizer often never realize how deeply a thoughtless remark can wound, or even cripple, the introspective Thinker or Mediator. Thinkers will often list time and stress management skills as areas for personal development.

Thinkers may be accountants, lawyers, academicians, writers, researchers, surgeons, artists, historians, scientists, underwriters, or engineers. Of the four personality quadrants, Thinkers will likely enjoy computers the most, and will often be found flourishing in this dramatically expanding field. While Achievers and Energizers are motivated by challenge and risk, the Thinker, like the Mediator, has a strong desire for security, stability, and tradition.

Bringing Out the Best in Thinkers

- Give them time!

- Avoid hyperbole and exaggeration.

- Allow them to ask questions.

- Make allowances for their natural caution.

- Include them, rather than dictate to them.

The Energizer

Energizers are the most popular people in any group. When you hear that someone is a real "people-person," you can make a safe guess that the individual being discussed is an Energizer. Blending and bonding with others appear effortless for them. A great many of the top salespeople you will meet have a dominant or secondary

Energizer personality. They are bright, articulate, and funny. Place them in a roomful of strangers, and the Energizer will move right out, shaking hands and making friends. Full of good cheer and easily enthused, Energizers exude the emotional pizazz the Thinker lacks. They do not dwell on the past, and the future plays little part in their thought processes, so Energizers are eternal optimists. Energizers, therefore, are most likely to clash with Thinkers, who are natural historians and who carefully consider the future consequences of every action. The Thinker distrusts the Energizer for being too impulsive, and the Energizer easily loses patience with the Thinker's quiet caution.

Energizers are highly imaginative and creative, and they love to develop, test, and discard new ideas. They respond with delight to new ideas, new people, and new challenges. "If it could be done, how would we do it?" is a question that resonates with the visionary Energizer. Details and planning, however, are not areas of strength, and the Energizer is easily bored by the very data that fascinates the Thinker. In fact, Energizers often struggle with overcommitment, because so many ideas are innovative and intriguing, and the busy Energizer genuinely wants to be involved with all of them! As a result, Energizers may find themselves racing frantically from project to project, juggling too many balls at one time. This situation is exacerbated by the Energizer's sincere desire to please everyone. They aren't particularly good at saying no. As a result, Energizers are the most likely to miss deadlines, show up late for appointments, and so on. When this happens, the Energizer is unfazed. He pushes on with his usual good cheer, assuming that all will soon be forgotten. The Energizer child begins reading the book assigned in school on Friday—and the book *report* is due Monday!

The Energizer and the Achiever both enjoy challenge and change, although for two different reasons. The Achiever wants to *manage* change and *conquer* challenges. The Energizer responds to challenges with delight because they are fresh and new. They like to turn things upside down and examine them in a new light. Unlike cautious Thinkers or Mediators, Energizers may move from job to job and experiment with several different careers. It's more fun that way! Similarly, Energizers usually have an enormous circle of friends, most of whom they would sincerely consider "close friends," which makes them tremendous networkers and promoters. Energizers are singularly suited for the world of politics, because they genuinely delight in meeting and talking to new people, and they do not dwell on the unpleasantness of the past. Although Energizers are discouraged by defeat, that unhappiness is quickly forgotten with the emergence of some new adventure.

In dealing with others, Energizers are genuinely surprised to learn that they are sometimes viewed with some distrust by the other personality groups. Thinkers are quietly envious of the Energizer's ability to relate to others or speak in front of groups of people, but they are irritated by what they see as the irresponsibility of overcommitment and tardiness and are alarmed by the Energizer's impulsiveness. Energizers have found that they can accomplish a great deal by the power of their personality, so when they make proposals to the fact-finding Thinker, the Thinker is likely to perceive their emotional approach as lacking substance. Energizers are almost always in a hurry, which violates the Thinker's need for a calm, rational approach.

Mediators are more introverted than the gregarious Energizer and envy the easy way that the Energizer relates to people, but sometimes the Mediator finds the Energizer too glib. The loyal Mediator does not develop as many friends, but forges deep relational bonds with close associates. The Energizer truly enjoys people and wants to spend as much time with as many of them as possible, emulating the bee in moving from person to person quickly. The more the merrier! The Mediator dislikes this apparent lack of commitment and bonding.

Words like *dogged* and *persistent* do not describe the Energizer, and this repels the Achiever. Achievers dive with equal enthusiasm into a new activity, but they "stick to it" until it has been mastered, long after the fun-loving Energizer has lost interest. The Achiever believes the Energizer lacks commitment. The Achiever wants to hear about the bottom line, the results. The Energizer excels at storytelling, and loves to paint all the humorous and emotional details into a word picture, which drives the terse Achiever to the point of apoplexy.

Bringing Out the Best in the Energizer

- Let them talk.

- Remember that Energizers are often highly creative. Listen to their suggestions.

- Don't bog them down with too many details.

- Be sure to follow up on them.

- Take some time for personal conversation before getting down to business.

The Achiever

If there were no Achievers, frankly, most of us would be standing in line outside a soup kitchen. Achievers are *doers,* the entrepeneurs and explorers. They are natural commanders, and most great military leaders are Achievers. If you want to motivate an Achiever, say "It can't be done," and then get out of the way! In any successful organization, the owner, the president, or whoever is responsible for "steering the ship" will most often be an Achiever.

Achievers are conquerors. They combine the Energizer's love for challenge with the Thinker's ability to plan. Where the Energizer envisions a castle in the air, the Achiever sees the same castle and is busy building the road that will carry her there. An Achiever has absolutely no qualms about taking charge of the construction crew!

Achievers are easily the biggest risk takers of the four personalities, which they combine with a dogged determination to succeed. Nobody hates losing like the Achiever. Many Achievers even have difficulty ever allowing their children to win at games they play together. One man told me recently, "I play basketball with my son, and I play to win. When he finally beats me, he's gonna know he beat my best." And if his son is also an Achiever, each successive loss will make him that much more determined to come back next time and win. The other personalities, however, would not respond so well. They might well grow to *loathe* basketball, and, far worse, the father who forces them to continue to compete at it.

Anytime a position requires the meeting and mastering of challenge, there will be a preponderance of Achievers lining up for the job. You will find them in management, sales, professional sports (both playing and coaching), government, and the starting up of tens of thousands of new business ventures every year.

Achievers must constantly work at developing their people skills. Of all four personality types, the Achiever group places the least importance on relationships. "Bonding" just isn't that high on their list of things to do! As a result, most Achievers are respected by those who work for them, and some are feared, but often they inspire no sense of love or loyalty. Regrettably, this is often true even at home.

Achievers often struggle with supplying positive reinforcement and encouragement. There is a combination of factors at work here. First, of all the groups, Achievers have the least desire for words of encouragement. Far more than any of the other personalities, Achievers draw immense personal satisfaction from achieving goals. One strong indicator of an Achiever personality is an office or den decorated with plaques, trophies, etc. Achievers *like* displays at work that indicate the top salesperson. Energizers like the applause and recognition that go with winning; the Achiever would rather see the results. The big bonus check that comes at the end of the month, along with her name on the plaque for "Salesperson of the Month," is all the reward that the Achiever needs or wants. I lost count long ago of the number of high-powered Achievers who told me, "I don't need somebody coming along, patting me on the back and telling me I'm doing a great job. I *know* when I'm doing well."

It is this very self-sufficiency that causes Achievers to totally miss the mark when they are trying to motivate others. They assume that everyone else thinks the way they do! (Don't we all?) So the results-minded Achiever may never praise those he lives and works with, *not* because he doesn't notice or care, but because he doesn't think *words* are important! To him, *results* count! Meanwhile, there are others on the team and in the home, particularly the relationship-minded Mediator, who will run through walls for a few kind words! But that praise is often not forthcoming. "I give them a paycheck every week," thinks the Achiever. "Hey, if they were doing a bad job, you can bet I'd let them know right away! What else do they want?" Again, this is not a result of coldness but a lack of awareness. Achievers, who draw great satisfaction from accomplishment, assume that everyone else feels the same way, and they are often truly puzzled to learn that they are considered "cold" and "unapproachable" by others.

This approach frequently operates at home, particularly among Achiever husbands. "I make a good living," he reasons, "we live in a nice house in a good neighborhood, the kids go to private school—what more does she want?" Well, of course, his wife wants a *lot* more: hugs, conversation, empathy, and an occasional kind word. One author has noted that Achievers tend to marry more introspective Thinkers or Mediators. These sensitive souls may find their self-esteem shredded after years of marriage, and the Achiever is often totally unaware of the intense emotional and psychological suffering their partner is enduring.

A second factor involved here is the mental toughness of the Achiever personality. As Vince Lombardi (a prototypical Achiever) once said, "Winning isn't the most important thing, it is the only thing."[2] Achievers are rarely cowed by defeat. In fact, losing just makes them that much more determined to come back to fight another day. They do not realize that the "sticks and stones" of life that bounce harmlessly off them may deeply wound others. Tell an Achiever, "You're no good," or "You can't do that," and they respond with a cold determination to prove you wrong. Other personality types may never forget it. Many will internalize a thoughtless remark, replay it in their memory, and begin to believe it.

Consequently, when an Achiever loses his temper (and Achievers can have *volcanic* tempers), they may say something that is cutting or cruel and forget about it quickly. But the recipient of their wrath may be deeply wounded or resentful. The Mediator, in particular, dislikes conflict and probably won't respond to an unjust remark, but he'll never forget it. This can be destructive in a marriage, *disastrous* in the emotional development of children, and damaging to professional relationships as well. Again, it boils down to a bad assumption that many of us make: that others react to situations the same way we do. The tough-minded Achiever lets a slight or a careless word roll off his back, figuring it is just one of the bumps in the rough-and-tumble road of life. He does not always pause to consider how deeply such a remark may cut or how long the wound may take to heal.

Another quality that can drive a wedge between the Achiever and others is impatience. Achievers can be ruthlessly self-critical and are natural "do it now" types. They have zero tolerance for their own mistakes (in extreme cases they may believe they never make them), and brook no procrastination within themselves. Some Achievers may hold others to the same exacting standards. You hear beleaguered staffers muttering darkly, "No matter what I do, it's never enough." Some of the other personalities, particularly the cautious Thinker, just do not react well to the kind of hard-charging pressure that Achievers thrive on. Achievers continually need to be reminded that some other personality quadrants do not wear well under pressure. As we mentioned earlier, the Thinker may actually *slow down* when rushed, in an earnest desire to make sure that they do *not* make a mistake.

Lastly, Achievers must guard against a tendency to react negatively to questions. The Thinker, in his desire for perfection, and the Mediator, wishing to avoid conflict, both tend to ask many questions, and some Achievers mistake these cautious queries for challenges to their authority. To avoid this problem, the Achiever must recognize others' needs for complete information.

Bringing out the Best in Achievers

- Don't waste time with small talk.
- You will have to help them delegate. (Remember that Achievers like control.)
- Don't let them intimidate you.
- Always, always set new goals and challenges.
- Show them how they will benefit professionally and financially.

The Mediator

Above all else, Mediators are motivated by a desire to bond with other people. You will find the highest percentage of this group in professions that require the giving of love and care: nursing, teaching, social work, religious leaders, personnel positions, and the like. Mediators are intensely loyal and are always on the lookout for people and causes to identify with and serve faithfully. While many of us will almost instinctively look at a new person or situation and wonder, "What can I gain?" the Mediator will likely think, "How can I contribute?" Mediators are *givers*.

Mediators are great listeners and demonstrate their love for others by listening carefully and empathetically, often to a complete stranger! My good friend Dan Philips, the director of training for my consulting firm, has strong Mediator tendencies. He genuinely, deeply cares for the people he serves. He bonds with them immediately. He'll often return to the office brimming with enthusiasm about the people he has met. On other days, I will find him troubled by the personal problems that someone has revealed to him during a confidential interview. He really and truly pours himself into the people he works with. He is a man who gives and loves.

Where the Achiever is motivated by accomplishment, the Mediator is motivated by kindness. Where the Energizer loves the roar of the crowd, the Mediator loves to hear, "Thanks. You really helped me." Where the Thinker desires to study and learn, the Mediator desires to encourage and contribute. One of the easiest ways to motivate Mediators is to show them how their efforts will benefit others.

Mediators are often some of the best team players in the organization. They are steady, loyal, always looking to encourage their coworkers, and willing to go the extra mile. A Mediator who is properly reinforced will often work very well under pressure. They are quite willing to sacrifice if their family, teammates, or the organization will benefit.

In dealing with others, the Mediator usually has the most difficulty with the Achiever. While it is *very* common to find an Achiever with strong Energizer tendencies, or vice versa, it is rare to find a true Mediator who possesses many Achiever characteristics. The two personality types don't mesh well. Of the four personalities, Mediators most dislike conflict and have a tendency to either surrender quickly or withdraw when tension begins to build. This has disastrous consequences when dealing with the Achiever, who often *enjoys* a good scrap and has little respect for someone who won't assert themselves. A vicious circle builds. The Mediator desires above all else to get along with others. The Achiever often pushes others hard to see when they will begin to push back, and the Achiever's respect actually increases for those who stand up to him! But when the amiable Mediator gets pushed, he'll often surrender, hoping that the other person will appreciate his accommodating spirit. Unfortunately, the Achiever perceives that cooperation as weakness, and will push even harder to see just when the unfailingly agreeable Mediator will finally push back!

The Achiever and Mediator are spurred by entirely different factors. The Mediator manager must remember that an Achiever is far more gratified by tangible rewards and recognition than he is, and the Mediator's well-intentioned words of encouragement do very little to spur the Achiever on to her highest and her best. Conversely, the Mediator who works for an Achiever must remember that the Achiever who offers little verbal reinforcement is *not* necessarily a "cold fish," but just doesn't recognize the Mediator's desire for emotional support. In fact, a Mediator in this situation would do well to review Chapter 3 to gain insight on encouraging his boss to provide him with the recognition he desires.

While the Mediator is not as outgoing as the Energizer, she is still very personable, always on the lookout for a new friend, and likes to talk and relate and bond. Therefore, the Mediator has to guard against a tendency to find the Thinker too quiet and standoffish. Where the chatty Energizer is not as easily rebuffed by silence, the Mediator may mistake the Thinker's silence for quiet disapproval. The Mediator and the Thinker often disagree on decisions, since the Thinker will make a decision based on information, where the Mediator is more likely to operate according to her emotions and make a decision based on feelings, hers and especially those of others.

It isn't uncommon to meet someone who possesses a number of Energizer and Mediator characteristics. These two types have a lot in common. Mediators and Energizers genuinely enjoy meeting new people and making friends (although the Mediator's friendships tend to run longer and deeper), and they are motivated more by their emotions than their intellect. So it comes as no surprise that these two groups tend to interact fairly well, but there are some areas in which they can conflict, as well. As I said previously, the Mediator may instinctively mistrust the Energizer, thinking that the Energizer is too much of a "love-'em-and-leave-'em" type of friend. The naturally cautious Mediator may see the Energizer as too glib and hold him at arm's length.

Mediators often need to deliberately work at improving their assertiveness. A Mediator manager may have difficulty reprimanding problem employees. They are happy to *encourage* the underachiever, but they aren't particularly good at confronting or counseling them. This can have unpleasant results for both parties involved. When the Mediator is finally forced to crack down, the other party in question may be furious because they feel they weren't given the proper warning signals. The Mediator, in a misguided effort to "be nice," may delay far too long before addressing an unpleasant problem. The other side of the equation is that the Mediator may become resentful when someone does not respond to her gentle, supportive approach. "I bent over backward for that person," you'll hear a frustrated manager say. "I encouraged them; I even took on extra work to help them keep their head above water, and *nothing* helped them! They just didn't respond! Well, I've had it. No more Mr. Nice Guy!" This Mediator did do everything—everything except confront the problem and lay out the steps needed to improve.

This tendency to "go along to get along" can be particularly dangerous in a marriage, where a long-suffering Mediator may stay with an abusive, alcoholic, or unfaithful spouse long past the point where the necessity for intervention would be considered blindingly obvious to anyone else. Another danger here is that the Mediator is the most likely to internalize the slights that are dealt them, year after year, until they finally reach the point of critical mass (which will be a point farther down the line than anyone else would go), and when they finally do explode, it is with a blind fury that eclipses even the Achiever's. At this point, the suddenly transformed Mediator will spew out *years* of anger and frustration, and may well say things that are so destructive that it is impossible to repair what has now become a gulf that separates them from the other party. Worse yet, some Mediators will *never* turn on the other party. Instead they direct their anger inward and destroy *themselves* through alcohol, drugs, or even suicide.

Bringing Out the Best in Mediators

- Give them time to adjust to change.

- Show them how change will benefit others. They love to contribute to others' well-being.

- Remember what motivates them. Your words motivate them!

- Know that values are important to them.

- Help them to meet and resolve conflict successfully.

A Symphony of Interrelationship

Think of the last time you heard a piece of music that touched you emotionally. Whatever the song or music that lifted your spirits, I'll bet all the instruments or all the voices weren't playing or singing the same note at the same time, were they? Once again, it comes back to the principle of unity and diversity. A choir, for example, will perform a particular song. They are unified by the tempo, the key structure, and the harmonic plan defined by that particular piece. Above all, the choir is unified by the purpose of supporting and expressing the music. At the same time, there is considerable diversity that exists within the performance of that one song. Different units may begin or end their singing at different times, different choir members may sing different words, some giving voice to rapidly moving parts that add fire and excitement, while others are voicing slow, sustained tones that provide harmonic support. This is what makes the song a beautiful one. *Beauty* lies in symmetry, balance, and harmony. These are the true elements of beauty. If all the voices were singing the same thing at the same time, or if all the musicians were playing exactly the same note, nobody would listen for long.

Simple beauty comes from simple relationships. Sophisticated beauty comes from complex interrelationship. Four-part harmony is a far more intricate relationship than four people singing in unison. For a brief period of time, that unison can have a dramatic effect. But it is harmony that gives texture and color to the song. You are *harmonizing* all the diversity that exists within that quartet. This produces *intense* beauty. The greater the interrelationship, the more intense the beauty. The artist who creates a beautiful painting knows how to harmonize the different hues. She brings them together in a unity of color and theme that is a visual feast. Our mind resonates to the harmonization of great complexity.

An intensely effective, massively successful team has tremendous harmony. In the introduction to this section, I defined *synergy* as "the maximization of collective potential." You look at a great team, and you can see their cooperation and how they interconnect in harmony with each other. Every member of the team sees the other members as being a crucial part of the symphony.

Once you have clearly gained an appreciation for your own personality with its particular strengths and weaknesses, you will be able to move forward with confidence and with love, fully liberated and fully alive to the awareness of the spectacular creation that is each and every human being. You will be ready to begin the process of personal and professional transformation with them. I can tell you with complete assurance that this is one of the most exciting journeys that you will take in this life! Enjoy it, savor it, rejoice in it!

Imagination Is Unlimited $\qquad$ 5

PERHAPS THE MOST fascinating gift that God has given us is the attribute of imagination. You only need to look around you to absorb the reality of God's imagination: each human being you meet is a living example. Walk into your local supermarket, and you will immediately experience the incredible profusion of diversity that is humanity: tall, short, thin, fat, dark, light, graceful, clumsy, cheerful, grumpy people! Even identical twins have distinct fingerprints and personalities. What delightful diversity!

Visit the library and flip through an encyclopedia of the animal kingdom. Who could imagine such magnificent creativity? From aardvark to zorille (a kind of weasel), there is a plethora of animals for every letter of the alphabet, including the xiphosuran (a type of crab). God not only has the imagination of the master Creator, but He also has a sense of humor, as well. I challenge you to look at an anteater, a manatee, an otter, a platypus, or a warthog and keep a straight face. You can't do it!

Let's go back to the very foundational premise of this book. Genesis 1:27 tells us, "God created man in His own image; in the image of God He created him; male and female He created them." God is imaginative, therefore *you* are imaginative. We are born with tremendous creative ability and imagination. Every person you meet is an artesian well, a shoreless, bottomless repository of imagination and innovation. There is no "unimaginative" person! Think back to when you were a child: you used to play for hours, using little more than your imagination. Those of you who have children have watched them frolick in the playground of their minds.

Unfortunately, what happens to many of us is that, over time, our imaginative powers atrophy from lack of use. A great deal of our education actually *stifles* the creative process! All too often, we're taught *what* to think, not *how to* think! In our desire to teach children disciplined, logical thinking, we discourage creative thinking. Even in art class and music class, which are supposed to encourage creativity and individuality, our schools teach children to remember the rules, the basics; they stifle innovation and ideation. We concentrate on learning rules and rote memorization, and the right side of our brain—the creative side—falls into disuse.

Just like any other muscle group, our God-given imaginative powers may become weak, but they can be restored through proper exercise. We can be trained to unleash our imagination in order to devise new solutions to old problems. In twenty-five years of writing and research on the subject of thinking and learning, I have never seen anyone who can approach the work of Dr. Edward de Bono. Edward de Bono affirms that every human being is fabulously imaginative. He believes that the mind must be trained to harness that creative ability through certain mental disciplines, which he calls Lateral Thinking. Dr. de Bono has developed more than one hundred lateral thinking skills that we can use to broaden the pool of thinking possibilities whenever we must make a decision.

Lateral and Logical Thinking

Dr. de Bono correctly points out that the thrust of our educational systems is to teach us to think in logical, linear progressions of mathematics and thought:

$$2 + 2 = 4$$

A ———→ B ———→ C, and following this progression will lead unerringly to X.

Lateral Thinking, on the other hand will often explore ways *around* these orderly progressions of thought. Lateral Thinking might ask, *"Why* must we go through C to reach X? Why couldn't we do it *this* way?":

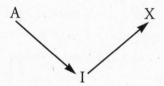

The purpose of Lateral Thinking is to *channel* our innate creative abilities toward a specific thinking *target,* and then allow our imagination to consider all the elements of that specific target. Most of us *do* use our imagination to a certain extent already, but what separates us from the truly inventive individual is that the effective thinker is able to combine "flights of fancy" with the ability to generate a specific *direction* or a *structure* within which to order those thoughts. I am going to teach you three of those structures, as I have learned them from intensive study of Dr. de Bono's superb book, *de Bono's Thinking Course.*[1] But first, let me lay out four ground rules for successful lateral thinking.

Ground Rule #1: Suspend Judgment and Emotion

We are all emotional people. We have already discussed the vital importance of *passion.* We can never, and *should* never, rid our lives of passion and emotion. Emotions are the amplifiers and appreciators of our lives. Just as we would never want to eliminate our sense of smell, which amplifies our enjoyment of the tangible things of life—such as the odor of wood smoke from a fireplace on a crisp fall day or the delicate perfume of wildflowers growing in springtime—we would never want to eliminate our emotions, which soak in the wonder of the intangible things in life: love, joy, and peace.

However, our emotions impede our success in life if they move from being enhancers to becoming *dominators* of our lives. We all know people who allow anger, for example, to become a dominating emotion in their lives, causing them to become unloving and unproductive. Similarly, emotions can cause our thinking to become stale and unprofitable. I recently heard Dr. Thomas Sowell, the brilliant educator and author, say during a radio interview that far too many of us have blurred the distinction between *thinking* and *feeling*. We use phrases like "soul-searching" to indicate that we have given careful thought to various issues. In reality, however, we have consulted our *feelings* about these issues, instead of examining them critically and dispassionately. The problem with this, of course, is that our feelings are not always trustworthy. Scripture warns us that "the heart is deceitful above all things, / And desperately wicked; / Who can know it?" (Jer. 17:9). If we don't make a conscious effort to block out our feelings about a matter, we're likely to let our hearts dictate to our heads what course of action we are going to take.

"Well, that certainly doesn't happen with me," you may quickly assure yourself. Really? Let's take a look at how our emotions can lead our thinking astray.

Take a look at the following diagram. When we are confronted with an event or an idea, most of us have a tendency to reach a decision about that concept very quickly. We tell ourselves, "I like that idea," or "I *don't* like that idea." We make that decision based on our knowledge and our emotions *at that moment.* It is important to realize that we will usually make that decision immediately. We call it "instinct," or "intuition." Some of you pride yourselves in your ability to make snap decisions. The point is, we actually expend very little mental energy on making that decision! We go with our "gut feeling," our *emotions*. We then expend a great deal of mental energy justifying, either to ourselves or to others, a decision we have already made. We can easily become so emotionally wedded to a particular idea that, rather than seeking to *learn* from the perceptions of others who may disagree with us, we seek to *defend* our idea from the insight of others. We expend far more mental energy justifying a decision we've already made, stacking up for ourselves an impregnable wall of reasons why we're right, *rather than using our formidable imaginative powers to explore the idea itself.*

Emotional Thinking

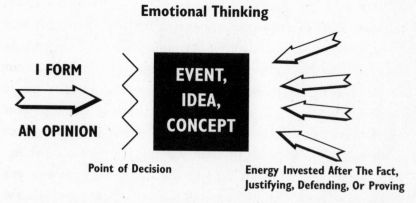

I FORM

AN OPINION

EVENT, IDEA, CONCEPT

Point of Decision

Energy Invested After The Fact, Justifying, Defending, Or Proving

What we should strive to do is to *delay,* to *suspend* that emotional decision, and allow our enterprising imaginations to enter into the idea itself, to play with the idea, and to consider it thoroughly. Our mental acuity should be focused on the myriad possibilities that can be generated by a particular concept, *not* on building an intellectual fortress *around* our idea that will repel all invaders. The second diagram gives an illustration of how delaying an emotional response allows us to utilize our imaginative ability. In this second case, we have expended the majority of our mental energy on the idea itself, not on the defense of our emotional reaction to it.

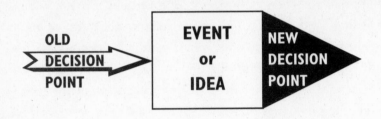

This first ground rule is, *Challenge the Known and Defend the Unknown*. All too often, we fall into lifeless, anticreative thinking, which says, "That's the way we've always done things around here," or "If it ain't broke don't fix it." We *defend* the known, and *challenge* the unknown! When someone comes along and says, "If it ain't broke, how can we *improve* it?" our comfort zone is threatened, we respond viscerally, and we immediately begin to poke holes in the newer, challenging (threatening) idea. We defend what we know, we protect what we are comfortable with, and we challenge that which forces us to reexamine our standard mind-set.

We can't possibly grow by standing still. If we're not growing, we're shrinking! If we're not improving, we're regressing! If we're not living, we're dying! Our life's focus should be on health and growth. If we're not moving forward, then we are slipping back. The *only* way to move forward is to *challenge* the limits we've always known and to *embrace* the improvements that will help us to hurdle those barriers.

Ground Rule #2: Focus

As I mentioned earlier, the beauty of Lateral Thinking is that it enables us to channel our creative abilities into a specific thinking *target*. This requires us to keep our focus on that target and to deliberately restrict ourselves from drifting away. Far from forcing us into a rigidity of thought that impedes our thinking processes, focus allows us to direct and concentrate our marvelous, God-given creative abilities in ways we had previously thought impossible!

Ground Rule #3: Quantity, *Not* Quality

Lateral Thinking benefits from the principle that is called "The Law of Requisite Variety," which simply states that *the greater the number of options from which I have to choose, the greater the likelihood of making a good decision.* If I am confronted by a decision and the range of options I have to choose from is very small, then I have only a limited chance of selecting a superior solution from within that small population. But if I can successfully expand my range of choices, and particularly if I can fill that newly expanded range of choices with bright, new ideas, then the likelihood of selecting a truly top-notch solution is dramatically improved!

In the early stages of these Lateral Thinking exercises, we should strive to generate as many ideas as possible, without worrying about their respective merits. This idea goes hand in hand with Rule #1, the suspension of judgment and emotion. During a Lateral Thinking session, the most heinous crime one can commit is to judge or ridicule the idea of another human being. The quickest way to abruptly turn off the spigot of creative energy is to tell someone, "Aww, you're crazy! That's the dumbest thing I ever heard of!" Rest assured that the person who is exposed to that kind of verbal assault will become *extremely* quiet; creativity will have been effectively destroyed.

Ground Rule #4: Have Fun!

Thinking should be fun! Most of us have suffered through interminable meetings where serious, sour-faced executives talk in deadly serious tones about dreadfully serious things that affect their extremely serious businesses. The individuals who conduct these somber affairs would look suspiciously at anyone who tried to inject levity into the situation. They would immediately assume that this humorous individual was a fluffy lightweight who didn't belong in their serious deliberations. It can all get a bit too serious!

When we attempt to "inspire" someone, do we not seek to invigorate them, to spark their imagination, and to trigger their natural ability? If that is true, then what part of "inspiration" involves sitting around a table with a group of people who look as if they've just bitten a particularly tangy lemon, making sure that every unsmiling word and deed properly reflects the gravity of the situation? May God save us all from this kind of funereal work environment!

So, please, have fun with these skills I am about to teach you. I used a phrase earlier in regard to children's use of their imaginative ability: to "frolic in the playground of the mind." I hope that you will use your natural, God-given creative talent to do precisely that.

The PMI (Plus, Minus, Interesting)

The first of Dr. de Bono's thinking skills is the PMI, which stands for Plus, Minus, Interesting. The object of the exercise is to consider a particular suggestion or concept, purposing to generate a list of all the positive aspects (Pluses) of the idea that we possibly can, a second list of all the negative aspects (Minuses) that we can think of, and a third list of all the innovative (Interesting) ideas that can be generated from the original suggestion. Let's see how the four ground rules of Lateral Thinking apply to the PMI.

1. Suspend judgment and emotion. This is essential to making better plans and building better relationships. We must strictly refrain from assigning any value judgments to the thoughts we generate.

2. Focus. We overcome our natural tendency to reach an emotional decision in large part by forcing ourselves to *focus:* in this case, we focus in turn on the Pluses, then the Minuses, then the Interesting factors that surround a particular concept or decision. A simple yet highly effective tool that helps us keep our focus is setting an arbitrary time frame for considering the three categories. The time frame might be very short, say, three minutes per group. Whatever time frame we select, we allow all three categories of thought (Plus, Minus, Interesting) the same amount of time.

For three minutes we consider *only* the Plus factors of the decision. What's good about this concept? What benefits will result from its implementation? What would I like about living with this idea? Then, at the end of three minutes, we shift our focus 180 degrees and concentrate with equal intensity on all the Minus factors of this concept. What's *wrong* with this idea? What would make me unhappy about living with its consequences? At the end of this second three-minute period, we reset our timer one last time and direct our attention to the Interesting or innovative ideas that the concept suggests. We discipline ourselves to work only within our parameter of focus for that particular time frame. If the ideas start to slow down or run dry before the time has elapsed, under no circumstances should we quit early and move on to the next category. We discipline ourselves to *focus*.

3. Quantity, not quality. This goes hand in hand with focus. During the time period we have set for each category, we determine to generate as many ideas as we possibly can. If the PMI is used in a group setting, and the Law of Requisite Variety strongly suggests that it should be, the leader should encourage *everyone's* enthusiastic input.

4. Have fun! This is particularly important during the time spent discussing the Interesting segment, but it is vitally important to have fun throughout the entire procedure. I'm not saying that we should be deliberately silly or frivolous, but we *should* strive to relax, and to create the kind of environment in which every thinker's contributions are celebrated and reinforced.

Let's take a look at how a PMI might work. Let's suppose a creative team is preparing to perform a PMI. The first order of business is to agree to suspend judgment and emotion. Next, they set a time frame. This group, for the sake of simplicity, chose a short time limit. In actual practice, I would never suggest a time frame less than three minutes.

Concept: Once a month, my company should hold a meeting for the entire staff to discuss concepts relating to unleashing untapped potential, and to evaluate how well we, as a group, are doing that.

Plus
- The meetings would improve communication within our company.
- People would get to know each other better, improving cohesion and teamwork.
- The staff would have a greater sense of involvement and self-determination.
- Discussing the skills necessary to unleash untapped potential would keep them fresh.
- Morale would improve.
- People would be excited to be invited to such a meeting.
- We would get good, "ground-level" feedback from the staff.
- We would obtain a better variety of ideas and perceptions.

Minus
- The meetings would take too much time.
- We already have too many meetings at this company!

- It would be difficult to schedule such a meeting.

- In a large group like that, too many people could sit in silence.

- People would get bored, sitting around talking about "touchy-feely" stuff.

- Managers might hold things people said against them. Staff would be afraid to speak.

- The meeting would probably dissolve into a gripe session. Nothing would get done.

Interesting

- Maybe we should hold the meetings only once every quarter.

- What if we held regular department meetings, which would allow greater focus?

- I like the idea of a smaller, rotating group.

- What if we formed a small, "motivational committee," almost like a booster club?

- What if we had a monthly barbecue or party for the whole staff?

- I like the idea of having awards ceremonies, with prizes for the top performers.

- Maybe we should concentrate on doing more to recognize and celebrate the staff.

- Maybe we should bring in a motivational speaker to these meetings.

Let's take a look at some of the factors of the short PMI that this group performed. One important thing to note is that the very factor that one member of the group thought was a Plus—"People would be excited"—another member saw as a negative—"People would get bored." This is perfectly normal and acceptable. The phrase "One man's meat is another man's poison" is a truism. How many times in your company was there a suggestion that the sales force thought was a brainstorm that accounting thought was a bust? That is the exact purpose of the "Quantity, not Quality" rule: we wish to unearth *all* the pluses and minuses of a particular idea.

Notice that in the Interesting portion of the PMI, the group wandered pretty far away from the original concept. Wonderful! The purpose of the Interesting section is to look for alternatives, to consider the unusual and the unconventional, and to have fun! During the Interesting section, we want to give our imaginative ability full freedom and delight in flip-flopping the idea, turning it upside down or inside out. We want to turn over every possible creative stone, looking to find grains of innovation under them.

The "Interesting" is the most exciting of the three sections. When considering a particular idea, begin your Interesting comments by saying:

- "Maybe we could revise the idea by . . ."
- "What if we could reverse it . . . ?"
- "What if we use this idea as a springboard to . . . ?"
- "Let's explore this particular aspect in greater depth . . ."
- "I believe there is a real spark of imagination in this portion of your thought . . ."
- "What if . . . ?"

During the Interesting portion of the PMI, we loosen our neckties, open our collars, relax, and let our imaginative ability run wild! Have fun! Let your creativity roam wherever it will. It is during this time that we will likely run across a truly original, dramatically different concept.

Do you see how it works? By the way, having done a PMI on this subject, I think it has real muscle! Why not take this book to work with you, share it with the leadership at your company, and see what they would like to implement at your workplace to unleash untapped potential?

Let me add a fifth ground rule for Lateral Thinking: Practice, Practice, Practice! It is true that some people who have learned Dr. de Bono's methods have enjoyed immediate success with them. But generally, as with any other new skill, you will need to use the PMI and the other Lateral Thinking skills on a regular basis before you begin to experience truly dramatic results. If you determine to practice Lateral Thinking regularly, you will soon find yourself using it automatically. I can't guarantee that you will always come up with the *best* idea each time, but I *do* guarantee that you will consistently make better plans and decisions each time you employ these skills.

I am providing two sample concepts for you to consider, to help you get started. Enlist some friends or family to work through these with you. Make it a point to encourage all the members of your creative thinking team to offer their enthusiastic input. You will become more adept at practicing Lateral Thinking as you teach it to others. You will also find the thinking exercises more exciting and enjoyable as you share and expand upon various new ideas with others.

Sample Concept #1: My family should sit down together and create a "Family Bill of Rights," designating the roles and responsibilities of each family member, and defining the consequences for failure to perform them. The Bill of Rights would outline the rights each family member enjoys, such as the right to be treated with courtesy and respect at all times, the right to have their accomplishments recognized and celebrated, etc.

Sample Concept #2: Everyone at my company should be assigned a corporate mentor. This mentor would help their "mentoree" move up the corporate ladder, learning new skill-sets and pursuing further education. When the mentoree's performance review occurs, the mentor would participate, detailing the mentoree's efforts to grow and improve.

Remember to suspend judgment and emotion, and approach this concept with a clean mental slate. Set a time limit for your group, and go for as many ideas as you can generate: first all the Pluses, then the Minuses, then the Interesting ideas. Remember Ground Rule #4: Have Fun!!!

You will find numerous opportunities each week to employ your newly developed imaginative skill. It might be something as simple as deciding what to do this Saturday night or something as complex as where to attend college or a career change. The more you look for opportunities to use Lateral Thinking, the more opportunities you will find! Be aggressive in your thinking! Have fun!

The CAF (Consider All Factors)

The CAF (it rhymes with "half") is an attempt to gather as many factors as we possibly can before we make a *procedural,* or financial commitment to a particular concept or plan. All too often, we'll commit to an idea *before* we consider all the factors we should. Later on, we discover that we omitted one or more crucial considerations that would have led us in a completely different direction. Then we groan, "Oh, if only I had known that, I wouldn't have done this!" We use the CAF to explore an idea as thoroughly as we possibly can *before* we pursue a particular plan of action, in order to eliminate poorly considered or hasty decisions that we may regret later.

Here is a simple illustration that emphasizes the importance of performing a CAF:

Concept: A young married couple are considering buying a house. They have included the following factors in considering their decision:

- Location
- Layout
- Price
- Color
- Proximity of schools for children
- Insurance
- Style of home
- Proximity to shopping centers
- Swimming pool
- Monthly mortgage payment
- Quality of neighborhood
- Realtor's reputation

Take two minutes and list some of the factors this couple have overlooked.

I'm sure you listed some factors that would dramatically affect this couple's decision. Just a few of these factors might be:

- Taxes
- Other children in the neighborhood?
- Proximity to work
- Condition of roof
- Termites?
- Quality of water

- Quality of schools

- Proximity to church

- Parking

- Homeowners association?

- Interest rate on mortgage

- Length of mortgage

Obviously, there are several factors that the couple left out that have a critical bearing on their ability to reach a better solution. In fact, the omission of just one of these, such as the condition of the roof, could have disastrous consequences!

The purpose of the CAF is to consider *all* the factors that could affect a decision. This is where Ground Rule #3 (Quantity, not Quality) plays a vitally important role in performing a CAF. We don't want to limit ourselves to merely considering all *important* factors. We want to give careful attention to *every* variable that might affect our decision. One seemingly unimportant factor could end up having a dramatic effect on our decision-making process.

We will benefit by drawing on the truth of the Law of Requisite Variety. We should involve other people in performing the CAF. A group that is encouraged to use their imaginative abilities to the fullest will invariably generate more ideas than one or two individuals. In theory, the CAF sounds quite a bit like what many of us call "brainstorming." When you add the Lateral Thinking ground rules, though, you have a more efficient thinking system.

Let's try a couple of sample concepts again, using the CAF Lateral Thinking skill. Enlist the help of friends or family. The focus of your thinking should be, "Is there anything we have overlooked here?" and "What else belongs on this list?" Keep the ground rules for Lateral Thinking in front of you as you work to ensure that you don't forget them. I'd suggest a three-minute time frame for both these exercises.

Sample Concept #1: Consider all the factors needed to maintain mutual trust and respect in a marriage.

Sample Concept #2: Consider all the factors that enable your company to meet and exceed the expectations of your customers.

The PMI and the CAF can be used on the same concept. They are entirely interchangeable. You might examine the Plus, Minus, and Interesting aspects of a particular concept, and then select one of those ideas and perform a CAF on it. Similarly, you may wish to select one of the items you listed in a CAF and subject it to further scrutiny by putting it through a PMI. A third option is to perform both thinking skills on the same concept.

The OPV (Other Person's Viewpoint)

The OPV is a Lateral Thinking skill that is designed to temporarily take us outside of our own mental and emotional framework and bring us into another person's parameters. The OPV is a superb tool for avoiding and resolving conflict. The OPV requires, as does all clear thinking, a temporary suspension of judgment and emotion. It is a deliberate attempt to see the situation or the problem that is under consideration from another person's point of view.

We use a lot of phrases in our day-to-day conversations that reflect the *idea* of the OPV: "Look at it from *his* point of view" or "Walk a mile in the other person's shoes." We *say* these things, but how often do we *practice* them as a deliberate skill? How often do we make a conscious, concentrated effort to suspend judgment and emotion and actually *become* the other person, to feel the way they feel and to think the way they think? The OPV is the very embodiment of the attitude that each and every human being, whether I agree with them or not, even whether I like them or not, is made in God's image and is deserving of my empathy and respect.

In order to successfully perform an OPV on another person, it is not enough for me to say, "Maybe she feels this way" or "Maybe he thinks that way." Rather, I make every effort to *become* the other person, and to consider, "Maybe *I* feel this" or "Maybe *I* think that." I want to make every effort to put aside my own thoughts and feelings and to think what the *other* person thinks and feel the way they feel.

Let me hasten to steer you away from two things that the OPV is not: first, the OPV is not an attempt to "get inside someone's head" for the purpose of manipulating him to behave the way I want him to. An OPV is intended to create a heightened level of awareness, *not* to give us a better negotiating position!

Second, the OPV does not allow us to superimpose our value judgments on another human being. It is not an exercise that allows us to say, "Maybe I (as the other person) do not respect the superior intelligence of the other person (me)" or "Maybe I'm just being unreasonable and hardheaded." The only way to effectively conduct an OPV is to put on the judgmental and emotional brakes and make a sincere effort to become that other person.

Let's take a look at a sample OPV:

Concept: You are the sales manager of a department of ten. It is becoming increasingly evident that a man and a woman in your department are arguing a lot on the job. The man has been with your company for several years and has always been a steady, if unspectacular, performer. The woman was hired just six months ago from a large company in a major city, and she is already attracting attention with her aggressive, "can-do" attitude. You recently overheard these two arguing again, and you know the situation is beginning to have a negative impact on the rest of the group. You have decided to speak with them both, but, first, you want to prepare yourself for the interviews by performing an OPV on both parties.

The man:

Maybe . . .

- I am resentful of being outsold by someone so new.
- the woman has been cutting in on my established territories.
- I believe she is using unscrupulous methods to become successful.
- I feel this woman is bossy and domineering.
- I dislike "city slickers" coming in and telling everyone how to do it.
- her success underscores my lack of it.
- she sold a big account that I wasn't able to close.
- my pride has been hurt.
- I believe she is getting an unfair advantage because she is a woman.

The woman:

Maybe . . .

- I'm a single mom who wants to send my kids to the best universities.
- where I used to work, we were taught to be extremely aggressive.
- I want to earn the respect of my peers by putting up big numbers.
- I'm not about to let anyone or anything get in the way of my success.
- I'm nervous about coming into a new workplace.
- I dated the man briefly, and now he's acting like a jealous teenager.
- I *am* a little flirtatious, but what's the harm in that?

- I am a veteran, professional salesperson, and I get good results.

- I've tried my best to be nice, but this man is *very* unpleasant.

The manager:
Maybe . . .

- I've been friends with the man for a long time. We're buddies.

- I'm disappointed the man has never performed up to his potential.

- I've never really liked the man.

- I'm irritated at having to referee a dispute that I find childish.

- I'm elated to have this fine, new salesperson on the team.

- I just want the best sales numbers, and I don't care how we get them.

- I gave the woman some top-billing accounts to help her get started.

- I'm intimidated by the woman.

- I think the man should mind his own business.

Even this very short OPV is a valuable reminder that there can be any number of unseen motivators that would cause us to behave in a certain way. By making a deliberate, determined effort to view the situation from the other person's point of view, we stand a better chance of uncovering common ground from which to reach a decision or resolve conflict.

I stated earlier that the OPV is a superb tool for conflict resolution. This exercise points out two ways in which this hypothetical manager could employ Lateral Thinking to defuse this situation. The first way is to do precisely what this manager did: suspend judgment and emotion and make a determined effort to reach a greater level of awareness for both individuals involved, as well as to take a look at what part he, the manager, might have played in helping to fan the flames of this conflict.

A great many leaders who are trying to resolve this kind of situation will call the two battlers into a meeting, either together or separately, and say, "Tell me what the problem is." The person involved in the conflict will invariably launch into a detailed explanation of what the *other* person has done to create the unhappy situation. The man in our previous example will explain exactly what the woman has done wrong, and the woman will list the man's shortcomings. The problem is, neither party is focusing on his or her *own role* in the problem. They are quite happy to perform an "OPF" ("Other Person's Failings"), but they have very little desire to examine how they, themselves, have been disagreeable or disruptive.

Imagine this scenario: the manager calls the man and the woman into his office and instructs them to perform an OPV on *each other* for the next three minutes. So, for the next three minutes, instead of pointing their fingers at each other, both parties are pointing their finger back at themselves. "How does this other person see me?" is the question they are asking themselves. At the end of the OPV, both parties then exchange papers and read the other person's suggestions. This can help accomplish tremendous progress toward eliminating misunderstandings and creating a commonly shared reality.

This will work beautifully with two friends, or with a husband and wife as well. It isn't necessary for there to be a conflict situation for the OPV to be appropriate. If a husband and wife were going to perform a PMI and CAF on the concept of buying a new home, they could perform an OPV on each other *first,* and then exchange papers. It might well be that the couple has not successfully communicated to each other what their reasons are for wanting a new home, or even if they really and truly *do* want the new home.

Here are two more sample OPVs:

Sample Concept #1: A mother is concerned that her fifteen-year-old daughter, who has always been a bright and vivacious girl, has become increasingly morose and uncommunicative. The mother knows that this is one warning sign for drug abuse, and she feels she must talk with her daughter and find out what is troubling her. Perform an OPV on both parties. (Three minutes for each person.)

Sample Concept #2: The CEO of a large corporation has always been happy with his executive assistant. This woman has always been efficient and reliable, but lately, she has made several "rookie" mistakes. At first, the executive wrote these errors off as "just having a bad day," but he now realizes that these events are occurring too frequently. Perform an OPV on the executive and the assistant.

We have seen that God created us in His image to use our words to build up human beings, and we have now learned that we can use our imaginative ability to forge better decisions and plans and to raise our level of awareness and understanding of others. Let me again encourage you to take every opportunity you can find to practice these new skills. The more you use them, the more comfortable you'll be with them, and the more proficient at creative thought you'll become.

Have fun frolicking in the playground of your mind!

You Are a Genius

6

I MAGINE A WORLD in which everyone made you feel smart. In such a world, you would awake every morning eager to begin the day because you knew everyone you met would honor your God-given mental abilities and make you feel important. We can create such an environment, maybe not throughout the entire world, but certainly within our own spheres of influence. The purpose of this chapter is to teach you how.

Dear Esteemed Reader, you have such phenomenal potential to learn! We live in a world system that incessantly mediates incompetency and promotes learned helplessness. You and I can reverse this trend by tapping into the true capacity for genius that we have all been endowed with and by helping others to discover the joy of lifelong learning.

Every time I look into another person's eyes and tell them from my heart how intelligent they are, I immediately see their eyes, which have been called "the windows of the soul," simply shimmer with joy. I intuitively know by their powerful, heartfelt response that few people have ever honored them in this way. Out of curiosity, I'll ask them, "Tell me, how many people whom you work with or for have told you how smart you are?" Far too often, the reply comes back, "No one."

I hope that after you have read and absorbed this chapter, you will set out to help me to stop this dehumanization and depersonalization that takes place in our homes, our schools, and our workplaces, the critical and creative contributions that so many "diamonds in the rough" *could* have made remain buried treasure forever. It has been said, "The price of education is paid only once, the cost of ignorance must be paid forever."

Let's look at this in the light of the foundation of all human motivation: the truth that we are created in the image of God. I am asserting in the strongest language I know that long-term, sustainable motivation must come from knowing who you are. This is your starting point, your philosophical given, from which you construct a life that is worth modeling. Each one of these secrets for unleashing untapped potential is an unveiling of a defining truth of our personhood, an illumination of what it means to be made in the image of God.

This chapter is titled, "You Are a Genius," and you *are* a genius because you are the image of God, the living, eternal God. He created us with a mind like His. We each possess a rational and logical mind with built-in moral frameworks. We have a self-conscious and highly imaginative mind. Our minds are capable of producing and processing symbolic and conceptual communication.

Did you know that the original meaning of the word *genius* is "to come into being"? So, by coming into being, by being born a human, which is the apex of all God's creation, you are a genius! You share this birthright with the other five billion geniuses who are all drawing breath on this planet!

I must hasten to add this disclaimer: we are not God. We are not all-knowing, as God is. He is infinite and perfect in all His attributes. We are finite and imperfect in all our thoughts and behavior. However, we do bear His image in a glorious, yet mysteriously limited way.

Since we have a mind like God's, created in God's image, and because that mind is an *immaterial* part of us, man will never be able to quantify human intelligence. How could we ever place a finite, limited value on something that is *immaterial*? Scientists have said that the human brain is composed of 100 billion neurons. This is their calculation of the material construction of the human brain. But what is the construction of the mind? How could we possibly measure it?

We have done a terrible injustice to humanity with our IQ tests. We believed the results of the test were an accurate indication of intelligence. Our current IQ tests are like an amateur astronomer's first inexpensive telescope. That telescope does help us to observe the heavens, but only in a very limited way. It is wholly inadequate for the observation or comprehension of the immensity of the universe that God created. Similarly, our intelligence tests measure only a tiny fraction of human intellectual ability. Using an IQ test to appraise intelligence is like attempting to ascertain the value and content of all radio transmissions by monitoring only signals found between 700 and 900 on the AM dial.

The terrible truth exists that for almost one hundred years people have been told that the results of this clearly inadequate test determined how they measured up intellectually. Educators would honor their profession and serve humanity more effectively if they would admit their limited ability to quantify the mental capabilities of human beings, and instead, spend more time honoring and expanding the God-given intelligence that each and every one of us possesses as our birthright.

Your Learning Languages

I am now going to share with you the secrets of peak mental performance. Let's start by a careful examination of *how* we learn. Here is a quick quiz that will help you determine how you process and retain information. Simply move through the sequence of questions and circle the answer that most closely matches your thoughts and feelings.

1. **When I think of my childhood sweetheart, the first thing that happens is**
   V. I see his or her face in my mind.
   A. I hear their voice speaking, laughing, etc.
   K. Some feeling (love, sadness, spite, etc.) comes to mind.

2. **When I remember the person from my past whom I most disliked, I**
   V. Visualize them doing that which I so disliked.
   A. Hear certain things they said.
   K. Become flooded with emotions (disgust, rage, fear, etc.)

3. **Regarding someone I like or dislike a great deal, one of these has the greatest initial impact on me:**
   V. Seeing them from a distance as they approach.
   A. Greeting and talking to them when we meet.
   K. The feelings I get when I sense we are about to meet, or when we actually touch, shake hands, embrace, etc.

4. **When I think of one of my favorite songs, I initially**
   V. Recall the concert or video where I originally saw the musician(s) perform the music.
   A. Hear the music in my mind.
   K. Become a part of the performance (sing or hum the tune, tap my foot, play "air guitar," etc.).

5. **At every level of education, I generally did best in classes in which**
   V. The textbook was highly illustrative or the instructor used the blackboard extensively.

A. The teacher was an effective, interesting speaker whose delivery made things easy to understand.

K. I learned by doing. These were hands-on classes, such as Home Economics, Drafting, Woodworking, etc.

6. **The aspect I enjoy most of a trip to the beach is**

V. Seeing the seascape, such as the breakers and whitecaps, boat sails on the horizon, sun glittering on the water, etc.

A. The sounds: waves breaking on the shore, the carefree laughter and play from others, the wind blowing, etc.

K. The feel of the sun warming my skin, the taste of salt spray on my lips, the feeling of well-being and serenity the setting provides.

7. **When I am faced with any challenge, my instinctive method of dealing with that challenge, and the way I get the best results, is:**

V. I imagine the parts, components, and whole of the problem in my mind. If a call comes to my work-station that a certain machine is malfunctioning, I visualize the machine and try to "see" the broken part.

A. I talk to myself as I work through the possibilities, seeking the best available alternatives. In doing this, I draw on what I've learned through education, texts dealing with the subject, shop manuals, and things I have either heard or stated concerning this particular situation.

K. I'm not much good at solving the challenge until I can "sink my teeth into it"—until I actually begin to work on the problem with my hands.

8. **When I telephone someone for whom I feel great love, and they tell me "I love you," my first response to those words is:**

V. I see the image of the loved one in my mind. I visualize "pictures" from the past as I remember that person in physical proximity and relationship to me.

A. Internal dialogue begins at once. I say to myself, "I feel so fulfilled! I am enjoying this!"

K. Feelings of great longing to be with that person sweep over me. I wish I could hug them or caress them. I rue unkind things I said in the past that might have caused pain. My emotional awareness heightens.

9. **When I go dancing with a friend or my spouse, I am inspired to get up and dance when**

V. Others around me get up to dance, and my mood becomes festive. I desire to join the fun that others are having. I am beckoned by the lowered lights, the dancing couples, and the animated showmanship of the band members.

A. I am content to sit until the band strikes up a song that I especially like. Hearing the opening strains of that song inspires me to get up and dance.

K. My initial reaction is, "I can't dance" or "I don't know how to dance." However, once I get out on the dance floor and loosen up, I get caught up in the mood of the music, and I really do enjoy myself. Though I don't think I dance well, once I move my body to the music, I find the motion pleasurable.

10. **First impressions are lasting ones. When you meet someone for the first time, what generally arrests your attention?**

V. Their appearance.

A. What they said and how they said it.

K. The emotions that person stirred within you.

11. **When I make a decision, my tendency is to**

V. Picture the alternatives in my mind, visualize my options, and make decisions based on what I see.

A. Carry on a running, inner dialogue that debates the pros and cons. I debate within myself and decide based on the answers to questions I have asked myself.

K. At times I find it hard to arrive at an impartial conclusion because of my emotions. I often get good or bad feelings about people and situations. My feelings often play a major role in my decision making.

12. **All of us have a circle of friends and casual acquaintances with whom we get along well. The people I enjoy generally have this in common:**

V. They communicate in animated form. They use metaphors, similes, and analogies well. They paint word pictures that are easy to see and understand.

A. They string their words together in a manner that makes for "easy listening." Anything they say, even if it is relatively unimportant, is interesting to me because of the manner in which they say it. I enjoy listening to them.

K. They touch my "hot buttons" when they speak. I am emotionally affected by their words more than I am by the words of most people. I find my mood is often altered after only a few moments with these people.

13. **When I need to memorize anything, it is easier for me to**

V. Write it down and study my 3 x 5 cards.

A. Repeat it over and over again in my mind until I know it.

K. Mentally act out the thing to be remembered.

14. **When I spell a word and then doubt the accuracy of the spelling, I generally**

    V. Question the spelling because it does not "look right" to me.

    A. Question the spelling because it does not "sound right" to me.

    K. I get an intuitive feeling that the word is wrong. In such cases, "something just tells me" that the spelling is incorrect.

15. **When someone relates a dramatic event to me and I wish to make a sympathetic response, I would normally say,**

    V. "I see what you mean."

    A. "I hear what you're saying."

    K. "I know how you feel."

16. **As a small child, I most enjoyed tales that**

    V. I saw at the movies or on television.

    A. Were told to me by a loved one, like a bedtime story.

    K. Were spiced by my imagination and feelings (fear, excitement, etc.), no matter what the source of delivery was.

17. **I tend to enjoy one of the following groups more than the other ones listed here:**

    V. Paintings, sculptures, monuments, beautiful sunsets.

    A. Music, sounds, the noises made by the wind, rain, or sea.

    K. Physical activity, such as aerobics, walking the dog, or working in the garden.

18. **I have, in the past, done a certain thing of which I am not particularly proud. Several things about this act sting my conscience, but chief among these is:**

    V. I see myself, in this instance, acting out of character with who and what I really am.

A. I hear my conscience speaking to me, either accusing or else excusing me from the responsibility of what I have done.

K. I feel deep remorse, shame, or indifference to my act(s); or waves of anger and/or other emotions sweep over me in conflict with each other as I consider what I have done.

19. The fondest memories I have of early childhood include

V. Scenes from the past, of loved ones and events that can't be duplicated.

A. "Fireside tales," or the gentle voice of instruction coming from now-deceased loved ones.

K. Being picked up, tossed in the air, tickled, or in some way being shown physical affection and attention.

20. What I enjoy most about going to church/synagogue is

V. The stateliness of the church building and the ceremony itself.

A. The content of the pastor/priest/rabbi's message.

K. The warm feelings I experience as I participate in the ceremony or service.

21. When I must learn a new assignment or job function, I prefer

V. To receive the instructions in written form.

A. That the instructions be given to me orally.

K. Being "walked through" the procedure (On-the-job training).

22. When any new thing is described to me, I seem to have better understanding of it when the person explaining

V. "Paints pictures" with their words that stimulate a sharp mental image.

A. Uses voice inflections, anecdotes, and compares and contrasts the thing to other things with which I am already familiar. (They might say, "It's similar to this, but not much like that," etc.)

K. Uses hand gestures and other body language and speaks with enthusiasm and emotion.

23. **Television commercials have in the past contributed to my selection of certain products. The major power of persuasion in commercials is**

V. The way a product appears and is presented to me. It looks like something I would like to have and own.

A. The commercial playing repeatedly until I not only know the message by heart, but also remember the advertised brand when I need to purchase that kind of product.

K. I have a good feeling and trust for the product as engendered by the commercial, and I am further influenced by the fact that others I know have a high opinion of it.

24. **When I am performing a task that does not require thoughtful attention as much as it does repetition (washing dishes, folding laundry, cutting the grass), my mind often wanders to more urgent, important, or interesting topics. At these times, I generally**

V. Find myself watching a "motion picture" in my mind.

A. Find myself in a running, internal dialogue with myself.

K. Find myself becoming emotionally involved.

25. **I am most distracted from what I am doing or thinking when**

V. Motion enters my peripheral field of vision.

A. Strange or unidentifiable sounds come to me.

K. I am physically uncomfortable.

Now, having answered every question on the quiz, go back and tally the number of questions you answered with V's, A's, or K's:

Write the number of questions you answered with:

V _____

A _____

K _____

What this quiz reveals is your preferred learning style, or if you like technical-sounding language, your *primary learning modality*. When you process new information, you tend to use this learning style first:

- If you answered more of the questions with the "V" answers, you are primarily a *visual* learner.

- If you answered more of the questions with the "A" answers, you are primarily an *auditory* learner.

- If you answered more of the questions with the "K" answers, you are primarily a *kinesthetic* learner.

I want to state, emphatically and categorically, that no one learning style is better or more effective than another. In fact, we *all* use all three styles. If you review your answers to the quiz, you will discover not only your primary learning modality, but also your secondary and tertiary modalities, as well. Your secondary modality is represented by the letter with which you answered the second highest number of questions, and your tertiary style is represented by the letter with which you responded the least often. Let me first explain the three learning styles.

Visual

Visual learners like to see visual representations, and they form vivid mental images in their minds. They'll often use visual language such as "It looks like this" or "I see what you mean." The old phrase, "a picture is worth a thousand words" applies to the visual learner. A visual person would be the most comfortable of the three watching TV with the sound off. They learn best by seeing demonstrations, dramatizations, movies, charts, graphs, pictures, and by reading.

If you were going to direct a visual learner how to drive to your home for the first time, the best way to do it would be to provide them with a map and a list of written directions. They aren't likely to remember verbal directions or messages as well. They like to remember and organize things through lists. E-mail and memos are their preferred forms of interoffice communication. The visual learner will remember faces well, but not names.

If a visual learner could make one demand of a teacher, it would be, "Let me *see* how to do it."

Auditory

The auditory learner wants to *hear* things. The auditory learner will soak in the traditional lecture format of the college classroom, and rather than forming mental pictures, they have an audible *voice* in their minds that helps them recall information. They use *auditory* language like, "It sounds to me as though . . ." or "I hear what you're saying." While a picture is worth a thousand words to the visual learner, the auditory learner would prefer to have something explained to them. They might well leave the TV on, but ignore the picture, being content to listen to the sound. They learn best by hearing explanations, cassette programs, sermons, etc. An auditory child will respond beautifully to rhyming, chanting, and singsong methods of learning, such as songs that contain the ABCs or the books of the Bible.

If you invited a primarily auditory friend to visit your home for the first time, and you offered the same map you drew for the visual learner, they'd say, "No, I don't need a map, just tell me." If you were riding with them to my house, they wouldn't refer much to written directions, but would say, "Jack *said* to take a right," etc. Auditory learners are often quite articulate both in written and oral communication. We have an old phrase for that. We say, "She has *an ear* for the proper use of language." They prefer verbal communication to written or electronic messages, and they like using the telephone. They often organize tasks by speaking aloud to themselves or by announcing to someone else what they are about to do: "I'm going to drive by the bank and cash my paycheck, then I'll stop at the supermarket, and on the way back I'll swing by the post office."

If the auditory learner could make one demand of a teacher, it would be, *"Tell* me how to do it."

Kinesthetic

The kinesthetic learner connects with something by *doing* or *feeling* it. Most of us cringe when we buy toys for our children that bear those dreaded words on the box: "Some assembly required." But while the visual learner would begin reading the directions ("show me how"), and the auditory learner would either ask for advice or begin talking to himself about how to do it ("tell me how"), the kinesthetic will pop open the box and begin slapping the toy together, only going to the directions when he runs into trouble. Kinesthetic students excel at art and shop classes, where they don't have to *watch* or *listen,* but actually get to *do.* In professional training programs, kinesthetics prefer role-play and action-oriented exercises. The kinesthetic learner will perform the most poorly in traditional educational environments, which demand that they *sit still,* something that kinesthetics of all ages don't do comfortably. Teachers who tell their kinesthetic students to "sit still. Stop wriggling. Look at me!" often don't realize that, far from listening, the kinesthetic learner's mind is now consumed by one urgent consideration: "When can I move again?" The kinesthetic is the one who, when asked if they like sports, will be most likely to respond, "I'd rather *play* the sport than watch it on TV."

Invite a kinesthetic to your home, and he'll merely ask you for the street address. "Let me give you some directions," you offer. "That's OK," replies your kinesthetic friend. "I'll find it." Who is the one who is *least* likely to stop at a gas station and ask directions? You guessed it. "We'll keep driving. I'll find it," insists the action-oriented kinesthetic. At work, the kinesthetic will prefer a face-to-face meeting and will prefer doing things like walking or eating while meeting with you.

As I said, many kinesthetics also learn by making an *emotional* connection. They react to people based on the emotions that others arouse in them. They are most likely to touch your arm or pat your back while speaking to you and are generally physically affectionate people.

If the kinesthetic could make one demand of a teacher, it would be, "Let me *experience* it."

Our Preferred Learning Patterns

Having described the three learning modalities, let me restate that each of us incorporates *all three* learning styles when we approach a new learning situation. What the quiz reveals is your individual *preferred learning pattern.* This is how it works.

Let's suppose a father is teaching his son Victor to ride a bicycle. Victor's preferred learning pattern is V, A, K. His primary learning modality is visual, his secondary learning modality is auditory, and his tertiary learning modality is kinesthetic. In other words, Victor first wants to *watch* his father successfully ride a bicycle, he then wants to *listen* to his father explain it, and then he'll be ready to actually *do* it. Victor may prompt his father through his preferred learning pattern by asking questions such as: "Will you do it, Dad?" Or "How did you make it turn, Dad?" or "OK, may I try it now?"

Victor will employ all three learning styles in the process of mastering the bicycle, but he will learn most effectively if he is allowed to absorb this new skill in the order of his *preferred learning pattern*, by first seeing a picture or demonstration (which allows him to form a mental image in his mind), then hearing an explanation, and finally, performing the task itself.

Ten years later, Victor, now a high school student, is ready to enter into the world of personal computers. His preferred learning pattern will be no different for this new skill from what it was for the physical art of riding a bicycle. Victor will want to watch someone operate a PC ("show me"), and to read some information about computers. Next, he will ask a teacher or friend some questions about operating the computer ("tell me"). Finally, he'll boot up the computer and begin work ("let me experience it").

Contrast Victor's preferred learning pattern with that of his brother Ken, whose pattern is K, V, A. Ken's primary learning modality is kinesthetic, his secondary modality is visual, and his tertiary is auditory. If Ken's father ignores this preferred learning pattern when teaching him how to ride a bicycle, confusion and frustration will follow for *both* parties. Ken will impatiently brush aside his father's attempt to *show* him how to ride a bicycle, because Ken needs to *experience* it first. Ken will want to hop right on the bike, try to ride it and fall off. Then, and only then, should his father provide a demonstration, then finally some verbal instruction *after* Ken has first tried it, then watched it. Likewise, when Ken enters the world of computers, he'll start hacking right away. When he runs into trouble, *then* he'll go to the manual, and lastly he'll ask for verbal instruction.

I said that ignorance of another's learning pattern can lead to frustration. There are two ways in which this is true. First, as I said, while the preferred learning style is obviously important to us, we still incorporate all three learning styles. Our secondary modality is absolutely crucial, because the *secondary modality provides the all-important link between the primary and tertiary modalities!* Without that bridge between the primary and tertiary modalities, our preferred learning pattern is interrupted, and we become easily irritated or confused. Let's revisit young Ken learning to ride a bicycle. He hops on the bike and wobbles around a bit before falling. "Let me see you do it, Dad," Ken suggests. But Dad replies, "Son, let me tell you what you did wrong." His father's instructions will not be particularly effective, because Dad has not provided the vitally important visual link between what Ken experienced and what he is now hearing. Ken wants Dad to *show* him what he did wrong! Ken needs *first* to form a visual image in his mind about the successful operation of the bicycle, and then hear about what he has just seen. If Ken has formed no mental picture, he cannot relate the instructions he hears to what he has done. In order to close the preferred learning loop, we need to incorporate all three learning modalities, and the secondary modality allows the primary and tertiary modes to integrate smoothly.

I firmly believe that a great deal of what we label "learning disabilities" are actually *teaching* disabilities! All across America today, in homes, schools, and business settings, parents, teachers, and managers display their inability to teach, and then berate others for their own inadequacy. We label our children "stubborn," our students "learning disabled," and our employees "unpromotable" when, in fact, we are simply not operating in harmony with the human mind! Children and adults are forced to sit through long lectures that will never release their will to win, broaden their belief, or increase their effectiveness. Others are told to "just *do* it," when simple demonstration and explanation beforehand would immediately transform them from dispirited drones to dynamos! Helping people learn is a matter of *flexibility,* of adapting to their learning styles, just as motivation is largely a matter of adapting your personality traits to someone else's preferred pattern of behavior.

There are six distinct preferred learning patterns that different human beings employ. In the chart below, I have outlined those six patterns, along with the way each pattern will internalize new information, as well as the way each learning pattern will express itself.

Preferred Learning Pattern	Order in Which They Like to Learn	Order in Which They Like to Express Themselves
V,A,K	Look, Listen, Do or Feel	Demonstrate, Speak, Act
V,K,A	Look, Do or Feel, Listen	Demonstrate, Act, Speak
A,V,K	Listen, Look, Do or Feel	Speak, Demonstrate, Act
A,K,V	Listen, Do or Feel, Look	Speak, Act, Demonstrate
K,V,A	Do or Feel, Look, Listen	Act, Demonstrate, Speak
K,A,V	Do or Feel, Listen, Look	Act, Speak, Demonstrate

To understand the chart, simply read across. The individual who prefers the V, A, K (Visual, Auditory, Kinesthetic) learning pattern will want to first look at how something is done; next, they want to hear how what they watched was done; at last, they'll want to do or experience the thing itself. When this individual is trying to express himself, he would prefer to show how something is done; then he'll give a verbal explanation of that he's just shown; lastly, he'll perform the task himself.

If we, as teachers, fail to recognize the preferred order of genius in other people, we are totally dishonoring the wonderful uniqueness that is our gift and our birthright from God. Dear Reader, please don't miss this: if I dishonor you, I am dishonoring myself. We're all in this together! We need each other to be successful. We do not act in isolation of others, but rather in community—communities that are formed by homes, schools, businesses, and churches.

A teacher needs her students every bit as much as the students need their teacher. The teacher needs the students to help her learn, and grow, and adapt her teaching style to the myriad, subtle needs of each of her individual students. Every teacher—whether she is a parent, a spouse, a manager, or an educator—faces a fundamental choice: Is she going to model high *command* and *control*? Or is she going to be a paragon of *elasticity* and *endowment*? Is she going to *frustrate* or *furnish*? Will she *constrain* or *contribute*? I will become a model of contribution when I operate in *harmony* with the preferred patterns of learning and behavior of others, rather than trying to impose my preferences on them.

Diversity in Action: Planning a Strategy

"Okay," you might well ask, "how precisely do I operate in harmony with others' preferred learning and behavior patterns? How do I operate in that kind of flexibility?"

The first step toward any problem solving or process improvement is *recognition*. Once I recognize that different individuals absorb new tasks and information in different patterns, and once I am aware that they will *express* that knowledge and ability in different ways, I am well on the way to creating an environment that will honor all the patterns of genius that God has created.

Every lesson should contain a seamless blend of reading and demonstration, verbal instruction, and hands-on activity. Too often, corporate training consists of hours of lecture, augmented by some slight visual reinforcement. This works well for those individuals whose primary learning style is auditory, but what about everyone else? Presentations should be reexamined to determine if there are enough role-play and interactive exercises to satisfy the need for kinesthetic learning. There should be plenty of skits, demonstrations, pictures, and charts to help visual learners form those all-important mental images.

Consider making meeting environments more "modality-friendly." Allow for as much interaction as possible among the participants. People should feel free to stand and pace if they wish. I think it is a tremendous idea to have a table off to one side with water and other refreshments, which provides an "alibi" for those primarily kinesthetic types who *need* to get up and move periodically.

Similarly, many process improvement teams perform their work according to the preferred learning pattern of the project manager, *not* the preferred patterns of the individuals. Different people can be assigned to work in the way in which they are most comfortable: some might diagram and create the visual representations and evidence of the problem at hand; others can be involved in discussion groups that talk through the problem statement and proposed solutions; while a third group would "get in there and do it," e.g., interviewing parties that will be affected by the group's actions, actually walking through the visual diagram that their teammates have created, physically implementing trial solutions, etc.

Take note of how people like to organize their work. Some like to make charts and lists, others will prefer to talk their way through procedures and plans, and another group will want to physically lay out their work in the way that they find logical. Help them to operate in the mode that is most effective for *them,* not the manner that works best for you.

Even something like teaching your kids to spell takes on the form of honoring their individual genius. One child will want to use flash cards and look at words to remember them, another will want to recite the words and letters out loud, and a third child will write out his spelling words to see if they "feel" right. Help them to utilize *all three* learning modalities and recognize that they have a pattern that works best *for them.* Some kids study perfectly well with the radio or television on; others need librarylike silence. Some kinesthetic children will pop up and down for water, to sharpen their pencils, and so on. Let them! My prayer, Dear Reader, is that you will let them learn.

True power is the art of making other people powerful. You will become truly powerful when you take the time to broaden your own belief in others to the point where you are willing, even eager, to consciously enrich their human spirit and release the untapped potential, the true *genius* that lies within each and every human being you meet. *Go for it!*

Good Health: An Immeasurable Asset!

ONE OF THE BEST-KEPT SECRETS in America today is the overwhelming evidence that the human body, far from proving the myth of evolution, is undeniable evidence of God's special creation. Dear Reader, there was a time in my life when I believed all the evolutionary myths that I had been taught in school. I had seen the pictures in textbooks showing monkeys gradually evolving into men, and it all looked perfectly logical to me. Even when I became a Christian and I desired to accept the Bible as the inspired, infallible, authoritative Word of God, I wondered what I was going to do about the scientific "fact" of evolution. Did the Bible contain Truth about other aspects of life, but only myth when it came to the subject of creation?

I told you that the author who totally changed my thinking on the field of human motivation was Dr. Mark Cosgrove, and his two books, *The Amazing Body Human* and *The Essence of Human Nature.* Mark was the man who helped me see and understand that *far* from being evolved from some genus of monkey, man's body is shining, irrefutable evidence of the handiwork of God Himself!

In *The Amazing Body Human,* Mark describes various physical characteristics that set human beings apart from all animals. He writes that "the body tells of our special design, of our personhood, of our glory."[1] Mark argues that we have overlooked the uniqueness of the human body because of an overenthusiastic support for the theory of evolution and the need to see humans as the descendants of apes. We have *assumed* evolution to be factual because it has been drilled into us since elementary school. We have *assumed* without asking questions, without really looking into the issue at all. Any fair-minded individual who will make even a minimal effort to investigate both sides of the issue will be fascinated to find a continual abundance of historical and archaeological evidence that supports the biblical account of Creation. Some universities even offer degrees in Creation Science, and there are schools of Christian Science springing up across America.

Mark Cosgrove has outlined an extremely important concept: the concept of "personhood." Personhood has been severely diluted, if not altogether annihilated, by the theory of evolution. If, indeed, we are no more than a higher species of ape, then the notion that we have a *spiritual* dimension, that we have a consciousness and a soul that is created in the image of God, seems flatly ridiculous. On the other hand, if we *do* have a Creator, who formed us for much more than physical survival and dominance, then we must dig a little deeper for evidence of the Creator's hand.

What's so remarkable about Mark's observations is that they make good, plain, common sense! Consider this tenet from evolutionary theory: those species that possess characteristics most useful for physical survival will remain, while those species with traits that leave them vulnerable will not survive. This is the critically important foundation of natural selection on which all of evolutionary theory rests. Evolutionists assert that these "vulnerable" traits will disappear as species evolve and become more highly suited for the interminable struggle for survival.

Yet, Mark observes, "many of the unique human features are even clear disadvantages to physical survival and are therefore not seen in the animal world. Changes in the human airway for speech and the nakedness of the human body are good examples of this."[2] I mentioned earlier that man's entire face and throat are uniquely suited for the formation of speech. Mark explains that man is the only creature who cannot drink and breathe at the same time. This is because the human throat has a uniquely complex design that leaves man at a *disadvantage* for physical survival, since it is far easier for a human being to choke to death on food than it is for an animal. So why does man, if he is the most highly evolved form of animal life, possess this characteristic that presents such a clear, physical inferiority to animals? Mark writes,

> The human throat exists fully developed only in man and speaks clearly of the gulf between humans and animals in the physical realm. . . . The function of the unique human airway revolves around personhood, since the human throat was designed for manufacturing the ingredients of a spoken language.[3]

Nothing about the human body suggests that it is an animal. Everything about the human body, even down to the tiniest details—the lips, the eyebrows, the eyelashes, the fingernails—speak of personal importance. Everything about the human body is intensely personal.

The Bible commands us to acknowledge God in everything that we do (Prov. 3:6), and we certainly want to acknowledge that we have been given a wonderful body that can run, jump, and play—a body that can afford us years of pleasure and delight, *if* we take care of it. The human body itself—which so many of us take for granted or even actively abuse through cigarettes, alcohol, drugs, overeating, and lack of exercise—is, indeed, the seventh secret for unleashing untapped potential.

Dear Reader, you have faithfully read through this book, and you are now armed with six secrets for turning ordinary people into extraordinary performers. You hold in your hands a veritable arsenal for becoming a master of human performance technology. But if you don't treat your body with the same kind of reverence and respect with which you should treat other human beings, you will never live long enough, or robustly enough, to be able to use the other six secrets to their maximum effect. We must honor our bodies and treat them with care. Our bodies are as much a source of untapped potential as our minds! The purpose of this chapter is to help you develop and maintain peak physical health and performance.

To begin with, let's talk about the absolute basics of life: water and oxygen.

Water: The Ultimate Nutrient

The human body is composed of 45 to 75 percent water. Water is absolutely essential for life and health. A human can survive for weeks on a diet that consists of nothing but water, whereas that same individual will die within just a few days if his body is deprived of fluids.

It is my firm belief that making a conscious, consistent effort to drink water will substantially improve the health of your body. For years, I have recommended that every man and woman should drink half their weight in ounces of water each day. A man who weighs 170 pounds should drink 85 ounces (that's just over five pints) of water each day. Drink water that has been purified or distilled. Too much tap water today carries chemicals in it that are not good for the body or the blood.

Many of you reading this *think* you're getting your proper intake of water through all the coffee, soda, and tea you drink. Did you know that all of these fluids I have just mentioned contain materials that are *harmful* to you? Coffee, tea, and most sodas contain caffeine, which acts as a diuretic to the human body. A diuretic acts to *expel* fluids from your body. You've noticed how you can drink coffee or soda, and just a few minutes later you're thirsty again? That's because your brain is sending you accurate messages that your body fluids are being depleted. Even though you're drinking a liquid, that fluid is actually acting to *dehydrate* your body! I've read research that indicates that a large percentage of the men and women you will meet today are walking around in a state of dehydration—and don't even know it.[4]

We Need Oxygen in the Brain and in the Blood

The second element that is essential for life and health is air—oxygen. Did you know that our brain comprises only one-fiftieth of our overall body weight, but the human brain demands one-*fifth* of all the body's oxygen?[5] Oxygenation of the brain and the blood is tremendously important.

As with water, too many of us take oxygenation for granted. After all, we breathe all day long! Surely our brain and our bodies are getting enough air. Unfortunately, that just isn't the case. Too many of us sit in office buildings all day, and the most strenuous exercise we'll perform all day will be a walk out to the parking lot to get in the car. When we are involved in this largely sedentary activity, we tend to breathe shallowly, and the brain and body are not getting their proper levels of oxygen.

Regular exercise, of course, is the best remedy for this situation, but even ten minutes of deep-breathing exercises each day have a terrifically invigorating and restorative effect. Throughout thirty years of teaching Kung Fu, one of the warm-ups I've had my students perform is ten minutes of the deep-breathing discipline I am about to share with you.

The object of the exercise is to take air into your diaphragm. I've found that the best way to do this is to breathe in deeply through your nose, rather than through your mouth. When you do, your stomach, *not* your chest, should expand. Inhale in a slow, deep breath, and then exhale through your mouth in the same kind of slow breath. Try to expel *all* the air you have taken in. Make your long, slow inhale last for five seconds, and make your exhale also last for five seconds. As you become more proficient at this, you will be able to increase your times substantially. My advanced students were able to inhale for *thirty seconds,* and exhale for the same period of time. Talk about an energy booster! This procedure is tremendous exercise for your lungs and heart, and provides much needed oxygen to the brain and to the blood. Practicing this kind of deep breathing also drops your heart rate to sixty beats per minute, which is an optimum level for good health. When you first begin this deep-breathing exercise, you may feel light-headed or dizzy. If you do, stop the deep breathing. Your brain is telling you, "Whoa! I'm not used to all this healthy, life-giving oxygen being up here all at once." This light-headedness is perfectly normal for someone who has not been practicing proper breathing techniques. When it passes, resume your deep-breathing exercise. In a very short time, you'll find that the light-headedness will not occur any longer. Deep breathing has a marvelously calming and therapeutic effect on the human body. The effects are similar to taking a Valium, without any of the negative side effects that come with taking a drug. Like drinking water, deep breathing will have almost instantaneous, noticeable, healthful effects on your body.

Exercise: Good for the Body *and* the Mind

All the experts agree that we need a bare minimum of twenty minutes of exercise at least three times a week. A great many people exercise simply to enhance their physical appearance, but there are so many more benefits to be derived from exercise besides that! First of all, exercise provides that all-important oxygenation of the brain and blood I just described to you. Of course, there are the obvious benefits of exercising the heart and lungs that come from exercise.

But did you know that regular exercise, far from fatiguing you, actually boosts your energy level and will improve your mood?

Bodily exercise produces the chemical serotonin into the body. Serotonin can be called the "feel-good" chemical. It actually makes you feel good about yourself. People take Prozac and other anti-depressant drugs precisely to produce more serotonin in their bodies. Serotonin works to reduce the debilitating effects of another body chemical, called cortisol, which is produced by stress.[6]

When we are suddenly frightened, our brain releases cortisol. It is part of the "fight-or-flight" syndrome. When we suddenly are confronted by danger, cortisol increases our awareness and attention, allowing us to meet the perceived threat and either fight or flee. The exertion that is produced by the ensuing fight (or retreat) causes the cortisol to dissipate. The problem is, in today's society, all too often the body reacts as if it is in a fight-or-flight situation when it really isn't.[7] For example, you're driving down the expressway when suddenly the car in the next lane veers over into your lane. You have to jam on the brakes to avoid a collision at sixty-five miles per hour. Suddenly, your heart is pounding, your palms are sweating, and your body is tense. Your eyes are wide open, scanning the road for any other danger. You have just experienced the fight-or-flight syndrome. The only problem is, you didn't have to fight or flee. Doesn't take much effort to stomp on the brake and whip the steering wheel, does it? Your brain has just dumped cortisol into your system to meet the danger, but there has been no exertion to dissipate it. (Shouting at the other driver is not the kind of "exercise" I'm talking about!) The cortisol remains at dangerous levels in the body. This kind of situation happens more often than you might think. People who go to watch movies like *Jurassic Park,* which cause entire audiences to cry out in fear, are producing cortisol in their bodies without the corresponding active response to danger. Even the anger that is produced by interoffice stress can and does produce cortisol in the body.

Stress, and the anger that accompanies it, actually shuts down the immune system. Rage, anger, hatred, and bitterness are all processed by our limbic system, which is also inextricably related to our immune system! The limbic system takes its cues from our minds. If our minds are busy with anger or hatred, the limbic system concentrates on these powerful emotions and ignores the functions of the immune system, i.e., fighting infections and disease. Hate actually destroys the hater! Our immune system functions at peak efficiency when our minds are focused on emotions like joy, peace, faith, thanksgiving, and hope.

God's word speaks directly to the truth of the bodies He created for us: "The spirit of a man will sustain him in sickness, / But who can bear a broken spirit?" (Prov. 18:14). About 1,900 years before Norman Vincent Peale wrote *The Power of Positive Thinking*, the apostle Paul encouraged the Christians at Philippi:

> Finally, brethren, whatever things are true, whatever things are noble, whatever things are just, whatever things are pure, whatever things are lovely, whatever things are of good report, if there is any virtue and if there is anything praiseworthy—meditate on these things. (Phil. 4:8)

Norman Cousins, who wrote *Anatomy of an Illness,* used laughter and Vitamin C to rid himself of a skeletal disorder. His book made the whole world stand up and take notice of the connection of mind and body in regard to physical health. Mr. Cousins bolstered his immune system with laughter. He flooded his limbic system with positive emotions, and his immune system responded accordingly.[8] Once again, Proverbs divulges this truth with simplicity and power: "A merry heart does good, like medicine, / But a broken spirit dries the bones" (Prov. 17:22).

The condition of *mental health*—our thoughts and our emotions—has a direct bearing on our *physical* health. But we can improve the state of our mental health through physical exercise, which produces the "feel-good" chemical serotonin.

Exercise Can Be Affordable and Fun

I am going to suggest some exercises for you that are fun, inexpensive, and tremendously effective. I recently celebrated my fiftieth birthday, and I can honestly tell you that I have the body of a man half my age. The exercises I am going to share with you have helped me develop and maintain that body. One word of caution: when you first picked this book up off the shelf, you saw there were no letters that looked like "M.D." after my name. I have, as a martial arts expert, done years of research on what types of physical disciplines are safe and effective. However, I am not your doctor. No one should begin any kind of program of intense physical exercise without first consulting his or her doctor. It only makes good sense to make sure that you and your physician are in agreement about what's best for your body. If your doctor disagrees with something I've said during this chapter, follow your doctor's advice. He knows a whole lot more about your body than I do. But I will say this: everything I am about to share with you is part of my regular exercise regimen, and it has never resulted in anything but increased health, stamina, and energy for me.

The triad of physical health that all of us should be aiming for is cardiovascular fitness, flexibility, and strength. One marvelous way to improve cardiovascular fitness is by walking. Many of us, as we get older, find that jogging is *very* tough on the knees. Walking does not subject the legs to the serious pounding that jogging does, as long as you've been careful to invest in a good pair of shoes. Furthermore, unlike jogging, walking allows you to *talk*. I walk for forty-five minutes every day with my wife. We walk together at the end of the day and enjoy the spectacular Florida sunsets. We walk, and we talk (how many couples would benefit from even *fifteen* minutes a day of that?), and we breathe deeply, supplying life-giving oxygen to our brains and blood. We also breathe in the pleasure of each other's company, bringing health to our home *and* our hearts!

Jumping rope is another marvelous form of exercise that doesn't put a lot of strain on the legs. It only takes a short time to get the hang of it, and you'll improve your sense of timing and coordination, as well as increase your cardiovascular health.

There are any number of exercises you can use to improve your flexibility. Stretching, of course, is vitally important. Go to the circus and watch the big cats in the cages. They're constantly stretching their muscles to keep them lithe and supple. So should you. Be sure to keep your back straight while stretching. Can you reach over and touch your palms to the floor? I can, and frankly, I love to see the look of consternation on the faces of men twenty years younger than I who can't do it! One thing that bothers me—too many people will bend over to touch their toes and bounce right back up again. That's tremendously harmful for your lower back! If you wouldn't lift a weight with your back all bent over, why would you want to lift your upper body's weight that way? It's all right to bend over to stretch, but then squat down, straighten your back, *then* rise, just as you would if you were lifting weights.

Twisting from side to side slowly but firmly is good for your back and stomach muscles. Tumbling is tremendous for your flexibility and agility, as well as for maintaining the suppleness and resiliency of your spine. I'll roll in a ball, back and forth, across the living room floor. This maintains the elasticity of your muscles, especially of your spine.

Another thing my wife and I like to do together is massage. I've learned through my Kung Fu training that massage increases circulation, improves flexibility, and improves emotional and physical health. A good, soothing massage releases healthful serotonin and reduces that stress-induced cortisol. Like walking together, giving each other massages is wonderful for the health of our marriage, as well!

For sheer strength building, push-ups and pull-ups are tremendous. Your body weight provides the resistance you need for building muscle mass. Pull-ups, in particular, are superb for the upper body. You can buy a piece of equipment that can be placed over a doorjamb for easy use, or you may suspend a bar from a tree in the backyard. Push-ups develop your chest, back, and shoulders. You can buy free weights if you want to, but the exercises I've given you here will help you build all the strength you could ever want in your shoulders and arms.

Another important exercise you should perform is the strengthening of the stomach muscles. There is no need to buy any kind of equipment to do this. You can easily perform "crunches" to build up the upper and lower abdominal muscles. If these muscles are not exercised, when you get older they will begin to sag, and you will develop back trouble. To perform crunches, just lie on your back with your legs bent so that your knees are pointing to the ceiling. Move your knees toward your face, while simultaneously lifting your head and neck toward your knees. Your buttocks should lift off the floor, but your back should not. The reason crunches are superior to traditional sit-ups is because of the stress that sit-ups place on the lower back.

Everything I've described to you requires a minimal investment of money. It's significantly less expensive than shelling out one thousand dollars or more each year for a membership at a health club or gym. Working on your coordination is important, so if you can afford it, spend that money on games like tennis, racquetball, golf, or bowling. These are all fun things you can do with friends and family that will improve your hand-eye and bodily coordination.

Whatever your exercise program, you want to be sure to involve the concepts of challenge, fun, and celebration. The key is to construct a program you can live with. You should be able to see progress or you will become bored and discouraged. It's also important to have fun! There is no eleventh commandment that says, "Thou shalt not have fun while exercising." Exercise should be something we look forward to and can get excited about.

Busy People Need R & R Too!

I want to point out two vitally important areas of your life that have nothing to do with physical exercise: rest and relaxation. A lot of busy parents and executives don't budget time into their hectic schedules for this, and it is absolutely vital!

Different people need different amounts of sleep. Some operate quite well on five to six hours a night, while others are dragging if they don't get eight to nine hours. The critical factor here is the need each of us has for R.E.M. (Rapid Eye Movement) sleep, which is the deepest stage of sleep. Studies have shown that people who exercise regularly enjoy longer periods of R.E.M. sleep, while people who use tranquilizers and sleeping pills enjoy *less* deep, healthful sleep. The same is true of people who use alcohol as a tranquilizer. You'll hear people joking about "passing out" from drinking, but their sleep is a drugged sleep, not one that gives health and replenishment to their bodies.

And since I'm on the subject, let me just say that nothing is more detrimental to mental, physical, and spiritual health than alcohol and narcotics. In my business, I meet thousands of people every year, and I long ago lost count of the tragic stories I've heard about promising careers and loving homes that have been eviscerated by these two monstrous marauders of the human spirit. Once again, I take you to Proverbs for God's clear and succinct warning to us all: "Do not look on the wine when it is red, / When it sparkles in the cup, / When it swirls around smoothly; / At the last it bites like a serpent, / And stings like a viper" (Prov. 23:31–32). I hate illegal drugs with a fury that I struggle to express in polite language. The

Bible tells us that man's great adversary, the devil, "walks about like a roaring lion, seeking whom he may devour" (1 Peter 5:8). Surely the father of lies has manifested himself in the horrible lie that is drugs, a lie that swallows whole families, leaving only the shattered lives of small children in its wake. I hope you'll forgive me, I just needed to get that off my chest! Alcohol, you see, is what killed my dad at age 54.

My right-hand man, Dan Philips, watched *his* father slowly strangle to death as a result of emphysema, produced by years of smoking cigarettes. While cigarettes do not destroy homes and careers the way alcohol and narcotics do, they are just as destructive to the human body. Unlike our parents, we all know how the tar and nicotine contained in cigarettes do violence to our circulatory and respiratory systems. People who smoke astronomically increase their likelihood of strokes, cancer, and heart and lung disease. Cigarette smoking can retard normal growth, cut stamina, and causes skin to wrinkle and age prematurely. I can spot most cigarette smokers immediately by the yellowish, sickly color of their skin. If that isn't readily apparent, the breath of a cigarette smoker can be detected several feet away. The stench of old tobacco befouls their clothes and hair and the air immediately surrounding them. Do you *really* want to be a stench in the nostrils of your friends, your coworkers, and your children? There are all kind of aids now to help people break the incredibly powerful grip of addiction to nicotine. There are nicotine gums, patches, and even support groups for "recovering" smokers. Dear Reader, if you smoke, I urge you: make a commitment to yourself *today* to quit this plague upon your body. You will be frankly amazed at how much better you feel physically!

Relaxation is a second critical ingredient for good health. Too many people believe they need a two-week vacation at Paradise Island in order to relax. Unfortunately, many of us don't have a schedule or a budget that will allow for that! Now, I enjoy vacations as much as the next man, but I don't believe that they hold the key to real relaxation. How many times have you heard someone say, only half-jokingly, "I need a vacation to rest up from my vacation!" Maybe you've said it yourself.

Relaxation is a decision. One wonderful way to relax is to learn to enjoy some of the great, classical music that was produced by the masters such as Bach, Beethoven, and Handel. These musicians strove to make beautiful music that honored God, and has a soothing effect on the entire body. In particular, the compositions that have sixty beats per minute have a marvelously therapeutic effect on the mental and physiological states. Listening to this classical music lowers the heartbeat, eases tension, and actually increases concentration. You will do yourself and your family a great service by introducing this slice of heaven into your home.

The Importance of "Superfoods"

Dr. Patrick Quillin has written a wonderful book, titled *Healing Secrets from the Bible*,[9] which discusses, in depth, the foods that bring maximum health to the human body. I'd highly recommend Dr. Quillin's book for your library. In it, he highlights certain foods, which he calls "superfoods," that actually help our bodies fight disease and promote good health. As with any other diet, you should always consult your own physician before making any radical change in the way you eat.

The three essential elements of any nutrition plan are proteins, carbohydrates, and fats. We need to keep these three in their proper balance. There is a hierarchy of foods that maintain the highest nutritional value. Fresh foods, of course, are best. If you can pick fruit from the tree in your backyard, or grow your own vegetables in a garden, these will have more nutrition than the produce at the grocery store that was picked several weeks before it was ripe in order to compensate for the long ride across the country to your store. The fruits and vegetables in the store are second best. Next comes frozen foods, and after that, canned foods.

All cabbages, cauliflower, and brussels sprouts promote the vitality of the body and protect our bodies from disease. Yogurt and carrots stimulate and reinforce the immune system. Legumes, as well as barley, are a high source of protein. Apples lower cholesterol. An apple a day really *does* keep the doctor away! Onions and garlic also contain tremendous disease-fighting powers. Soybeans are a tremendous source of protein and have been shown to reduce the incidence of prostate and breast cancers. Another benefit of soybeans is that they help the body retain calcium, which maintains the health of the bones.[10]

People often ask me to recommend specific vitamins or minerals. I have discovered a breakthrough technology in vitamin absorption. Kare Mor vitamin and mineral spray is a new item that has recently been developed. I once read that nearly one out of every ten people are unable to swallow regular vitamin pills. These new spray vitamins are a wonderful supplement to a well-balanced diet for these people. I also advise a consultation with your doctor before any changes in your diet or regular vitamin routine are made.

As much as you can, avoid processed sugars and starches, such as white sugar and white bread. Sugar, in particular, is damaging to the human body. Sugar feeds and nourishes yeast overgrowth, which causes all sorts of infections and allergies, and generally weakens the immune system. Even learning disabilities have been traced to yeast overgrowth.

Generally speaking, the whole foods—foods that God put together—give us tremendous energy and super nutrition. A good example of these are the fruits and vegetables that God created to grow on the earth. These foods are also very easy for the body to digest and don't disturb our rest. A steak, on the other hand, as good as it tastes, can take hours of furious effort for the body to digest, which can actually interfere with our deep sleep.

God has given us a unique, personal, physical body to feed and care for. I've spent years studying the ways to do that most efficiently and effectively, and I've done my best to pass along the fruits of those labors to you. When we are physically healthy, we can fully concentrate on developing a healthy mental platform, as well. The next five chapters of this book reveal the secrets that will allow you to do just that.

Greatness Is Based on Goodness

8

IMAGINE BEING IN THE PRESENCE of Patrick Henry and hearing his declaration, "Give me liberty or give me death." He was prepared for the hour at hand, brimming with passion, meaning, and resolve, because a mighty fortress of God-centered truth had been established within his soul. The "liberty or death" speech given in St. John's church, one year before the signing of the Declaration of Independence, stirred action and resistance against the British Empire. At the end of the speech Patrick Henry thundered, "Why stand we here idle? What is it that gentlemen wish? What would they have? Is life so dear, or peace so sweet, as to be purchased at the price of chains and slavery? Forbid it, Almighty God! I know not what course others may take, but as for me: Give me liberty or give me death!"[1]

The power and impetus that evening were not in artillery, rifles, and armies; the power was in Patrick Henry's living words that were drawn from a magazine filled with God-centered values. No one motivated him to present such captivating and powerful truths. The power and challenge did not originate from the outside; they freely flowed from his inner core, from a plumb line of eternal truth centered deep within his soul. He was compelled to articulate deep meanings so full of force and effect that if there had been no human response, the animals of the world would have lined up to march against the British Empire. One individual operating from a God-centered core was the dynamic impetus for freedom. He was the spark that set the colonial hearts ablaze with the fire of truth and righteousness.

Patrick Henry had learned to release a bottomless storehouse of untapped potential and serves as an outstanding model of greatness *based on goodness.* Living core values provide the personal power to act. If all is going wrong, and no one agrees with you, yet the cause is right and just, internal core values enable you to stand before the masses and declare, "Give me liberty or give me death." It has been said that one person filled with conviction and resolve can rout an army of ninety-nine armed with only an interest. When we live by truth, our mind-set is firmly fixed on the mission. God-centered core values are the very backbone of our existence. They are our code of conduct, our constitution, our nonnegotiable and unshakable resolve.

More Than a Blank Slate

Every chapter in this book points to the fact that we are made in God's image. We are a reflection of God in the respect that we are moral agents created by His hands. At birth, God inscribed in us a living moral framework. This sense of right and wrong is not progressively transmitted by the vacillating and relativistic values of society; it is written by the Giver of all value, and it is present in us at birth. We have a sense of "ought" from birth because He placed it within our being. We often refer to it as our "conscience."

However, I must unequivocally warn you that our conscience is not a trustworthy barometer of truth. Jeremiah 17:9 warns us that "The heart is deceitful above all things, / And desperately wicked; / Who can know it?" What makes our internal sense of "ought" reliable is the word of Truth. Psalm 119:105 declares, "Your word is a lamp to my feet / And a light to my path." If we live removed from this light of truth we can easily become misdirected and flounder aimlessly.

Outliving of Inliving Values

God-centered values provide the means to be responsible and responsive. When we operate from this firm foundation, we will reap harvests of clarity, exhilaration, freedom, power, and passion. When we become occupied by these living values and direct our fixed and steady attention on them, the more we will become transformed into their likeness. We will be an outliving expression of these inliving core values. Our values are the moral landmarks signifying what is truly important in life. Living values will enable us to be wise stewards of our valuable time, talents, and treasures. They serve faithfully as the anchor and compass for our journey in life. Values define who we are, what we are, and that for which we stand. We are exceedingly wise when we stand for something, because if we don't stand for something, we will fall for anything.

The Binding Force of People and Nations

What was the binding force that held the Jewish people together during the diaspora (dispersion)? Without question it was their God-centered values. They had been taught, as outlined in the book of Deuteronomy, to live by the Word of God moment by moment and day by day. They were admonished, in Deuteronomy 4:40, to keep His statutes and commandments; "that it may go well with you and with your children after you, and that you may prolong your days in the land which the LORD your God is giving you for all time." Again and again, the Israelites were admonished to "be careful to do as the LORD your God has commanded you; you shall not turn aside to the right hand or to the left" (Deut. 5:32).

Alexis de Tocqueville, the French statesman and author, visited America in the 1830s. As he traveled across the new nation and interviewed hundreds of Americans, he observed:

> I sought for the key to the greatness and genius of America in her harbors . . . ; in her fertile fields and boundless forests; in her rich mines and vast world commerce; in her public school system and institutions of learning. I sought for it in her democratic Congress and in her matchless Constitution. Not until I went into the churches of America and heard her pulpits aflame with righteousness did I understand the secret of her genius and power. America is great because America is good, and if America ever ceases to be good, America will cease to be great.[2]

What de Tocqueville discovered was God-centered values embraced by the people of this country! The strength of America, with all her greatness, power, and genius, was not in physical or material resources but in spiritual resources—her values. John Witherspoon, one of our Founding Fathers, declared, "A republic, once equally proved, must either preserve its virtue or lose its liberty."[3] It is painfully obvious, to even the most casual observer, that we have not passed the torch of values on to the next generation, and as a result, we Americans are now paying a heavy price for our loss of virtue.

Why Develop Our Core Value System?

Our core values should be timeless, universal, immutable principles that guide and govern our attitudes and actions. These values serve as our moral and ethical boundary lines. They will preserve us from the enslavement of a bankrupt, unprincipled life and simultaneously empower us to pursue truth and personal integrity in the accomplishment of our loftiest goals and highest ambitions. When we are undergirded by truth and live our lives on the basis of solid, biblical values, our thinking, actions, and attitudes will be governed by a most noble framework.

When values are embraced as our own personal constitution, they provide a stable foundation. Values will not remain dormant: they produce positive results such as consistency, productivity, and a sense of fairness. Values preserve the moral and spiritual strength of individuals, families, and nations. Core values provide a reason to believe, a reason to achieve, and a reason to celebrate. As we interact with others, perform tasks, and complete projects, we should always be aware of the operation of underlying values. Values are our reasons for long-term success and cohesiveness. Our values are the foundation stones for goodness, contribution, and caring.

If we wish to possess values that are vibrant, active, and alive, they must be identified, clearly written, and memorized. Our core value system should then be discussed with our family and friends. A living values document has increased meaning for families when it is framed and proudly displayed in the home. When core values adorn our walls, this family constitution serves as a beacon of truth pointing every family member to that which is right and good for the individual, for the family, and for our country! What joy we share when every family member embraces these core values and organizes their lives around them!

What is the enabling power that breaks the chains of mediocrity and catapults the individual into magnificence? How may we fully leverage the incomparable human spirit? Maximum leverage for the highest and best is to live our lives built on the basis of solid truth. A more superior basis from which to live a dynamic and purposeful life does not exist.

From Pleasure to Pain, or Pain to Pleasure?

The highest possible degree of energy and passion is aroused when we operate from a sturdy platform of core values. Our forefathers pledged everything important when they signed the Declaration of Independence. They immediately put at extreme risk their lives, their possessions, and even their families.

In today's freewheeling society we often hear, "We must first please self." Our own pleasures appear to command the greatest attention. The pleasure principle, moving from pain and discomfort to pleasure, is a major means of motivation for a large segment of our society. This form of motivation was foreign to our Founding Fathers because they, most certainly, were not moving away from pain toward pleasure. Rather, they were moving from pleasure to pain, they were moving toward sacrifice because of a deep sense of meaning and purpose—a meaning and purpose so noble that it transcended inconvenience, discomfort, and pain. The all-consuming goal of our forefathers was not pleasure. They understood that *happiness is an outcome, rather than the objective, for doing right things for the right reasons.*

Seeds of Greatness

Imagine for a moment the beginning of our great country, when God-centered values were shared by the overwhelming majority of the people. Then follow our decline, as we disregarded those values, and evaluate where we are today as a nation, socially and morally. The present American condition is at one of the lowest points in our history. Violent crime is on the increase, and almost every category of good social behavior is declining. We have abandoned goodness, and therefore, greatness is found wanting. At our own peril, we are rapidly abandoning such values as restraint, goodness, and the sense of "plain old right and wrong."

Imagine that you see a family leaving Great Britain to move to America. Notice that they are taking the very best seeds from crops that have produced abundantly for hundreds of years. These seeds have been perfected generation after generation and produce the most nutritious food possible, food that nurtures strong and healthy bodies. This family carefully transports these "good seeds" to America. With great joy, the fertile seeds are planted with the knowledge that seeds from these new crops will be passed on from generation to generation, here in a new country. The nutrition produced by these crops will be even better, and the seeds that will be passed on to the future generations will also be better.

The parallel is quite clear, as we relate the seeds to our country's values. The tragic mistake America has made for far too long is that we have not taken the values of our Founding Fathers and passed them on to future generations. We are not involving our family members in the process of developing a family values statement. The word of truth (values) should be clearly displayed in our homes:

> You shall teach them diligently to your children, and shall talk of them when you sit in your house, when you walk by the way, when you lie down, and when you rise up. You shall bind them as a sign on your hand, and they shall be as frontlets between your eyes. You shall write them on the doorposts of your house and on your gates. (Deut. 6:7–9)

Perhaps we are not taking sufficient time with our family members to focus on the importance, benefits, and results of living according to an unshakable set of core values. It takes precious time to sit down with a child and say: "Let's discuss the values our family has lived by for many, many years. These are the values your grandmother and grandfather lived by, and your great-grandparents too. These core values made the difference in every life in our family. Shouldn't we live this way too?" These are precious words, communicated in the most important arena to the inheritors of our nation's values. Let us be diligent as to how we handle this most vital responsibility. I am convinced that the survival of our families and our nation depends upon it!

Developing the Skill-Set

Previously I mentioned that mind-set precedes skill-set, belief precedes behavior, philosophy precedes performance, and theory precedes practice. Thus far in our journey we have considered the mind-set and the philosophy. Now, we will develop the skill-set—the practice and application of what we know.

An illuminating and exhilarating exercise is to assemble and polish a personal values statement. Proverbs contains a great arsenal of human values and virtues, so strong and practical that, if adopted and exercised, it will sustain this nation and its families for thousands of years. It is from this book that we will develop a living, practical, and workable list of values. The selected values should be so important that you not only live by them but are willing to die by them. If you haven't discerned what you would die for, neither can you know what you would live for! I want to urge you to take sufficient time to complete this exercise, to help you obtain clarity as to how your life is conducted in comparison to your internal core values. Upon completion of the exercise, you will be able to step back and measure what you must do in order to realize alignment and congruence in your life. What an inspiring challenge!

Let's begin with a careful review of the list of values, which is taken directly from the book of Proverbs and emanates from God's nature. The first step is to select, from the "Values Shopping List," at least ten of the values you most value.

Values Shopping List

1. Wisdom	18. Faith	35. Patience
2. Understanding	19. Peacemaking	36. Loyalty
3. Spirituality	20. Obedience	37. Gentleness
4. Justice	21. Harmony	38. Giving
5. Discipline	22. Dependability	39. Compassion
6. Emotional stability	23. Responsibility	40. Kindness
7. Listening	24. Independence	41. Forgiveness
8. Learning	25. Virtue	42. Friendliness
9. Righteousness	26. Hope	43. Vision
10. Judgment	27. Trust	44. Authenticity
11. Purpose	28. Teaching	45. Respect
12. Confidence	29. Social growth	46. Honesty
13. Power	30. Patriotism	47. Morality
14. Humility	31. Graciousness	48. Family
15. Love	32. Support	49. Fear of the Lord
16. Purity	33. Integrity	50. Financial responsibility
17. Industry	34. Flexibility	51. Physical health

When we examine this list of values we are focusing on what God Himself values; this is true because all values emanate from His nature. He is the Originator of all values. Without God there is no value! So let us begin the creation of our own personal values statement by incorporating the values of our Creator into our own written code of ethics. Never forget values form thoughts, thoughts create actions, actions develop habits, habits mold character, and character determines destiny.

Step One: Carefully review the "Values Shopping List" and select at least ten (10) that are uncompromisingly important.

1. _____
2. _____
3. _____
4. _____
5. _____
6. _____
7. _____
8. _____
9. _____
10. _____

Step Two: Arrange those ten values in numerical priority, with Number One being your most important value. (You can use the chart set up below for Steps Two and Three.)

1. _____
2. _____
3. _____
4. _____
5. _____
6. _____
7. _____
8. _____
9. _____
10. _____

Step Three: (a) Describe what each value means.

(b) Describe what each value does *not* mean.

Example:

Value: Giver

Meaning: (a) As a giver I like to contribute.

Does not mean: (b) I am selfish.

Value	Meaning	Does not mean
1.		
2.		
3.		
4.		
5.		
6.		
7.		
8.		
9.		
10.		

Step Four: For the sake of convenience, recopy the ten critical values you identified in Step One. Then, in Step Five, estimate how much time you actually spend living the ten values. How much of an investment of your actual time and effort do you make in living these vital values?

Step Five: (a) Review the ten values in Step Two.

(b) How much time do you spend on each value?

1. _____

2. _____

3. _____

4. _____

5. _____

6. _____

7. _____

8. _____

9. _____

10. _____

You can now easily compare the time currently expended on living the values identified in Step Two. If the first value in Step Four is love and it is farther down, or not on the list in Step Five, then your time is not dedicated toward what you value most. In this event, there is no congruence, and you are floundering in a world where the greatest degree of balance and stability is required. It is certain that unless we are intact internally we cannot be at our best externally. We must learn to schedule our priorities and not simply prioritize our schedule.

Step 6: If you had only six months to live, what five values would be most important? (Are your "top five" values *really* your top five?)

My values, with only six months to live:

1. _____

2. _____

3. _____

4. _____

5. _____

The North Star

When I decide, up front, that what is important to God is important to me, and then determine to live my life in a manner that manifests God-centered values then I am successful. Why? Because, I am examining the essentials and nonessentials, and I have decided to embrace that which is right and good and true. With resolute determination, I am choosing to turn from those things that cause me to spiral downward. When I do this, I am embracing that which is of eternal importance for my country, my family, and me.

The sextant is a critical navigational instrument that allows seagoing vessels to maintain a fixed course. In the beginning of the journey, a course and destination are established. During the journey, the seaman manning the rudder strives to keep the ship on course, but small variances in steering, along with boisterous winds or angry waves, can knock the ship off course. If no adjustment is made, the ship will not reach the predetermined destination. It will zigzag, hopelessly and aimlessly, wandering alone in a vast, indifferent ocean. The sextant readings properly align the ship with its intended destination. The sextant points to the North Star, and the ship's bearing is adjusted as many times as necessary to stay on course. The sextant consistently defines the proper direction in spite of winds, gales, or the roughest of seas.

If we are to maintain a fixed and steady bearing toward personal growth and responsibility, our lives must be aligned with True North. The sextant, pointing to the North Star, serves as our reminder to live from a God-centered perspective. The storms and winds that we encounter during our course in this life can push our vessel far from our intended destination. The rudder that steers the ship represents our choices. We may vacillate, choosing to veer right or left, and lose our bearing; or we may sail straight and true. To hold a steady course through the turbulent winds of change and the storms of pain and loss requires an unerring fix on the North Star.

Our North Star of excellence is always there, ready to help us accurately adjust our course headings. It has never moved and may be trusted completely. We are successful when we are aligned with the North Star, because the Lord of the Ages is the North Star. God placed the North Star in the heavens so that we might safely navigate every storm and end our course at the desired destination. The North Star of Glory, the Lord Himself, is our North Star for yesterday, today, and tomorrow. You will never lose your bearing nor veer off course when you follow His light and steer His course to glory. This is wisdom, this is stability, this is life!

You are now equipped to live victoriously and powerfully from a God-centered values system that proclaims that greatness is based on goodness!

Humans Need
Meaning and Purpose

9

IN A SERMON HE DELIVERED to his congregation, Dr. D. James
Kennedy painted a vivid portrait of a man who lived a life that
was wholly and completely focused on the accomplishment of a
mission. The sermon recounted the story of David Livingstone,
whom Dr. Kennedy referred to as "the greatest missionary in the
past five hundred years—the apostle to Africa." It was to this man
that Henry Stanley said, "Dr. Livingstone, I presume." Here is an
excerpt from the text of Dr. Kennedy's sermon:

> Livingstone was asked to speak at the University of Glasgow. He
> perhaps would have declined had he known what was waiting for
> him. It was the custom of the undergraduates in those days to heckle
> speakers that came, and they were well prepared for this preacher.
> They had peashooters, as any good university student should have;
> they had toy trumpets, rattles, and noise makers of every description.
> Livingstone walked out onto the platform with the tread of a man
> who had walked eleven thousand miles. His left arm hung limply at
> his side, having been almost ripped from his body by a huge lion
> which crushed his shoulder to splinters. His face was a dark, leathery
> brown from sixteen years in the African sun. It was furrowed with

innumerable lines from the bouts of African fever which had racked and emaciated his body. He was, as he described himself, a "ruckle of bones." He had been attacked by savages and by the Turks who plied their vicious slave trade. His body was wasted; he was half deaf from rheumatic fever and half blind from a branch that had slapped him in the eyes in the jungle.

The students stared, and they knew that here was a life that was literally being burned out for God. Not a rattle moved, not a foot shuffled. A hush crept over that vast auditorium and they listened with rapt silence as David Livingstone told them about his journeys in Africa and about the tremendous needs of this vast African population.[1]

Just as David Livingstone's battered body proclaimed more forcefully than any spoken message the evidence of his commitment, God's creation bears irrefutable testimony to the truth of God's existence and His sense of mission. God's creation *screams* of meaning and purpose. There is nothing in nature that is random or mindless. As I said during our discussion of passion, a work of art is not the result of someone taking a bucket of paint and throwing it, willy-nilly, onto a piece of canvas. A true work of art reflects self-conscious conversation, planning, design, and thought. I challenge you to show me something in creation that has no purpose.

If you carefully study any ecosystem, you'll discover there are no "throwaway" parts in it. Every member of that environmental system is interconnected, highly significant, and pregnant with purpose. Creation gives thunderous evidence that God is a *meaning* Being. Any artistic masterpiece reflects the artist's intention and design. The masterpiece is, indeed, a reflection of the artist's personhood. Everything in nature is a reflection of the Creator's *purpose*.

We see the personal nature of God in the construction of our bodies. Consider DNA, which is like an advanced medical textbook containing all the codes and instructions for the human body. We are just beginning to comprehend the significance of DNA. But one thing is absolutely certain: each and every human being has his or her own personal DNA "textbook." It is unique to that individual, and it is a testimony to God's purpose and meaning that eclipses even a stark message like the broken body of David Livingstone.

When you think about it, the only mindless, random activity you'll witness in all creation is the behavior of a man who has *rejected* the truth of God's existence and believes that life is merely a jumble of purposeless, unconnected events. This man may suddenly snap and commit some senseless, unconscionable act of violence. By using adjectives like *senseless* or *meaningless,* we are saying the man's actions *make no sense to us,* because they have no apparent purpose. A man who climbs a tower and begins sniping at passersby when the whim strikes him, or a woman who drives her car into a lake with her children still sleeping within are not behaving in ways that evidence any sense of *purpose* to us. These lost souls see no logical outcome to the totality of creation or their own isolated actions, and therefore, they are "like a wave of the sea driven and tossed by the wind" (James 1:6). Their lives are aimless, purposeless, and their only motivation is to satisfy whatever sensual hungers animate their consciousness at that particular moment. Their mind-set has preceded their action: they see the world as random, without meaning or sense, and therefore they behave nonsensically.

Unleashing Untapped Potential Is the Result of *Purpose*

Let's quickly review the philosophical construct that underlies this entire book. I started with the bedrock that God—a personal, powerful, Holy Being—exists. The personal nature of God is the model for all mankind and all creation. It is reflected in everything we see.

Second, I stand on the truth of God's Word, the Bible, that God created man in His own image. Every human being, therefore, is a reflection of God Himself. We reflect God's purpose. My mind and body were created by *intention*. My very soul is constituted to seek meaning, to live in harmony with meaning, and to live out meaning and intention. Dear Reader, you were designed to live with a constant sense of purpose and destiny!

By learning about the essence of the personal nature of God, I learn how my Creator intended for *me* to live. By following God's blueprint for my life, I can live in harmony with who I am—which is a reflection of who *He* is! If I am to be truly successful, personally and professionally, I need to align myself with God's purpose.

Meaning in the Workplace

There are essentially three types of companies that operate throughout the world today. You recognize them by what their mission is. Far too many organizations are *profit*-driven. They focus on the collection and maximization of profits. Regardless of any fine-sounding words posted in the lobby for visitors to read, there is very little recognition and celebration of the human spirit in these organizations. There is virtually no passion, since it is impossible for a workforce to be passionate about profits that are generated for someone else. The energy level in these organizations is invariably, inevitably low.

The second type of company is the *customer*-driven company. At this level, you see the first glimmerings of *synergy*, which, literally translated, means "together energy." The customer-driven company strives to create a sense of contribution, and the energy level there is significantly higher than in those companies who focus on the bottom line.

However, to truly maximize the collective potential of every human being in the workplace, to elicit a sense of passion and commitment, there is a third level to which the truly successful organization must aspire, and that is to become a *meaning*-driven company. As Dr. Baum said, only *meaning* truly arouses energy. No job is big enough to house the human spirit. If leaders desire to be truly successful, both on the top line *and* the bottom line, then they must broaden the borders of the job with meaning. Otherwise, people won't be effective, productive, or competitive. Without meaning, we feel insignificant, fearful, and disconnected. Human beings are meaning seekers and meaning makers. We are eternal question boxes (this is especially true of children), constantly seeking to bring a sense of meaning to everything we see. When we can attach meaning to what we do, we feel significant, confident, and *connected* to the organization and to our coworkers.

What truly extracts excellence is to have a job that is meaningful, not "money-full." You need no further proof of this than to look at the many professional athletes, entertainers, and musicians—many of whom make astronomical paychecks—whose lives degenerate into a morass of divorce, drugs, misery, and despair because they have no sense of destiny or meaning. Ask O. J. Simpson if a big paycheck brings happiness.

The human spirit is greater than any company. There is no expiration date on the human soul, but there *is* an expiration date on every company. When we absorb this truth, we reach the inescapable conclusion that the human soul is worth *infinitely* more than all the profits that any company could ever earn! You hear a lot of folks talking about "value-added," but *meaning* is the ultimate value-added experience.

Every person in every organization needs to feel that who they are and what they're doing have significance. There are no little people or little places. This is not a nice-sounding slogan, but a fact that reflects God's love toward all mankind. Jesus asked, "Are not two sparrows sold for a copper coin? And not one of them falls to the ground apart from your Father's will. But the very hairs of your head are all numbered. Do not fear therefore; you are of more value than many sparrows" (Matt. 10:29–31).

It is essential that this truth of the significance and worth of every individual is communicated with sincerity and spirit to all. People need to know that they are not "performance puppets," but powerful, purposeful partners connected to a meaning greater than the individual tasks they perform. The operative word here is *connection*. There must be a connection with a higher purpose. When a leader imbues a job with meaning, then the task can broaden to meet the dimensions of the human spirit. The constant theme of any and all communications within an organization should be "Why are we here?" and "What are we trying to accomplish?" I have visited far too many companies that seem preoccupied with "What's wrong?" and "Who did it?" One of the most crucial and vital tasks facing any superior leader is to help every person who walks into a job connect what they're doing with the overall purpose of the organization. This is the difference between an organization that is powerful and dynamic and one that is unanchored and ineffectual.

Meaning unifies us! In an environment where meaning is clear, there is no fragmentation. There is a sense of connection. A company that has labored to communicate a sense of shared meaning provides harmony and creates purpose partners, rather than a staff that is in conflict and competition. Meaning creates clarity; clarity formulates power; power generates sustained energy; and sustained energy produces high productivity and high satisfaction—for customers *and* employees.

Another word for "power" is one which we've spent some time with already: passion. Passion springs out of meaning.

A Worker, a Builder, and a Creator

You've probably heard the story of a man who was walking down a street that led him past three men who were laying bricks. Curious, the man stopped to talk to one of the workers.

"What are you doing?" he asked the man.

The workman looked up at him with some disgust. "I'm building a wall," he replied shortly.

The man was still curious, so he stopped and asked the second man, "What are you doing?"

The second worker was more forthcoming. "I'm building a church," he replied.

Curiosity satisfied, the man was about to go on his way, when he noticed a third worker slapping bricks along the string line with alacrity. This workman was whistling cheerfully as he worked. The pedestrian was drawn by this man's good cheer. He asked the third man, "What are you doing?"

The third worker looked up with a bright smile. "I'm building a cathedral," he replied, "a place where lives will be changed. This is a building in which marriages and families will be strengthened, the bonds of addiction will be broken, missionaries will be funded and encouraged, and people will lift their hearts and their songs to heaven. The members of our community who walk in here will leave with a real sense of truth and destiny, and with a greater knowledge of our Lord of glory."

These three workers are a wonderful microcosm of the three types of companies I have just described. The first man was only building a wall. He was entirely *profit*-driven, just laying bricks for his employer. His leaders had not taken on the responsibility to infuse his job with meaning. Leadership is not something that is printed on a business card. It is something that has to be *lived,* something that requires a sense of contribution. Every human being, made in God's image, must know and believe that they make a difference. *There are no mundane or menial jobs when your life's compass is magnetized to a meaningful mission.* Only meaning extricates man from mediocrity and propels him into magnificence. So-called "leaders" who do not bother to provide a sense of purpose to the work they are directing are robbing everyone around them of the very essence of their humanness.

In their book *Why America Doesn't Work*, Chuck Colson and Jack Eckerd recounted the horrific story of a group of Jewish prisoners during World War II who had been sent to forced labor by their Nazi persecutors. The prisoners were forced to do loathsome work, made even more miserable by the knowledge that the factory they had been sent to was aiding the Nazi army. "Yet month after month the laborers survived on meager food and disgusting work," the book reports. One night the factory was destroyed in an air raid. What happened next is appalling, but it provides a stark lesson in the destructive effects of aimlessness:

> The next morning the guards ordered the prisoners to one end of the charred remains where they were commanded to shovel the debris into carts and drag it to the other end of the compound.
>
> *They're going to make us rebuild this wretched place,* the prisoners thought as they bent to their labor.
>
> The next day they were ordered to move the huge pile of debris again, back to the other end of the compound.
>
> *Stupid swine,* the prisoners muttered to themselves. *They made a mistake and now we have to undo everything we did yesterday.*
>
> But it was no mistake. Day after day, the prisoners hauled the same mountain of rubble back and forth from one end of the camp to the other. After several weeks of this meaningless drudgery, one old man began sobbing uncontrollably and was led away by the guards. Another screamed until his captors beat him into silence. Then a young man who had survived three years of the vile labor that supported the oppressors' cause darted away from the group and raced towards the electrified fence.
>
> "Halt!" the guards shouted. But it was too late. There was a blinding flash . . .[2]

The authors go on to describe how, as the meaningless work dragged inexorably on, more and more prisoners went mad, many of them actually following the first prisoner's example and hurling themselves to their deaths on the electrified fences surrounding the camp. This hideous experiment had actually been ordered by the camp commander, who had wanted to see how human beings would respond to living lives that were utterly devoid of purpose. The results were madness and death.

Of course, in the workplace, you would never see the kind of terrible results that resulted from the Nazis' ghastly mental manipulation. But you *will* see workers with no joy, no passion—workers who put forth malicious obedience, much like the first worker at the cathedral site. It is not enough that workers be able to *infer* meaning from what they do. They must be told. They must be encouraged to discover the significance of their every action.

All of us are searching for meaning. Each of us is born with a ladder in our hands, and we spend our formative years looking to find which wall to rest our ladder against. We may well lay our personal ladder of meaning against the wall of pleasure, or prosperity, or power, or performance, or pulchritude. So we spend our lives climbing the ladder of success, and at the end, we discover we've laid it against the wrong wall! You'll never see a U-Haul following a hearse.

I was a pastor for ten years. During that time I sat with scores of people who were in the final process of dying. Not one of these men and women, who were acutely aware that the end was approaching, ever told me that they wished they had more vigorously sought after all those "P's." What they talked about was faith, family, and friends. On their deathbeds, they finally figured out what was really important in life. Why can't we grasp it sooner?

The second bricklayer was *customer*-driven. He was building a church, and rather than merely working for a paycheck, he was connected to who his customer was. As a result, his attitude was better than the first man's, and his productivity was correspondingly higher, as well.

The third worker, however, was the only one who was *meaning-driven*. He was a passionate purpose partner. He did not merely see a wall, or a building, but he saw the ultimate purpose behind his work, and he was filled with a sense of destiny and contribution. He was working for the glory of God and for the edification and uplifting of all the people who entered the cathedral he was helping to erect. This man obviously was more committed to excellence.

The more meaning that we can inject into our work, and into the work of those around us, the more competitive and productive our companies will be! We all desire to make a contribution to something that is larger than ourselves. We want to reflect a strong sense of contribution and purpose. A person who is tied into this kind of grand vision can cope with change, conflict, and crisis far more easily than an individual who feels disconnected from any sense of higher purpose. When we have purpose and meaning in our lives, we experience contentment. We have fulfillment and a sense of completeness. We learn up front why we're alive—what our purpose in life is—and we develop life skills that help us accomplish that purpose. We organize our lives around that center. We live our lives in light of that central purpose.

The philosopher Seneca said, "If a man does not know what harbor he is making for, no wind is the right wind."[3] If a person has no harbor, no sense of destiny or purpose, if there is no orientation toward mission and meaning, then that individual is left alone to founder in a sea of subjectivism. The winds and waves of change and crisis will toss this person to and fro like a chunk of driftwood.

Every man and woman alive is, either consciously or subconsciously, searching for a faith fit to live by, a purpose fit to live for, and a self fit to live with! Only meaning can provide all three. The common element that unites these three quests is *relationships:* our relationship to God, to ourselves, and to our family and friends. All of life revolves around the quality of our relationships. We should rest our personal ladder of meaning against the wall of *people*.

My teacher, my personal mentor, invested his life in people—not in prestige or power. He certainly wasn't focused on pulchritude: Isaiah 53:2 tells me that he wasn't even a particularly handsome man. He didn't have a Gucci robe or designer sandals. He told me that the most important mission in life was to "love the LORD your God with all your heart, with all your soul, with all your mind, and with all your strength," and to "love your neighbor as yourself" (Mark 12:30–31). Jesus Christ's definition of success was to *love God* and *love people.* This is where He invested His energies.

The Personal Drives the Professional

Sense of purpose is ultimately derived from our core values. When you have a solid, unyielding foundation of values, external changes in circumstances and direction will not rattle you, because you will remain on purpose. Whenever I begin our six-month, in-house training with a company, the first assignment I give to every participant is to take an inventory of precisely what their personal core values are. I want them to examine what their foundation is, what kind of ground their feet are planted on. This is where it all begins. How can I possibly hope to provide meaning and direction to others if I am unsure what is meaningful to me?

Here is a wonderful, quick exercise for married couples. Sit down with your spouse and write down, each on your own individual sheet of paper, what you believe the top five purposes of your family should be. You may not feel that you are accomplishing all of them right now. You may not even feel that you are *trying* to accomplish all of them right now! Don't let that discourage you. The important thing is not to collaborate with each other in developing your five purposes for your family. Each of you silently write down the top five purposes that *you* believe your family should be striving for. When you have both done that, rank them in order of importance, still without consulting each other. You are both developing a *purpose hierarchy* for your family. When each of you has prioritized your five purposes, then go ahead and compare your lists.

Your spouse may begin reading his list by saying without reservation, with great resolve of soul, "My Number One purpose for our family is . . ." and that item isn't even on your list! And you've been married for fifteen years! You look at your spouse's Number One priority, and you nod your head. "You know," you say, "I really like that. That's truly commendable. I'm going to make that *my* Number One, too." Now you are coming to alignment.

Parents, let me ask you what might be a disconcerting question: If *your* purpose is not in alignment, if *your* values are not clear and strong, how can your kids' purpose and values be clear to them?

I was once brought in to conduct a training program for the Department of Revenue for one of our great southern states. I had been asked to work with twenty-five managers who were responsible for the guidance and direction of nine hundred people who represented the entire revenue department for that state's government, and I conducted a very similar exercise with them. I asked them to write down, individually and with no conversation, the five purposes for their department, and then to develop a purpose hierarchy.

I asked those twenty-five managers, "How many of these five top purposes do you think will agree?"

They answered, "Probably none of them."

My response was, "If *we* aren't agreed on the five most important purposes for this department, then what kind of alignment do the nine hundred people have?" The room was silent.

Writing a Personal Mission Statement

I have never seen anything that does more to extract excellence and unleash untapped potential than teaching someone to create her own personal mission statement. There are several excellent reasons why this is true:

A mission statement creates clarity of purpose for your existence. Such a statement enables you to remain focused on what is really important in your life's journey. Your mission statement springs from your core values, which we discussed in the previous chapter. You will be ready to create a mission statement when you have first identified your God-centered core values.

A mission statement is a compass for your life. It is your North Star, your universal reference point for true success. Your mission statement is your compass, one that is reliable and trustworthy, because it is magnetized to a meaningful mission.

When I was in the Boy Scouts, we were taught how to read a compass. We learned that the compass would tell us at a glance if we had drifted off course. In the same way, a mission statement is a reference point for meaning and fulfillment. If I have to make a midcourse correction in my life, the mission statement keeps me focused on my overall destination. It is a constant reminder of why I'm here and what I'm trying to accomplish.

A mission statement eliminates menial and mundane moments. Every moment becomes packed with meaning. As I said before, only meaning extricates mankind from mediocrity and leads us into magnificence. A mission statement provides fulfillment, contentment, and completeness for your entire life.

A mission statement enables you to cope more effectively with change, crisis, and conflict. With a mission statement, you're always working with a higher purpose in mind. When the waves of adversity are beating against the bow of your ship, you remain focused on your North Star, your higher purpose. You have developed resolve.

Purpose enables us to *cope.* Without a sense of meaning, we have no real coping skills. In his book, *Man's Search for Meaning,* Dr. Viktor Frankl described the abominations of the Nazi death camps during World War II. He reported that the survivors were not, as a rule, the physically strongest specimens, but those who had the strongest sense of purpose. The prisoners were stripped of everything that represented individuality and personhood. Their clothes were taken, their heads were shaved, even their names were replaced by a number. The only thing left was one's individual meaning and resolve.[4]

A mission statement helps you express, in written form, what your ultimate reality is. You will have spelled out what you value most and how you will organize your life around that truth. A mission statement allows you to live with a constant and abiding sense of destiny.

A mission statement fuels a greater sense of commitment. You will have more personal power, be more productive, and perform with greater passion!

Three Elements of a Successful Mission Statement

As you set out to compose your own personal mission statement, keep in mind these three essential features that will help you to produce a compelling document.

Step One: Specify Your Transcendent Truth

The first step in crafting a mission statement is defining ultimate meaning. This becomes your center point. This transcendent truth was specified in the list of core values you developed during Chapter 8. This is the truth by which you organize your life and interpret all events and information.

What you value most springs from how you define ultimate meaning. For example I, Jack Lannom, organize my life around the transcendent truth that God exists, God is holy, and God is personal. I have centered my life around the reality of a loving, infinite God who orders the entire universe and all of its affairs according to His perfect purpose. This is my center point, like the bull's-eye on a target. Just like the concentric circles on a target, the other elements of my mission and vision are grouped around the central, transcendent truth of God's existence and personal nature.

Your personal concept of transcendent truth is the beginning point for your thoughts and behavior. It is your prime driver and mover, from which the rest of your attitudes and actions radiate outward. In creating your personal mission statement, you must begin by aligning yourself with Truth, which, ultimately, is God. Once you have established your central, abiding core of meaning, you are ready for the second step.

Step Two: Clarify Your Central Purpose

Here you identify, based on transcendent truth, what your central purpose in life is. Your mission is your *raison d'être,* your reason for being. In this second step, you are essentially stating, "Because *this* [your transcendent truth] is true, I live to accomplish *that* [your mission]. Mission gives me a purpose that is life-consuming. It is my overall and overarching reason for living."

As a Christian man, my Truth is God. Based on the fact that God exists and that you and I are made in His image, my overarching mission in life is to glorify God and enjoy Him forever. I organize my life around a desire that others would want to know God and would be excited about God because my love for Him and my excitement about His truth and power are so evident.

This is why I said that a mission is like a compass. With this overriding mission, I simply check my course in everything I do by asking myself: "Will what I am about to do give glory to God? Will other people be more or less excited about God if they know He is my motivation for doing this?"

Another way of expressing this idea is that I can assess anything and everything I do by measuring it against how someone would respond when I answered their question: *"Why are you doing this?"* If I helped an elderly man who was struggling with several bags of groceries to load them in his car, and he asked me, "Why did you do that?" I could answer, "Because I am in love with God. I wanted to show you His love through my actions." It would be my hope that God was honored by my behavior, and that the man would want to know more about God.

But if I performed some mean, bullying act, like sitting back and laughing at his struggles with the shopping bags, and he asked me plaintively, "Why are you doing that?" how would I respond? I certainly couldn't tell him I was trying to express God's love. Would that elderly man want to worship the God of a man who has just demeaned him? Would he be excited about God? Hardly.

An example of a radically different viewpoint was expressed by the character of the unscrupulous millionaire, Gordon Gecko, who was portrayed by Michael Douglas in a movie some years ago. In the movie, Gecko explained his view of truth at a stockholders' meeting: "Greed is good." This was Gecko's core. In light of this "truth," Gecko's mission was to make money. This was the overarching purpose of his life. Everything was measured against it. If a business venture, a possession, even another human being would assist him in his mission of making money, then it (or they) became a part of his life. Everything was measured against the ultimate mission of acquiring money.

Mission, therefore, is the first ring on the target around the bull's-eye of meaning. Everything else springs forth from this central plan. The last step, which expresses the remaining circles on the target, is to develop the vision.

Step Three: Unpackage Your Central Purpose

This is vision. Vision answers the questions, "Based on my core of transcendent truth, and in light of my mission, what am I going to *do?* What do I want to accomplish in light of these values? How will my life reflect my central meaning and mission?" Vision is how you demonstrate and express the truths you expressed in Steps One and Two. It is the outliving of the inliving values.

This book is an expression of my vision for my personal and professional life. I believe that since you and I are created in God's image, we should treat each other that way! Everything I do radiates outward from that vision. This is how my belief in the Truth of God and my mission to glorify God express themselves. Jesus Christ said:

> Come, you blessed of My Father, inherit the kingdom prepared for you from the foundation of the world: for I was hungry and you gave Me food; I was thirsty and you gave Me drink; I was a stranger and you took Me in; I was naked and you clothed Me; I was sick and you visited Me; I was in prison and you came to Me. . . . Assuredly, I say to you, inasmuch as you did it to one of the least of these My brethren, you did it to Me. (Matt. 25:34–36, 40)

That is the essence of Jack Lannom's mission. I strive to do it all for His glory, and to express His glorious, unfathomable love to every single man and woman with whom I come in contact.

In 1996, I challenged Dan Philips to create his own personal mission statement. As usual, Dan's response was enthusiastic and affirmative. Dan didn't let any grass grow under his feet! The next day he called me back.

"Wow," Dan bellowed into the phone. "I had no idea I was going to enjoy this so much! What a marvelously crystallizing effect this had on my mind. This mission statement really helped me zero in on what matters. You know, you could use a mission statement to help plan your day! When you're laying out your daily plans and goals, you could ask yourself, 'Does this support my mission and vision? Will this activity reflect my central core of meaning?' Jack, I'm so glad you encouraged me to do this!"

I recently asked Dan if I could share his mission statement with you. I thought you might like to see what one looks like. We were talking about it on the telephone, and even a year after he had written it, I could hear Dan's voice grow rough with emotion as he read it to me. What a delightful human being he is! You don't need to ask Dan what he's thinking or feeling: you see it in his eyes and hear it in his voice. Now all of you can read what he holds in his heart. This is what Dan Philips uses to guide him:

Personal Mission Statement—Daniel Judson Philips

I. *Meaning: What is Truth?* The Truth is that "in the beginning God created the heavens and the earth" (Gen. 1:1) and "God so loved the world that He gave His only begotten Son, that whoever believes in Him should not perish but have everlasting life" (John 3:16).

II. *Mission: Why am I here?* I am a Christian man. Jesus gave us the two greatest commandments: "Love the Lord your God with all your heart, with all your soul, with all your mind, and with all your strength," and "Love your neighbor as yourself." These awesome responsibilities extend into every area of my life—personal, spiritual, and professional. I need to honor God in each of these three areas.

III. *Vision: What does it look like?* In my personal life, my goal is to model the behavior of my Lord Jesus as a man, a husband, and as a father. I am aware that, to a great extent, I provide my sons, Marcus and Shane, with their mental model of God. I must be a source of love and encouragement to my boys. I am to love my wife, Cheryl, "just as Christ also loved the Church and gave Himself for her" (Eph. 5:25). And my behavior should be above reproach, so as to make my neighbors curious to know, "Who is this Jesus?" I will endeavor to embody the beauty described in 1 Peter 3:4: "Let it be the hidden person of the heart, with the incorruptible beauty of a gentle and quiet spirit, which is very precious in the sight of God."

In my spiritual life, I must exhibit the fruit of the Spirit: "love, joy, peace, longsuffering, kindness, goodness, faithfulness, gentleness, self-control" (Gal. 5:22–23). I must not allow myself to be "conformed to this world, but be transformed by the renewing of [*my*] mind" (Rom. 12:2). This will take constant, consistent effort, to which I will dedicate myself every morning through prayer and the study of God's Word. I must be alert for opportunities to serve my church, and be willing to cheerfully volunteer where needed.

In my professional life, I must strive for excellence in all my affairs. I must continue to hone and improve my teaching and speaking skills. Honoring God as a professional means to pray regularly for Jack, both as my employer, and as my mentor and friend. I am to honor Jack in every way, by my own quest for excellence; by being consistently helpful, cheerful, and honest; and by making the extra effort to aim for excellence every time I write, every time I speak, every time I do anything in the name of Lannom, Inc. It is never enough to merely do an adequate job.

"The greatest of these is Love." It is not enough for me to strive for professional excellence, for without love, "I have become sounding brass or a clanging cymbal" (1 Cor. 13:1). Christ's love must burn in my heart and shine from my eyes. I must love everyone with whom I come into contact, even the unlovely and the unlovable. That love should further inspire me to practice and prepare for every workday.

Dan's mission statement is a long one. He would be the first one to tell you with a smile that he will "never use five words when fifteen will do." I told him his mission statement should be no more than a page, and he told me he struggled mightily to hold it to that limit, and I don't think he was joking! Not all of you will want to develop such a lengthy document.

My family sat down together to create our own family mission statement, and it is significantly shorter. We framed these words and hung them on the wall, as a reminder to all of us that we are mutually responsible for creating the culture we agreed our family would thrive in.

Lannom Family Mission Statement

Our family mission is grounded in the triune, infinite, personal God. The love, righteousness, and grace of our Lord Jesus Christ is the exemplary model for our family purpose. Therefore, our primary mission is to faithfully respond to God's truth by loving God and loving each other. In fulfilling this family mission, we will mutually create and sustain a Christian culture that upholds God-centered values which will govern our attitudes and actions. These values include taking mutual responsibility for modeling: mutual respect; trust; honoring and encouraging one another; nurturing and forgiving; caring and sharing; learning, laughing, and listening; beautifying, visioning, achieving, believing, honesty, contribution, and godliness.

These Christian values will guarantee each family member equal significance, support, security, and stability. Consequently, we will lovingly contribute to each other's growth—mentally, physically, spiritually, emotionally, socially, and financially. By means of this balanced growth we will individually become responsible, productive, and caring Christians. The end result of this family mission is to glorify God, and to develop a Christian family legacy that is worth modeling for future generations.

Dan used the three-step format to create his mission statement; we employed a narrative style, although you will recognize the same three points in both. Dan's statement is several paragraphs long; ours is only two. You might create a mission statement that is only a few sentences long. The most important thing to remember in putting together either a personal or family mission statement is that it doesn't matter what it looks like or how you put it together. What matters is that you *do* it and that you *live* it! I would strongly encourage you to create your own personal mission statement, and then to collaborate with your family on a family mission statement as well. Then you will be firmly locked on course, and neither you nor your family will be easily rocked by the crises that inevitably occur in life.

The Mission Statement as a Constitution

Thomas Jefferson once said, "Our peculiar security is the possession of a written Constitution."[5] The Constitution of the United States is a truly remarkable document. Our republican form of government has flourished for more than two hundred years, due to the meaning, mission, and vision that our brilliant founders provided for us that hot summer in Philadelphia. Other countries have endured the tragic and bloody horrors of the coup d'etat, but "The American Experiment" lives on. Our Constitution has given us a unique sense of stability and direction.

A mission statement is our own personal constitution. We each need to lay down our personal plumb line, our individual measure for stability and direction. Our mission statement grounds us in why we're here and where we're going. And, as Dr. Baum assured, once we have supplied our daily lives with *meaning*, we will arouse energy, power, and passion. This is doubly true for your family. Imagine, for a moment, that instead of being gathered around the television (with Hollywood's increasingly violent and amoral values being beamed into the hearts and minds of your children), your family was gathered around timeless, universal truths, like faith, hope, and love. A family that is united by such a document and committed to making it a reality will weather any storm.

How about the workplace? What do you think the atmosphere in your company would be like if every person in leadership wrote his or her own personal mission statement, sat down with their families to create a family mission statement, and then they showed their two mission statements to everyone who worked with them and for them? Would those leaders be living models of transparency and contribution? Do you think that synergy—"together energy"—would dramatically increase throughout the organization? Absolutely! There would be such a sense of *connection* in the organization that passion would just glitter throughout the workplace, and productivity would skyrocket! The staff would know exactly where their leaders are coming from, and having modeled what a person who is focused on *legacy* looks like, the leaders could then encourage everyone on the staff to develop their own personal mission statements that would guide and direct each individual.

Too much of what we teach in corporate America is not rooted in *life* skills. We forget that the personal drives the professional. We concoct fine-sounding corporate mission statements, that are obviously well thought-out, *but if a mission statement is not linked to a person on an individual basis—if it doesn't touch them on a personal, emotional, visceral level—it is virtually useless!* It is meaningless! Our companies sterilize our humanity with slogans and mission statements that are chock full of corporate language and buzzwords, but speak little, if at all, to the hearts of people.

I firmly believe that if you truly wish to unleash untapped potential at your company, you should train and challenge everyone in the organization, part-timers and full-timers, from the CEO to the janitor, to draft their own personal constitution, their own declaration of excellence. People could declare to God, to themselves, and to other people: "This is who I am; this is why I'm here; and this is what I'm going to accomplish."

Imagine what it would be like if you were walking down the hall of your company, and everyone you met had their own individual and corporate (family) mission statement, and they couldn't wait to share it with you! Better yet, they couldn't wait to help you accomplish your personal mission statement. *Nothing* could possibly create more synergy! But before it can be effective on the macro level, it must be effective on the micro level.

Change begins from within, not from without. You might be tempted to read these chapters and think, "Well, it's up to _____ [fill in the blank: "my spouse," "my boss," "my parents," etc.] to start this. It's _____'s job to take the initiative!" Dear Reader, I hope, by now, you have seen that the message of this book is not to fall into the mind-set of powerlessness, but of power. You are created in the image of God, Himself, the *all*-powerful Creator! He *spoke,* and the world came into existence. King David, the man after God's heart, exulted:

> When I consider Your heavens, the work of your fingers,
> The moon and the stars, which You have ordained,
> What is man that you are mindful of him,
> And the son of man that You visit him?
> For you have made him a little lower than the angels,
> And you have crowned him with glory and honor. (Ps. 8:3–5)

You have been "crowned with glory and honor"! *You* are a champion of change! The very fact that you purchased this book, entitled *Untapped Potential,* indicates that you want to bring out the best in yourself, your family, and the people around you. *Don't* transfer to anyone else the tremendous personal power of choice and decision that God Himself has bequeathed to you as your birthright. You can begin to make an enormous, dramatic, dynamic difference—at home, at work, in your church, and in your community. But first, you must formulate a plan. Before you read any farther, I urge you to stop right here and put together your personal mission statement.

Purpose in your heart, right now, to be that champion of change you are intended to be. You can start by drafting *your* personal mission of excellence and meaning on the next page. I'll provide you with the format Dan Philips used to create his personal constitution. Yours can be as long or as short as you want.

My Personal Mission Statement

Step One: Specify Your Transcendent Truth. Write down the central, core truth of your life. What is the truth by which you organize your life and interpret all events and information? If you need to, go back and refer to the work that you did during Chapter 8, and then write your core of meaning below:

_____

_____

_____

_____

Step Two: Clarify Your Central Purpose. In this second step, identify, based on what you believe to be transcendent truth, your central purpose in life. What is your mission, that which gives you a purpose that is life-consuming? What is your overall reason for living?

_____

_____

_____

_____

Step Three: Unpackage Your Central Purpose. Based on my core of transcendent truth, and in light of my mission, what am I going to *do?* What do I want to accomplish in light of these values? How will my life reflect my central meaning and mission?

_____

_____

_____

_____

Step Four: The First Draft. This is where you combine Steps One through Three into one single statement. You probably will want to work through more than one draft before the finished product will say exactly what you want it to. I would encourage you to keep it short enough that it can be easily read, certainly no more than one page.

When you have completed your final draft, type or print it neatly, frame it, and hang it where you can read it every day. Show it to your spouse, your friends, your peers, and your supervisor, and ask them if they can suggest any amendments to your personal constitution. Make this a document that will inspire and encourage you to your highest and your best!

Without a Vision, People Perish

10

MOST OF YOU ARE FAMILIAR with the name and the face of H. Wayne Huizenga, whose Florida Marlins won the 1997 World Series in such dramatic fashion, with Game 7 going into extra innings before Edgar Renteria delivered the game-winning hit. Wayne also owns the Miami Dolphins and the Florida Panthers, the hockey team that went from infancy to the Stanley Cup finals faster than any other team in NHL history. Wayne has already built and sold two hugely successful business ventures, including Blockbuster Entertainment, and is now in the process of creating a third. One national business magazine recently called Wayne Huizenga the number one entrepreneur in America.

When I first met Wayne, he had just announced his dream of bringing major league baseball to South Florida. He invited me to fly to London with him and his staff, and we all spent five highly enjoyable hours together learning the secrets of unleashing untapped potential. Naturally, I was fascinated to talk to one of the most visionary men you or I are ever likely to meet. Wayne Huizenga had a dream for a family entertainment empire, and when he sold Blockbuster, it employed more than 20,000 people! That was the result of that particular vision. Sixty-five thousand people jammed Pro Player Stadium to see Wayne's dream of owning a world champion baseball team become a glorious reality. The Miami Arena is sold out every time the Panthers take the ice to pursue what has become an annual hunt for the play-offs.

You and I and everyone we meet share a quality that Wayne Huizenga has in abundance: we are all visionary human beings. We are visionaries because our Creator is a visionary, a planner.

> Your eyes saw my substance, being yet unformed.
> And in Your book they all were written,
> The days fashioned for me,
> When as yet there were none of them. (Ps. 139: 16)

Everything you see in all creation existed in the mind of God before it came into being. Creation is the outliving expression of the inliving eternal reality that exists in the mind of God. God has an eternal vision—an eternal plan. We will discuss one of God's major plans—His for mankind—in Chapter 12.

Just as everything you see in creation is a result of God's vision, every manufactured thing you see, everything you use—clothes, tools, your wristwatch, the car you drive, the home you live in—was a vision, a dream, in someone's mind before it was built. We're all born with an internal dream box. Some of us just need to turn that box back on again. We need to reinvigorate our dreamer.

The Triad of Human Transformation

This chapter is the third member of what I call the triad of human transformation. We've discussed values, mission, and now we're going to look at vision. I want you to view these three chapters as one synergetic unit. Each one is powerful on its own, but when you combine the three in harmony, you achieve extraordinary transformation!

A values statement proclaims to the world who I am and what I stand for. Values provide a stable foundation. A mission statement gives me a meaningful purpose. The mission statement tells the world, "This is the reason for my existence." A mission statement is a proclamation of what I am trying to accomplish.

This chapter was written to help you tap into the visionary aspect of your personhood. Vision speaks of the future. A vision statement identifies what you want to become. Far from operating in isolation, vision is an outgrowth of my values and mission. Vision produces values-based, mission-guided, goal-oriented behavior.

As I have said in previous chapters, in order to define what something is, it is also essential to define what it is *not*. When I speak of vision, I am *not* talking about some New Age concept that suggests that you can create reality merely by envisioning it. This kind of thinking has even infected some portions of the Church, taking form in "Name It and Claim It" theology. I could not disagree more passionately with these notions!

Because we are human beings made in the image of God, we should first look to God with a desire to reflect His glory. "Unless the LORD builds the house, / They labor in vain who build it," Psalm 127:1 asserts. God created us to dream and to plan, but we must always bear in mind that "a man's heart plans his way, / But the LORD directs his steps" (Prov. 16:9). Everything I do begins with my transcendent truth, that God exists and is highly interested and active in all our affairs.

However, in order to accomplish things, I must first have a dream. We need a vision before we can translate it into a concrete goal. Tom Watson, the founder of IBM, was once asked when he had become a success. His reply: "Really, it was when I first conceived it." Vision gives me a worthy, well-defined destination. If a vision is based upon my God-centered core values and is harmonious with my mission, it is worthy of my wholehearted and energetic pursuit.

I want to encourage you to dream! We all need to encourage each other to take the talents that God gave us and put them to their fullest use! We mustn't drag each other down with negativism and defeatism. We want to lovingly challenge each other to our highest and our best. We want to redefine excellence for each other and for ourselves. We should all dream great dreams—not self-serving dreams, but lofty, worthy goals.

Prairie Chickens and Eagles

Many people don't dream great dreams because they have become discouraged. We've been told, "You can't do that. You aren't [good enough, strong enough, smart enough, powerful enough, etc.] to accomplish that." People tell us, "You're not an eagle. You're a prairie chicken. You should be content to nose around in the dirt to find whatever worms or bugs are available to you there." No more of that! We have been outfitted in prairie chicken costumes by small-minded people whose vision is too narrow to take in the panorama of the sky where eagles soar. Einstein said, "great spirits have always encountered violent opposition from mediocre minds."[1] Just like Clark Kent removes his reporter's suit to reveal his Superman costume beneath it, we, too, can take off the prairie chicken costume that others have tried to fit us in and reveal the eagle feathers beneath. We were created and designed to soar in excellence!

You have seen this happen time and again throughout history. When slavery ended, men like Booker T. Washington flatly refused to accept second-class status. "Just because I'm black," men reasoned, "doesn't mean I'm destined for slavery. I am a human being created in the image of God! I am destined for greatness!" One hundred years later, Martin Luther King Jr. boomed out, "I have a dream!" He clearly saw that blacks' humanity had been *defined down,* but he knew that they possessed the same dignity and worth as any other man or woman.

Whether it was expressed in the cause of women's suffrage or children's slave labor, people defined humanity as something unique because it is created in the image of God Himself. The embryo in the womb, that tiny body that was "fearfully and wonderfully made / . . . And skillfully wrought" by God (Ps. 139:14–15), was designed for visionary greatness. We are not, never were, never will be intended for inertia and mediocrity. We are designed to dream, to build, and to accomplish!

In 1870, Bishop Milton Wright intoned, "The Millennium is at hand. Man has invented everything that can be invented. He has done all he can do."

Someone stood up in the back of the church and challenged Bishop Wright. This man was a visionary. He stated, "I believe that some of the greatest inventions are yet to be seen. In fact, I believe that in the next fifty years, man will learn to fly."

"Blasphemy!" Bishop Wright thundered. "Don't you know that flight is reserved for angels?"

The man's prediction was off by seventeen years. In December 1903, two young men launched the very first aircraft at Kitty Hawk, North Carolina. You know their names: Orville and Wilbur . . . Wright! They were the visionary sons of the myopically minded Bishop Wright.[2]

Fall Down Seven Times, Get Up Eight!

The major impediment so many of us face when trying to realize our dreams is fear of failure. Fear grips us: *"What if I try, and it doesn't work? What if I look ridiculous trying? That would be too awful!"* I like to say that fear is merely Fraudulent Evidence Altering Reality. We just can't allow ourselves to lapse into that kind of timidity! We have to redefine the meaning of failure. We *must* stop viewing failure as something to be avoided at all costs, and rather see failure as a stepping-stone to success.

The first pencil we ever received in school had an eraser on the end. There's a message in that! No worthwhile goal was ever accomplished without effort, toil, and, yes, failure! There is an old maxim: "Life is a grindstone: either it will sharpen you up or grind you down." We must truly accept in our hearts the truth that failure is not awful. Failure is a learning opportunity. Failure is fortuitous feedback.

You, dear Reader, are a natural born risk taker. You learned to walk by failing! You tried to walk and you fell down. But you got up again. And again. Walk into an elementary school. How many kids do you see without scratches, cuts, and skinned knees? All children take massive risks every day and give it no thought. Failure will either strengthen us or destroy us. It is all a matter of whether we fall backward or forward!

Everyone remembers Babe Ruth for his 714 home runs. For years, before his record was broken by the great Henry Aaron, "the Babe" was home run king. But did you know the "Sultan of Swat" also struck out 1,330 times during his illustrious career?[3] He swung for the fences and *missed* a lot more often than he succeeded! But Babe Ruth was a risk taker. He learned the game of baseball through his successes *and* through his mistakes.

Someone once told Thomas Edison, "You're really a great inventor. Why, you have more than one thousand patents in your name!"

"Thank you," Edison replied, "but I'm really not the great inventor you believe I am. Only one of those ideas was truly my own. That was the phonograph. All the other ideas belonged to men who had tried to make them work, failed, and then gave up. Before I created a working light bulb, I had more than 1,200 failures."

"1,200 failures!" His listener was astonished. "Didn't all those failures discourage you?"

"No," Edison coolly replied. "I successfully discovered 1,200 ways *not* to construct a light bulb!"[4]

Thomas Edison had learned that failure is the most important aspect of the innovative process! He was *positively eliminating* the ways that wouldn't work, with each failure moving him closer to success. We successfully learn to do something by discovering how *not* to do it. It is not what happens to us, but how we *respond* to it that makes us or breaks us. At the core of the hard shell of every failure exists the seed for greater growth potential. Every growth opportunity is marvelously masked as an impossible situation. It is only in the fiery furnace of adversity that our faith is forged into unconquerable character. Faith is a Fearless Attitude Inspiring Troubled Hearts.

- John Creasey, the great English novelist, had some experience with failure. He received 753 rejections! But he also had 564 books that were published.[5]

- Ernest Hemingway rewrote *The Old Man and the Sea* eighty times, before he had the finished product he believed was the right one.[6]

- Abraham Lincoln had eleven major failures in his life before he finally won election to the presidency in 1860,[7] only to face what might have been the darkest hour in American history: the Civil War. Abraham Lincoln went on to become one of the most famous and best-loved presidents in the history of our republic.

- R. H. Macy failed seven times before his Macy's store became a major success in New York City.[8]

- There was another man who was called "crazy" for his vision of working with vulcanized rubber. Only his wife believed in him, encouraged him, and worked with him to develop the concept. His name was Charles Goodyear.[9]

- Albert Einstein failed his first college entrance exam, at a college in Zurich, Switzerland.[10]

- Robert Fulton's steamboat was scornfully nicknamed "Fulton's Folly."[11]

The men I just described to you saw failure as *inspirational dissatisfaction*. It has been said, "If you can see the invisible, you can accomplish the impossible." But there will always be critics and naysayers who will try to pull you back down to their level. You have to be careful whom you share your dreams with. Some folks would prefer to relegate you to permanent prairie chicken status. This has been called "mediating incompetency." It is learned helplessness. Schopenhauer wisely quipped, "Every original idea is first ridiculed, then vigorously attacked, and finally taken for granted!"[12]

We all have a sign hung around our neck that reads "Under Construction." We are all works in progress. To play on the title of a recent book, "I'm not OK, you're not OK, but that's OK!" A sculptor creating a granite statue of a human being might well describe his art as the process of taking his hammer and chisel and knocking off the pieces that don't belong to the man. In a similar manner, when I fall down, I discover what doesn't belong to me. I wasn't designed to crawl, I was designed to walk and to run! We are made in the image of the Creator of the universe! It is *antihuman*—a contradiction of who we are—to go through life and not dream great dreams. It is a tragedy. We are sculpted for nothing less than excellence.

I love the phrase *carpe diem* that was glorified in the movie *Dead Poets Society*. "Seize the day," Robin Williams's character urged. "Let your lives be excellent!" Dreams are infectious. They are contagious. Let the people you live and work with catch your vision of excellence. Seize the day!

Creating Your Own Vision for Success

I'm going to teach you how to create your vision for personal and professional success. Turning ordinary people into extraordinary performers means putting people in touch with their own inner dreamer and showing them how, in a concrete way, they can turn their dreams into reality. We begin to accomplish this by writing out vision statements that are supported by objectives, goals, action steps, and follow-up.

There are ten areas where we need to develop a vision for the future that is undergirded by a concrete plan to arrive there:

1. Spiritual (Faith in God)
2. Intellectual (Learning and education)
3. Physical (Physical fitness and overall health)
4. Family (Relationship to spouse, children, parents, relatives)
5. Social (Friendships and associations)
6. Emotional (Exercising emotional responsibility)
7. Financial (Stability and responsibility)
8. Professional (Career goals)
9. Cultural (The arts, music, etc.)
10. Recreational (Travel, hobbies, etc.)

I'm going to walk you through the visioning process and give you an example of what a completed vision statement looks like. Let's select two of the ten areas I've identified—Family and Professional—and we'll work through the process together. There are five steps to the creation of a vision statement: Vision, Objectives, Goals, Action Steps, and Follow-up.

I. Vision

The first step is to define your vision for each area. Vision is the end product. Vision answers the question, "What will this look like when I'm finished?" In essence, we're beginning with the end in mind. We establish what we would like our intellectual life, for example, to look like when we have accomplished everything we would like to. Then we work backward from there.

When Tom Watson first started to build IBM, the first question he asked himself was, "What do I want this company to look like when it is complete?" He began with the end product—International Business Machines—in mind. Vision is the big picture.

You might, for example, have this vision for your family: to build balanced, spiritually mature lives, and to pass on a lasting, Christian legacy. At the end of your life, then, you want to look back at the lives of your spouse, children, and grandchildren and be able to say honestly that your vision statement has become a reality.

As a professional, you might develop this vision for your career: to create an Incredi-ball environment at work, in which people are enthusiastic and excited about coming to work each day, and to exceed the expectations of our customers. This is your vision of the end product. Constructing a concrete vision for the future creates a *forward* pull for us. The vision pulls us toward a worthy destination. By beginning with the end in mind, with an exciting vision, we infect other people with our desire. Vision is contagious, and it draws us into the future with new determination and vigor.

2. Objectives

The second step is to develop objectives that support the vision. Objectives are more specific than your initial vision. Your major objective(s) will bring about the reality of your vision statement. A woman whose intellectual vision is to be a "well-read person" might establish an objective to read all the classics. A man whose physical vision is "a body that is fit and healthful in every way" might set an objective to use a combination of diet and exercise to lose weight until he reaches his ideal weight. Objectives are the completed steps that will carry you to the shining reality of your vision.

Let's create an objective for each of our two sample visions:

Family Vision: To build balanced, spiritually mature lives, and to pass on a lasting, Christian legacy.

Family Objective: To develop quality relationships with each family member and contribute to their personal and spiritual growth.

Professional Vision: To create a profitable, Incredi-ball environment at work, in which people are enthusiastic and excited about coming to work each day, and to exceed the expectations of our customers.

Professional Objective: To employ the techniques outlined in *Untapped Potential.*

There may well be more than one objective that must be accomplished in order to realize your vision. For example, you might set other family objectives that all of your children will attend four years of college, that all family members would actively support your church, and that every member of the family would enjoy at least one healthy hobby. I suggest that you set no more than four major objectives that you believe will make your dream a reality. In the interest of space and time, I'm going to stick to only one objective for each vision.

3. Goals

The third aspect of realizing your dreams is to create the goals that will allow you to make your objectives a reality. These goals will define the roles and responsibilities that will lead you to the realization of the objectives you have set. Once again, you are narrowing your focus and starting to come closer to who you must *be* and what you will *do* to realize your vision.

Let's go back to our two sample vision statements, and add goals to the vision and objectives:

Family Vision: To build balanced, spiritually mature lives, and to pass on a lasting, Christian legacy.

Family Objective: To develop quality relationships with each family member and contribute to their personal and spiritual growth.

    Goal #1: To be the best husband I can be.

    Goal #2: To be the best father I can be.

    Goal #3: To be the best son I can be.

    Goal #4: To be the best brother I can be.

Professional Vision: To create a profitable, Incredi-ball environment at work, in which people are enthusiastic and excited about coming to work each day, and to exceed the expectations of our customers.

Professional Objective: To employ the techniques outlined in *Untapped Potential.*

    Goal #1: Develop a better awareness and understanding of my peers' personality styles.

    Goal #2: Improve positive reinforcement by the use of encouraging words.

    Goal #3: Incorporate the use of the three lateral thinking skills at the management level.

    Goal #4: Create and share with coworkers my personal and family mission statements.

4. Action Steps

This is the step during which we commit to exactly what we will do, on a step-by-step basis, to realize our goals and objectives, in order to make our vision become a reality. The term *action steps* implies the use of verbs in their creation. "To become a more understanding husband" is a lofty goal, but it implies a quality, as opposed to action.

Action steps, then, are the specific procedures that must occur in order to accomplish each individual objective. Your action steps should be S.M.A.R.T. ones. They should be:

S pecific
M easurable
A chievable
R ealistic
T ime-bound

This is an acronym that I have heard used by various consultants for more than twenty years. I don't know who created it, but this is a widely popular method for determining what a successful action step will *look* like.

Specific. Action steps must be clearly defined. "Help my children do well in school" is not specific. *How* well should they do? All passing grades? Honor roll? Valedictorian? What does the phrase "do well" actually mean? "*To create a list, with the help of my pastor, of the one hundred most important books ever written, and to read four of those books each year*" is a highly specific action step that also answers the second condition, that action steps should be measurable.

Measurable. Action steps should be created that can be measured. Reaching your ideal weight is a measurable step. So is reading four books each year. "I want my kids to be happier," or "I want to feel more spiritual" cannot be measured or quantified in any way. There should be some objective form of measurement that will identify the successful completion of your action step.

Achievable. Action steps should be achievable *by you*. These should be things over which you have direct control. An action step stating "that my boss would be more supportive" is not specific (*how* supportive?); it isn't measurable (how do you measure "more supportive"?); and it is totally out of the visionary's control. How will he cause his boss to become more supportive? Select goals that you, yourself, can achieve.

Realistic. I don't ever want to discourage you from dreaming great dreams. But neither should you create action steps that you can't reach, thereby causing you to lapse into frustration. Action steps can and should be challenging and ambitious. But it is easy to turn "stretch goals" into "impossible dreams." Take care to devise action steps that challenge you to your highest and your best, but that are truly attainable.

Time-bound. Action steps should be bound by a completion date. "I will lose twenty pounds in four months," "My son will make second honor roll by the third marking period," and "I will read through the entire Bible in one year" are good examples of time-bound action steps.

Let's go back to our sample goals, and develop action steps for one of them.

Family Vision: To build balanced, spiritually mature lives, and to pass on a lasting, Christian legacy.

Family Objective: To develop quality relationships with each family member and contribute to their personal and spiritual growth.

Goal #1: To be the best husband I can be.

Action Steps:

1. Talk to my wife over Sunday dinner about what I need to do to improve our relationship.

2. During that conversation, I will create a written, prioritized list of the things she suggests. This list will have three categories: things she would like to see more of . . . same of . . . less of.

3. Call my pastor tomorrow and ask him to suggest the best book he knows for building a stronger marriage. Purchase (or order) the book tomorrow night after work, and then read a minimum of six pages each day until it is completed.

4. Seek out a happily married male role model at church and ask him to mentor me. I will identify and contact this individual within two weeks.

5. Ask close friends to give me feedback on how they have observed how I treat my wife. Three weeks to complete this step.

Professional Vision: To create a profitable, Incredi-ball environment at work, in which people are enthusiastic and excited about coming to work each day, and to exceed the expectations of our customers.

Professional Objective: To employ the techniques outlined in *Untapped Potential.*

Goal #1: Develop a better awareness and understanding of my peers' personality styles.

Action Steps:
1. Tell my peers about *Untapped Potential,* and outline the benefits of knowing how different people are motivated. Tell them I am going to use this knowledge to help me be a more effective manager. One week.

2. By the end of the same week, I will perform an OPV on each of the five individuals on my management team and try to identify their predominant personality pattern.

3. Week two: Ask the other five managers to complete the "What Are Your Tendencies?" test from Chapter 4. We will share the results with each other and discuss the four personality quadrants in detail. Two weeks to complete these meetings.

4. During these meetings, I will ask for feedback from each member of the team about how *they* like to be motivated. Does the Achiever want new challenges? Does the Mediator desire more kindness?

5. Proactively integrate the insight gained during these conversations with the knowledge gained from Chapter 4 into a more personal, innovative approach to motivation. Three weeks.

5. Follow-up

The last step in realizing your vision is to create follow-up for your action steps that allows you to determine when you have completed them. This follow-up allows you to ensure that your action steps are truly specific, measurable, realistic, and time-bound. So for example, follow-up steps for the family actions steps we created look like this:

Follow-up on "Family" Action Steps:

1. Six weeks from our initial conversation, I will sit with my wife for our first follow-up conversation. During that conversation, we will review the list of prioritized suggestions she gave me, and she will tell me what progress I have made and what areas she may feel have not yet been addressed. We will make a date for our next formal follow-up conversation, two months hence.

2. Review my progress on reading the book about marriage. If I have been reading six pages a day for the last five weeks, I will have completed 210 pages. If I am behind, then I will immediately schedule the time necessary to get caught up. When I have completed the book, I will immediately talk at length with my wife about what I have learned.

3. Make sure that I have, indeed, created a strong accountability relationship with a married man to mentor me. I should have set a schedule with this man that allows us to talk at length at least once a week to check my progress.

4. Recontact the personal friends whom I had involved in this endeavor and ask for their candid observations about what improvements they have or have not seen me make.

An accomplished vision statement, then, will have one *vision;* one or more *objectives* that support that vision; *goals* that will outline the roles and responsibilities necessary to realize each objective; *action steps* that detail the physical action necessary to accomplish each goal; and *follow-up* that will ensure the actualization of each action step.

Some of you may be reacting with some dismay: "Jack, are you saying that I should develop ten vision statements [Spiritual, Intellectual, Physical, Family, Social, Emotional, Financial, Professional, Cultural, and Recreational] with objectives, goals, action steps, and follow-up for each one? Then I actually have to accomplish all that? That's a huge job! How will I find time to do it all?"

First, please remember that we are talking about a *life* vision here. You are not going to accomplish these in the space of just a few months or even a few years. We are building lives and passing on legacies, and that isn't an undertaking you breeze through quickly! You are crafting a lifelong road map, not a six-month project. You are taking time to be the engineer of your life.

Second, bear in mind that it has been said that 85 percent of what you write down actually becomes a reality. If you merely write out complete vision statements for the ten areas of your life and begin concentrated work on *one* of them, you'll have taken giant strides ahead of almost everybody on the planet! You will have become a *visionary* person. Better to set a lofty, ambitious goal and accomplish only half of it, than to set *no* goal and accomplish all of it.

Most people have no written goals. If you doubt it, take an informal survey of everyone you work with. Ask them if they have a written values, mission, or vision statement. I guarantee you that no more than one out of a hundred people you ask will answer in the affirmative. It is astounding to me how few people will even put in writing what they hope to accomplish in a week, much less in a lifetime! If there is no vision, there is no forward movement. If there is no movement, there is no energy and no growth, only inertia. Thomas Edison once said, "Opportunity is missed by most people because it is dressed in overalls and looks like work."[13]

Last, and perhaps most important, it is a demonstrable fact that the most laborious undertaking (and constructing a life vision is an exciting task, not a laborious one!) is proven to be a simple undertaking when it is broken down to its simplest unit. Even though the job may look like a large one, it can be accomplished by patient, persistent effort. The *Mona Lisa* was painted one brush stroke at a time. A journey of one thousand miles begins with one step. I've always enjoyed the old question: "How do you eat an elephant?" Answer: "One bite at a time." A life that becomes a shining legacy for the generations to come is built one action step at a time.

Don't be dismayed! Start thinking of yourself as "diligent," "indefatigable," and "steadfast." You can make a glittering difference in your own life and in the lives of the people you love and influence by drawing your personal road map for success and then starting down the highway, one step at a time. What a buoyant and breathtaking journey it will be!

I'd like to help you take the first step on that journey. Before you move on to the next chapter, let's put together your vision statement for the first area on the list: your spiritual life. I've provided the format for you to do this on the following pages. Remember nothing becomes dynamic until it is specific.

Spiritual Vision Statement Worksheet

Spiritual Vision: (At the end of your life, when you look back on your spiritual life, what will it look like?)

_____

_____

Spiritual Objective: (What major objective[s] will allow you to accomplish your vision?)

_____

_____

Spiritual Goals: (What roles and responsibilities will lead you to the realization of the objectives you have set?)

Goal #1: _____

Goal #2: _____

Goal #3: _____

Action Steps: (What specific steps must you take that will enable you to accomplish your goals? Remember to create S.M.A.R.T. Action Steps!)

Action Steps for Goal #1:

1. _____

2. _____

3. _____

4. _____

Action Steps for Goal #2:

1. _____

2. _____

3. _____

4. _____

Action Steps for Goal #3:

1. _____

2. _____

3. _____

4. _____

Follow-up: (What will you do to measure and ensure that you have actually completed your action steps?)

Follow-up on Action Steps for Goal #1:

1. _____

2. _____

3. _____

4. _____

Follow-up on Action Steps for Goal #2:

1. _____

2. _____

3. _____

4. _____

Follow-up on Action Steps for Goal #3:

1. _____

2. _____

3. _____

4. _____

There! You did it! You haven't just taken the first step on your journey, you've completed the first mile! Have fun! Keep going!

Power Means Passing It On

11

DAN PHILIPS IS THE DIRECTOR of training for my company. Dan is, quite simply, my right hand. He fills in for me whenever and wherever I need him, whether it is for a speaking, meeting, or writing commitment. I pick up the phone, tell Dan what needs to be done, and then I don't give it a second thought. He represents me beautifully. This very book you are reading would not be a reality without Dan's hours of research, writing, and editing. Much of what you have read is a triumphant expression of Dan's effort and enthusiasm. God truly blessed me the day He brought Dan Philips and me together.

Having said all this, let me also tell you that I thought twice before I hired Dan. When I met him, I honestly questioned if he would be able to fill the role of corporate trainer that I originally envisioned for him. Dan had just seen his first marriage end in divorce, and his self-confidence was in tatters. At thirty-eight years of age, he was beginning to seriously question if he had any kind of a meaningful future ahead of him. He looked and sounded like a beaten man. At the same time, I saw a spark of greatness there. I've told audiences that a true leader is not the person who looks at an apple and sees the seeds within, but someone who can look at the seeds and see the apple orchard that will grow out of them. That's what meeting Dan Philips for the first time was like. He was a diamond in the rough, with the emphasis on "rough"!

I made a decision: I hired Dan, and I made an investment in him. I invested *myself* in Dan. I spent countless hours with him, a great deal of it outside the professional arena. Some of that time was spent in professional training, of course, but by far, most of our talk was *contribution*. I poured myself into Dan. I poured my belief, my confidence, and my passion into him. A man I used to work with once told me: "If you don't have enough faith, borrow some of mine." I lent my faith to Dan. I let the Pyramid of People Power cascade from my lips in all of our conversations. I made sure, however, that my praise was sincere and specific. Dan is an extremely intelligent man, and he would have sensed in an instant if I had been simply trying to flatter him. When Dan first started to "fly solo"—working with some of my clients by himself—I would call after he had left to check on how Dan was doing, and to be sure my customers were happy. Invariably, the feedback I received was positive, and I would immediately pass that along to Dan.

I have enjoyed few more satisfying experiences in my life than watching Dan Philips grow during the last three years. I have seen his confidence, his enthusiasm, and his love for God and people multiply exponentially! Two years ago, when I sent Dan on a new assignment, I would ask him, "How do you feel about this situation?"

"Well, I'll do my best, Jack," he would respond. I could see the worry in his eyes and hear the uncertainty in his voice. So I'd pump Dan up. I'd lend him my faith. I'd remind him of his past successes and assure him that new ones were just around the corner. I told him how much I believed in him, how proud I was of the strides he was making, and of how excited I was about his future with the company. Off Dan would go, and then he would report back to me, fairly bubbling with delight (and I think, initially, some surprise), "You were right, Jack! Everything went just fine!"

Today, I'll ask Dan the same question—"How do you feel about this new situation?"—and I want to laugh aloud for joy at his response. "No problem, Jack," he'll reply warmly, with no hesitation. "I can do it." Dan's rise through my company has been nothing less than meteoric. He is my purpose partner, and I am proud to introduce him to you as my good friend. My initial investment in Dan has paid off in ways I had never dreamed possible!

The Power of Choice and Decision

I had a choice to make about Dan Philips, and I made the right one. It would have been easy to "take a pass" on Dan, and instead hire someone who had all the outward appearances of professional spit and polish. The choice I had to make was this: Would I hire someone "safe," who would come in and do an above-average job, represent me well, and demand only a minimum of attention? I chose, instead, to take a calculated risk. I knew that in Dan Philips I was assuming some extra responsibility, but I was confident from the day I met him that, if I made that investment of time and attention, I would have a representative who would never be content with "above average." In Dan, I had found an extraordinary person who wanted to be, and has since become, an extraordinary performer. I chose the diamond in the rough, and he has truly turned out to be a precious gem. In mentoring Dan, I confirmed another great secret of human transformation, and it is my delight to share this truth with you.

The purpose of this chapter is to introduce you to the eleventh truth, which is that *real power is the power of making other people powerful.* This is our power of choice and decision. The power of choice is our volitional attribute; it is another defining element of our personhood. Our self-determined attribute is expressed in self-governance and autonomy.

Moreover, our self-determination is a reflection of the personal nature of God. God is a sovereign Being. Consequently, all of His actions are free and self-determined. "You did not choose Me," Jesus told His disciples, "but I chose you and appointed you that you should go and bear fruit" (John 15:16). "Blessed . . . [are] the people whom He has chosen as His own inheritance," Psalm 33:12 exults. "You are a chosen generation," Peter told the believers of his day (1 Peter 2:9).

God's sovereignty and self-determination are expressed in His creation. "He gives to all life, breath, and all things. And He has made from one blood every nation of men to dwell on all the face of the earth, and has determined their preappointed times and the boundaries of their habitation" (Acts 17:25–26).

Since we are made in His personal image, with the attribute of volition, we have been bequeathed the privilege and the duty to *choose.* We have been given the power of choice and decision. We do not operate on instinct. Geese do not *decide* to migrate every winter, their nature compels them to. Human beings, on the other hand, can choose to perform well . . . or poorly. "If you do not do well, sin lies at the door," God admonished Cain "And its desire is for you, but you should rule over it" (Gen. 4:7). Cain *should* have ruled over sin, he *could* have done so, but instead he slew his brother in a moment of horrible jealousy and rage and bore the mark of his crime for the rest of his life.

"Why?" you might well ask, indignantly. "Why does God allow such terrible things to happen?" The answer is cause for rejoicing! God did not create us to be automatons, thoughtless creatures who behave with no forethought or decision. Instead, He created us to make our own choices! We can choose to walk toward God or away from Him. We are not animals, which means we are not instinct-driven. We are responsible human beings, given the power of choice.

The Pilgrims *chose* to come to the New World so that they could worship God in their own way. Our Founding Fathers *chose,* against all odds, to rebel against England, which was the leading world superpower of their day. Thomas Edison *chose* to work and sweat and create when other men had given up in mediocrity and despair. We can choose to create a better life for ourselves, or we can choose to drift aimlessly towards an indeterminate future. Clearly, choice is the very center of life. Excellence is a choice. Love is a choice. Happiness is a choice. Life is what we make of it! No one *makes* me angry, just as no one *makes* me happy. I choose my thoughts, my feelings, and my behavior! Abraham Lincoln once said, "Most people are about as happy as they choose to be."[1] This is truly one of the most profound statements I have ever heard, as it makes *me* responsible for my attitudes and actions. I have a choice!

In fact, the very essence of extraordinary performance springs forth from discretionary effort, which is the disposition of our minds, regulated by choice. Our sense of self-determination enables us to embrace life with dignity and delight. Quality of life is my birthright . . . my heritage . . . my inheritance. We are all intended, designed, and equipped to live a fulfilled, contented, and complete life—one that is based on our wise choices.

We were not created to be negative, irresponsible people. A quality life is based solely on quality choices. The fact that we are responsible for our own quality of life is not bad news: it's great news! It allows *me* to be in control. It allows me to exercise my personal power of choice and decision and to reclaim my dignity as a human being, made in the image of God. I do not have to surrender my will to any other person or outside circumstance. When I abdicate my personal power, I have voluntarily stripped myself of my worth, my self-respect, and my human dignity!

A person who has become an extraordinary performer understands this and models behavior based on this concept. The extraordinary performer understands that life is 1 percent what happens to us . . . and 99 percent how we interpret and respond to it! When an extraordinary performer is handed a lemon (the 1 percent), he chooses to make lemonade! He has internalized the truth that he can either *sulk* about what he *can't* do and what is wrong, or he can *celebrate* what he *can* do and what is right! The extraordinary performer knows the same resolute determination expressed by an old Scottish soldier, lying wounded and bleeding on the battlefield, who said: "Lay me down and bleed awhile, I am wounded, but not slain, I shall rise to fight again." Yes! Fall down seven times, get up eight!

A true story I love to tell is about an incident from the 1936 Olympics in Germany. This is one of the finest reflections of human greatness that I have ever heard. Jesse Owens, who would go on to win four gold medals that year, was in serious danger of not winning the third. He was twice disqualified for inadvertently stepping over the starting line as he began his broad jump. With only one attempt left, Owens stood before the crowd, dejected and uncertain. At that very moment, a German athlete named Luz Long sensed Jesse Owens's discomfort. Luz Long made a choice. He told Owens, "I will place my towel in front of the line, and you can use it for your take-off point." Jesse Owens took the towel, followed Luz Long's advice, and went on to win the gold medal.[2]

It's important to note that Luz Long was not just any athlete. He was one of Jesse Owens's competitors in that same event! Luz Long made a choice. He knew that winning was important, but it wasn't everything. For if winning is everything, then how you play means nothing! Who do you think was the very first person to embrace Jesse Owens after he won the gold? The very same man who understood that the quality of life is determined by the quality of choices we make. Luz Long knew that by helping Jesse Owens, he would be improving the quality of his own life. He believed that *true* quality is *the* quality of *every* quality at its highest point. Luz made the decision to serve someone else . . . and by doing so, he served himself. Luz Long had thoroughly embraced the truth that real power is the power of making other people powerful!

"How Do I Get Others to
Exercise Their Personal Power?"

Perhaps the most common question I will hear from people in leadership positions in Corporate America today is this: "How do I get people to think and act independently? I work with them, I train them, but when all is said and done, they still won't make a decision without coming to me first. I want them to take responsibility for their own areas, not come running back to me to OK every little decision! Jack, how do I get them to *do* that?"

Let's start to answer this question by reviewing the three stages of growth that occur within an organization:

1. *Total dependence.* The newly formed company is totally dependent on the entrepreneur or chief executive. All direction and innovation come from this one individual. The entrepreneur's daily presence is vitally necessary for keeping the organization on track and on purpose.

2. *Growing independence.* As the company grows, "the boss" can no longer oversee every little detail, so managers and department heads are installed to ensure the success of daily operations. They make any number of independent decisions. However, they still meet regularly with the entrepreneur to receive affirmation, guidance, and notices of course corrections. The chief executive is still solely responsible for the bulk of inspiration and innovation. In some organizations, there is a dollar figure that is prescribed beyond which a department manager cannot spend without authorization. In other companies, the "line of empowerment" is a more hazy one. In either circumstance, the managers know there is a certain point past which they dare not stretch the limits of their authority. The vast pool of talent, knowledge, experience, and skills that have been assembled beneath the entrepreneur remains largely untapped and underutilized.

This is the point of critical mass! There is a danger that a corporate entity may remain stuck at this intermediate stage and never advance to the pinnacle of competency, which is the third and final stage of growth.

3. *Interdependency.* The level of peak performance. Each individual employee sees himself as an integral part of the organization. Staffers are keenly aware of the unique contributions they make to the team. At the same time, they are also aware of the combination of abilities that lies within each coworker. There is an amplification, a multiplication of strengths, an accentuation of abilities. There is no thought given to the taking or holding of positional power, none of the debilitating "turf battles" that plague other organizations, only an ongoing commitment to excellence.

The chief executive is still involved in the decision-making process and still retains the right and the responsibility to approve or veto the suggestions of the staff. However, the CEO is no longer responsible for being the sole source of creativity. The managers, and even the frontline employees, have been transformed into passionate purpose partners who are busily engaged in the process of identifying areas for improvement and creating the processes that will ensure perpetual innovation and competitive advantage. The organization is constantly discovering and developing paradigm pioneers at all levels and from all departments.

I believe that a great many top-flight leaders truly wish to develop this kind of a peak environment, and they believe they are encouraging it, but they are deeply frustrated that it hasn't become a reality at their companies. Perhaps you are one of these leaders, and you're nodding your head this very minute, saying to yourself, "Yeah, that's right, how do we break out of that kind of inertia?"

Let's consider those folks whom we feel aren't taking enough initiative. Many of them are top-flight people, as well. Remember? That's why you hired or promoted them in the first place! They aren't timid or indecisive by nature. However, just like anyone else, they do possess a good, healthy desire to survive, and "empowerment" is truly a double-edged sword.

Middle managers in most organizations are aware that their leaders want them to "take the ball and run with it." But they are also clearly aware that, somewhere out there, is a line over which they dare not step. Their leaders tell them, "I want you to act independently." But in far too many companies, "empowerment" *really* means, "You're completely empowered, *until* you make a big mistake, and then you're in big trouble!" Let's be honest: we all know that line exists. The problem is, do we know exactly *where* it lies? Can I make a ten-dollar mistake? Probably. But can I make a ten-*thousand*-dollar mistake? Will I lose my job if I do?

Many middle managers feel like they have been set down in the middle of a big field on a pitch-black night. Their leader is standing next to them, but it's so dark, the middle manager can't see her, they can only hear the leader's voice, saying, "I want you to start walking. Walk quickly, confidently, and well. You've been walking for years now, and I know you'll do a good job. Just one thing. Somewhere out there is a sheer cliff. If you walk over the edge, it's a ninety-foot drop to the rocks below. You'll be killed for sure."

"But it's pitch black out," the middle manager protests nervously. "I can't see where the edge of the cliff is!"

"Don't worry about that," the leader replies. "If you walk over the edge, you'll know soon enough!"

It might sound silly, but this kind of conversation actually takes place every day, in organizations all over the country. The language may be slightly different, but the basic message, whether spoken or implied, is exactly the same. As a result, too many managers are operating with a sense of fear. It isn't any wonder they keep going back to their supervisors to get backup for their actions and ideas. They're trying to find out where the cliff is!

There are two things that leadership can do to help relieve this kind of fear. First, by all means, make every effort to shine searchlights on the cliff! No one should have to guess where the boundaries are. Dr. James Dobson has written of an experiment that an educator tried with a group of young children. The educator was concerned that a fenced-in playground restricted the children's sense of freedom and imagination. He removed the fence, in the hope that a removal of barriers would cause the children to truly move out into the world, so to speak, and realize their full potential for play and, ultimately, for life. The actual results were just the opposite. The children clustered together near the center of the playground. Far from striking boldly out into the unknown, the kids *voluntarily* restricted their movements even more dramatically than when they knew where the barriers were.[3]

Adult professionals behave in much the same way! If they don't know where the boundaries are, they'll be even *more* cautious, even *less* likely to act independently, because they have no clear idea where the limits of their empowerment really are. This is true of Thinkers, who are often intensely self-critical and dislike making mistakes; it is true of Energizers, who want to be liked and don't want to make waves; it is true of highly ambitious Achievers, who don't want to hurt their climb up the career ladder with a mistake; and it is true of Mediators, who fear conflict and don't particularly want to stand out from the crowd. Therefore, it is important to clearly delineate what the lines of demarcation are, so that people can expand their horizons up to that point.

Second, and even more important, leaders and companies who truly want to encourage an environment of empowerment must take every opportunity to *recognize* and *reinforce risk!* Generally, our society only celebrates *successful* risk takers. For example, late in a football game, a team faces a fourth-and-one situation in their own end of the field. The safe, conservative call ("the way we've always done it") is to hand off to the team's best running back and let him pound up the middle of the line. If he hammers out the one yard, the offense has four fresh tries to move the ball downfield. Everybody in the stadium expects this call. The defense expects it, too, and they crowd the line with tacklers looking to stop the run.

The quarterback decides to gamble. He goes for the play-action pass, faking the run and throwing to a wide receiver streaking deep down the field. The crowd roars when it sees the ball in the air and then groans when the ball lands just beyond the straining fingertips of the receiver.

Immediately, the second-guessing starts: "That dumb call cost us the ball game!" or "If that idiot had just played it safe, we could have won!" And so on.

On the other hand, if the pass is completed for a touchdown, the quarterback is the toast of the town! Everyone calls the quarterback, "brilliant," "gutsy," and "fearless," instead of "an idiot."

As leaders, we need to reinforce risk, even when our manager *doesn't* hit the big pass to win the game. In fact, the pass may be intercepted and run back for the touchdown that *costs* us the game! Nevertheless, leaders need to hold that *effort* up for approbation. Instead of calling the manager into a closed-door session to warn him, "One more mistake like that, buster, and you're gone," we need to celebrate the *behavior* in front of the entire team. *"This* is the kind of boldness, the aggressive attitude that we're looking for! Sure, the results weren't what we would like, but it's this can-do, will-do attitude that is going to put us miles ahead of our competition! This manager is a model of excellence!"

Imagine a bright, young manager who is trying to pursue an aggressive marketing strategy for a new product line, and in so doing, makes a mistake that is going to cost her company $100,000. She was doing her best, but she miscalculated the market response. She doesn't sleep well the night after the mistake comes to light. She figures she'll be fired the next day.

Sure enough, when she arrives at work, there is a message that the CEO wants to see her at 10:00 A.M.

When she arrives for the meeting, the CEO says to her, "I understand we've had a setback on the New Project campaign. Tell me what happened."

"Yes," the nervous manager replies, "and it's all my fault. I'm so sorry. I really thought this new approach would be a profitable one. You see, I—"

The CEO interrupts her. "I didn't call you in here to lower the boom on you. I just want to know what happened."

The woman continues, as if she really hadn't heard what was just said: "I'm just sick about the whole thing. I'm so sorry it happened. I truly believed we were going to gain a significant competitive advantage. This is all my fault."

To her amazement, the CEO actually *smiles* at her! "You still aren't hearing me," he gently insists. "I didn't call you in here to fire you, or to reprimand you. The way I see it, this company has just invested $100,000 in your education. I want to see what kind of return on investment we've gotten. What have you learned from this? More important, what can we as a company learn from this?"

Rather than cutting this woman off at the knees, the CEO realized that her $100,000 mistake might one day earn the company millions, because this ambitious trendsetter has forced the company to look in directions they had never considered before. The CEO is using a finger that *could* have been pointing toward blame and shame to point toward a bright, new, innovative future. During the previous chapter, I spent some time talking about a champion's attitude toward failure. We unleash untapped potential in others when we see failure as the means for positively eliminating the ways *not* to do something. The CEO looked at the manager's $100,000 mistake and thought, "Let's do a PMI (Plus, Minus, Interesting) on this mistake. What are the pluses of the manager's idea? Where could it lead us? What can we learn from it?" Just as important, the CEO considered what positives in the manager's behavior should be reinforced, even though the results weren't the desirable ones.

Too many organizations will define themselves as being strictly "this," and as a result they paint themselves into a corner. They restrict themselves from exploring "these" and "that" and "those."

The manager who made the expensive mistake had the gumption to raise her vision above her company's comfort zone and look toward a bold, new future.

It is only through the taking of risk that we can explore new horizons! The people who don't *fear* the future are the ones who *create* the future! There are those in an organization who ask questions like "Why?" and "What?" But the leaders who will take us into the twenty-first century are those who aren't afraid to ask, "Why not?" and "What if?"

The Freedom of Values

Our values are the foundation that sets us free to be prudent risk takers. If our central, core value is that we are all made in God's image, then we *honor* people, we know that every human being has limitless potential. The human mind is infinitely upgradable! We were made and created for risk taking. Every individual is an artesian well of ideation, innovation, and imagination. *This* is the philosophy that creates an environment that encourages independence and empowerment.

We are made to redefine excellence, moment by moment. Our whole planet is screaming for "More, better, faster, cheaper, smarter!" It is a constant demand. Increasingly, our companies are in global competition. As a result, we must be able to reexamine our methods almost constantly. We must think differently this year than we did just last year! We are constantly redefining excellence and taking fresh risks.

If our values tell us that there are no little people and no little places; if we don't allow ourselves to succumb to "Big I" and "little you" thinking; if we see each and every individual as *vitally* important, as an image-bearer for the company; *then* we are able to break out of "What?" and "Why?" thinking, and we burst into "What if?" and "Why not?" innovation! Then our competitors watch us go sailing by them on our way to record-setting profits, and they wonder "Why? Why didn't I think of that?" The answer is, because they didn't allow the people in their companies to *operate in harmony with who they are!*

Clearly, the secret of this chapter, the secret of our power of choice, is expressed in the title to this chapter: *Power Means Passing It On.* We need to recognize and reinforce the risk takers in our companies and our communities. When they exercise their personal power of choice and opt to take the bolder path, we celebrate them! Even if they don't quite get the right results, we celebrate their courage! Encourage them to *choose* to reach for the stars! Celebrate them even when they fall! Then, and only then, will we unlock the true greatness that lies within our homes, our businesses, our schools, and our nation.

Every human being is worthy of the utmost honor and respect. Each and every man and woman you meet is the possessor of a titanic worth and dignity that are completely beyond the ability of science to measure, because science is incapable of defining and measuring the magnificence of the human spirit. We have each been granted the right to make choices that are *powerful* or powerless. We can adopt the mind-set of a champion of change or a victim of circumstance. It is our choice, an election to be influential or ineffectual. We can choose to be winners, or whiners.

Dear Reader, *you* are a winner! You would not have worked your way through this book if you weren't a man or woman of conviction and perseverance. Use that personal power of choice to build a life that is worth modeling. I have developed a quick "Checklist of Choices" for you to review.

Checklist of Choices

- I *choose* my internal conversation. My self-talk buoys me up or brings me down.

- I *choose* my response to every situation. No one and nothing *make* me respond.

- I *choose* my attitude towards my job.

- I *choose* the way I treat other people.

- I *choose* what I will do about my physical health.

- I *choose* what I will eat and drink.

- I *choose* how happy I will be.

- I *choose* to maintain emotional control. I *choose* to act response-*ably*.

- I *choose* to grow spiritually.

- I *choose* what I will learn (or if I will learn).

- I *choose* how much money I will earn, and how many hours I will invest earning it.

- I *choose* how much of my time, talent, and treasure I will give to others.

Don't Make a Bad Choice!

Some of the "new" morality teaches us that we are not responsible for our choices, that our decisions to become alcoholics or killers or moral and spiritual failures are not the result of choice, but rather the result of our genes. Some of these purveyors of pop psychology have gone so far as to claim that because some animals in the wild kill their offspring, that a human being who commits infanticide is merely acting according to the call of their evolutionary ancestors.

Don't let yourself fall prey to this kind of polluted, poisonous, empty thinking! Let's all claim the right to our personhood and human dignity by making quality decisions, and let's take responsibility for every decision we make. Let us not be spectators of our own lives. Let's be participants!

After God had delivered the Israelites out of slavery in Egypt, He set before them the most important choice of all: "I have set before you life and death, blessing and cursing; therefore choose life, that both you and your descendants may live" (Deut. 30:19). We *choose* to live meaningful, magnificent lives of caring and contribution, or we can elect to meander through a maze of meaninglessness and mediocrity. *We* choose. *We* decide.

Dear Reader, I have one last secret to share with you. It is the single, most important truth that will enable you to truly *"choose life,"* and to live it to its fullest. Come with me for the unveiling of this last, most powerful secret!

Our Greatest Wealth Is Our Spiritual Strength: In Search of Ultimate Meaning

12

Now you have come to the twelfth secret for turning ordinary people into extraordinary performers. This secret is the truth that will truly enable you to become totally human and alive totally. This secret ties the whole book together and gives power, freedom, and fulfillment to the other eleven truths. The first eleven secrets wired you with truth; now this twelfth secret throws the energy switch. The physicist David Bohm says, "Only meaning arouses energy."[1] The twelfth secret challenges our mind to explore ultimate, final meaning—*truth*. I know that if I were to leave this chapter out, the book, in the final analysis, would be meaningless. I would be doing you a great disservice because I would be leaving you floundering in a sea of subjectivism. Even though we have covered many good things in this book, the good can be the enemy of the best. Your being is hardwired for the best, and what we are going to expose you to in this chapter is the best of the best.

Motivation Without Meaning

Dear Reader, for years I read every motivational book I could get my hands on, and those books always left me with an emptiness. I knew within my spirit that there was something missing. The authors told me how great I was and that all I needed to do was tap the power within me; I had all I needed within me to solve all my problems. Yet, their instruction never delivered what I really needed, which was inner peace. Socrates said, "You will never know a line is crooked unless you place a straight one beside it."[2] The straight line, the discerning plumb line of all reality, is truth. Only truth affords peace for all time and eternity. Truth always causes us to search the spiritual dimension of life, and that is the purpose of the twelfth secret: to examine where you are on your spiritual journey.

My Search for Truth

After studying the eleven major religions of the world, one of the religions captured my attention. No one had ever taught me the uniqueness of this religion. Then I discovered it isn't really a religion after all—it is a relationship. What I am referring to is Christianity. The source book for Christianity is the Bible. My quest for truth ended when I learned that the Bible is the only book among the eleven major religions of the world that is an inspired, prophetic book.

No book in human history prophetically writes about and names specific nations, events, people, and places, hundreds and thousands of years before these prophecies became a reality, like the Bible. Let's look at just one area of biblical prophecy.

Three Hundred Prewritten Prophecies About Jesus Christ

If I handed you a book that had been written hundreds of years before Abraham Lincoln was born and this book foretold more than 300 specific prophecies about his life, wouldn't you think that book was divinely inspired? Well, that is exactly what the Bible does concerning the birth, life, death, and resurrection of Jesus Christ.

There are more than 300 Old Testament prophecies that were written hundreds of years before the birth of Jesus Christ. And all 300 of those prophecies became a historical reality in the historical Person of Jesus Christ. When I first read this in Josh McDowell's book *Evidence That Demands a Verdict,* I said that if I were a betting man I would place all my chips on Jesus Christ as being who He said He was—God in the flesh.

Think about this. Has what I just said sunk in yet? Jesus Christ fulfilled *all* 300 Old Testament prophecies. Do you realize that no religious leader in all of human history can claim that kind of prophetic fulfillment? What would be the odds of Jesus' fulfilling all 300 of those prophecies? The odds are beyond any stretch of the imagination that they could have been possibly fulfilled *by chance.* Let's look at just 8 of these 300 prophecies and then consider the odds of fulfilling those 8.

1. It was prophesied that He would be born of a virgin. *Prophecy:* Isaiah 7:14 *Fulfilled:* Matthew 1:23

2. It was prophesied that He would be born at Bethlehem. *Prophecy:* Micah 5:2 *Fulfilled:* Matthew 2:1

3. It was prophesied that He would come from the tribe of Judah. *Prophecy:* Micah 5:2 *Fulfilled:* Luke 3:23–33

4. It was prophesied that He would have a ministry of miracles. *Prophecy:* Isaiah 35:5, 6 *Fulfilled:* Matthew 9:35

5. It was prophesied that He would be resurrected. *Prophecy:* Psalm 16:10 *Fulfilled:* Matthew 28:6

6. It was prophesied that His hands and feet would be pierced. *Prophecy:* Psalm 22:16 *Fulfilled:* Mark 15:24

7. It was prophesied that His name would be Immanuel ("God with us"). *Prophecy:* Isaiah 7:14 *Fulfilled:* Matthew 1:23

8. It was prophesied that none of His bones would be broken.
Prophecy: Psalm 34:20 *Fulfilled:* John 19:33

Professor Peter Stoner, in his book *Science Speaks,* states that according to the laws of probability, for Jesus to have fulfilled just these 8 prophecies the chance would be 1 in 10 to the 17th power. That would be the number 10 with 17 zeros behind it: 1 in 100,000,000,000,000,000. Think about that: Jesus had one chance in one hundred thousand billion to pull that off. That alone proved to me that the Bible is truly God's Word.

Professor Stoner goes on to look at the probability of fulfilling 48 prophecies. He said that the chance would be 1 in 10 to the 157th power. Let me help you visualize this number to get the full impact of it:

1 in
10,000,000,000,000,000,000,000,000,000,000,000,000,
000,000,000,000,000,000,000,000,000,000,000,000,000,
000,000,000,000,000,000,000,000,000,000,000,000,000,
000,000,000,000,000,000,000,000.[3]

This should really get your attention! The amazing thing about this is that we are only examining 48 prophecies out of the 332 prophecies He fulfilled. That leaves us with 284 prophecies that we could submit to the science of probability for its mathematical analysis. Can you imagine what the probability would be for Jesus' fulfilling an additional 284 prophecies? It is as if God said, "I am going to write a Book like no other book on this planet, and when anyone studies My Book they will know beyond any doubt that it is a miracle Book. And when they compare My Book with other books written by men they will know only My Book teaches *absolute, total, and final truth.*" I hope by now you are saying to yourself that you must start reading the Bible and embrace its truth into your soul.

How to Know the God of the Bible

The God of the Bible—the only God—has made it very easy to know Him. He has established only one way to know Him. That is very good news because we don't have to figure out our own way to come to God. We don't have to guess and discover which way is the best way. He has already devised a plan by which anyone can know Him for certain. He clearly lets us know in the Bible that He accepts people on His terms and not on their terms.

The God of the Bible Became the God-Man

The plan God created in order for us to know Him is the most personal way I ever heard of in my life. No other religion can claim the personal uniqueness of this plan. It is called the "plan of salvation." What is the profound uniqueness of this plan? It is that the God of the Bible became the God-Man. You can't get any more personal than that: God became one of us. In this book I have been showcasing who we really are: we are the zenith of God's creation because He made us in His intensely personal image. Therefore, it makes perfect sense that the personal God of the universe would not do anything less than come up with a plan to show Himself personally to the ones He created in His personal image. His heart's desire is to have a personal relationship with you.

Are you ready for the verse that settles forever how to come to God on His terms? In the fourth book of the New Testament the apostle John quotes the very words of the God who became flesh: "Jesus said to him, 'I am the way, the truth, and the life. No one comes to the Father except through Me'" (John 14:6). You just read it—that is the only way to know the God of the Bible. Jesus did not claim to be *one* of the ways or *part* of the truth or a life teaching that will help you on your individual path to the Father. He made a mind-blowing claim like no other religious leader in history. He said He was THE WAY, THE TRUTH, and THE LIFE and that there is absolutely no other way to come to the Father unless you go through Him.

What a claim! In that claim, He said, "I am God." He claimed to be the fountainhead of all reality. That all truth was His truth. That He was the Wonder of all wonders. That He was the Origin of the universe. Now we must examine something very closely. If Jesus said that He is God and the Father is God, do we have two Gods?

Is Jesus God?

In the first chapter I introduced the theistic concept that we are created in God's image, and I quoted Genesis 1:26: "Then God said, 'Let Us make man in Our image, according to Our likeness.'" Notice what God said: "Let *Us* make man in *Our* image, according to *Our* likeness." If you are Jewish you would immediately respond and say there is only one God, not two or three Gods. And you would quote Deuteronomy 6:4, in which the God of the Bible taught Israel to say: "Hear, O Israel: The LORD our God, the LORD is one!" And I would agree that there is only one God. However, the Hebrew word for "one" is the word *echod,* which means "a plural unity"—not an absolute unity, but a composite unity. The New Testament speaks of God as being a tri-unity. God is three Persons in one Godhead. As you read the New Testament you will read about God the Father, God the Son, and God the Holy Spirit. Not three different Gods, but one God in three Persons.

Therefore, in order to know God the Father you must believe that Jesus is God also. If you don't believe in the deity of Jesus then you have embraced false spirituality. Dear Reader, believing in the deity of Jesus is the only door to knowing God the Father. Let's look at the New Testament and see if Jesus really claimed to be God.

Jesus Claimed to Be God!

As I read the New Testament, I found it fascinating that wherever Jesus was teaching, Jews were standing around with stones in their hands. Why? Look at John 10:30–33 and you will see why. Jesus said,

"I and My Father are one." Then the Jews took up stones again to stone Him. Jesus answered them, "Many good works have I shown you from My Father. For which of those works do you stone Me?" The Jews answered Him, saying, "For a good work we do not stone You, but for blasphemy, and because You, being a Man, make Yourself God."

The Jews knew exactly what Jesus was saying. He was claiming to be God. What was the central message behind everything Jesus said? It was always His deity. Why did the Jews want to stone Him to death? Because He constantly hit them in the gut with His claims of deity.

Why did the Jews finally crucify Him? Because, under oath, Jesus told the whole world in strong language that He was God in the flesh. Listen to this historical record of what Jesus said under oath, found in Mark 14:61–62: "But He kept silent and answered nothing. Again the high priest asked Him, saying to Him, 'Are You the Christ, the Son of the Blessed?' Jesus said, 'I am. And you will see the Son of Man sitting at the right hand of the Power, and coming with clouds of heaven.'"

There you have it, dear Reader, the historical record that states that Jesus believed He was God. We must look at another great passage in which Jesus drove home His deity to a group of unbelievers: "When Jesus saw their faith, He said to the paralytic, 'Son, your sins are forgiven you.' And some of the scribes were sitting there and reasoning in their hearts, 'Why does this Man speak blasphemies like this? Who can forgive sins but God alone?'" (Mark

2:5–7). Scribes, you got it—only God can forgive sins, and that is precisely what Jesus was saying, "I am God, and I am the only One who can forgive sins."

The uniqueness of Jesus screams at us from every page of the New Testament. Have you ever read of any religious leader claiming sinlessness and making it the central issue for his ministry? Jesus is the only One who ever made that claim. Jesus said in John 8:46, "Which of you convicts Me of sin?" Can you imagine that? He basically said, "Show Me one time when I sinned." That is a bold statement unless you are God. No one could step forward and say, "Well there was one time when Jesus did something bad." Not one of His critics could dispute His claim to sinlessness.

Who Do You Think Jesus Christ Is?

Dear Reader, it is time for you to make a decision. Let me ask you the most important question anyone can ever ask you: Who do you believe Jesus Christ is? Do you believe He is God? You know what I believe. I believe with all my soul that Jesus is God Almighty, and I have received Him as my Savior.

Jesus warns us of what will happen to us if we don't believe that He is God. Listen, like you have never listened before, to the eternal warning of Jesus Himself: "Therefore I said to you that you will die in your sins; for if you do not believe that I am He, you will die in your sins" (John 8:24).

When Jesus used the title "I am" in this verse, He was referring His listeners back to Exodus 3:14, when Moses asked God, "What is Your name?" "And God said to Moses, 'I AM WHO I AM.' And He said, 'Thus you shall say to the children of Israel, I AM has sent me to you.'" Dear Reader, we are standing on holy ground. God has just given you great truth about Himself. The I AM of the Old Testament is Jesus of the New Testament, and He is inviting you to trust Him as your Savior.

God's Plan of Salvation

Do you remember earlier when I mentioned that God has a plan of salvation? God has a simple plan, and I want to reveal that plan to you right now. The reason there is a plan of salvation is because we are sinners and we need a Savior. So far in this book I have said that we are God's image: we are rational, personal, and created with a moral nature. However, there is a spiritual dimension of this I have not discussed. The next section will help you understand why you are a sinner and why you need a Savior.

Only Persons Made in God's Image Can Sin

When God first made Adam, God made him as an indefectibly righteous, holy, and sinless being. Then Adam sinned against God and he lost that original sinlessness. Consequently, we still bear the wonderful image of our God, but it is a sinfully marred image. If we had completely lost that image in the Fall, with Adam, then we would be impersonal animals and we could not sin. Only persons made in God's image are capable of sinning. All sin is personal. All sin comes from personal choice. There are no victims when it comes to sin; we are personally responsible for every sin we commit. Therefore, all sin is a personal affront to the Holy Being of God. So, if we had lost our personhood in the fall we would not need a Savior; but we didn't lose that personhood, and we do need a Savior.

Don't you feel it inside you, that you don't live up to what you know you should? That there is something tragically missing within your being? What is missing is sinlessness and fellowship with God. Everything about us is designed for righteousness, excellence, and greatness—and not sin. Sin destroys us. When we sin we walk around with an unbearable burden of guilt and shame, and a deep sense of alienation. Our conscience points a finger at our soul and relentlessly seeks to condemn us. When we sin we know we are not the kind of persons we are supposed to be. Just read the newspaper or listen to the news on television: we are a spiritually sick race.

Why We Are Sinners, and Why We Need a Savior

Let's continue looking at why we are sinners and why we need a Savior. God's plan of salvation started in a garden thousands of years ago, according to the Bible. The Bible says in Genesis 2:15–17, "Then the LORD God took the man and put him in the garden of Eden to tend and keep it. And the LORD God commanded the man, saying, 'Of every tree of the garden you may freely eat; but of the tree of the knowledge of good and evil, you shall not eat, for in the day that you eat of it you shall surely die.'"

Eating of the tree of the knowledge of good and evil was the one thing Adam and Eve were told they could not do. And if they did, they would die spiritually, resulting in eternal separation from God. I used to think, "How could just eating of the fruit of one tree send Adam and Eve to hell forever? It's not like they burned down the garden or killed all the animals, they just ate a piece of fruit!" In my ignorance I thought like this, until I came to understand the personal holiness of God and the nature of sin.

The Nature of Sin, and the Holiness of God

Dear Reader, really think with me on this: It is not so much what Adam and Eve did but whom they sinned against. They sinned against an infinitely holy, personal Being who demands infinite satisfaction for any sin committed against Him. Therefore, any sin (e.g., eating from the forbidden tree, lying, stealing, murder, or evil thoughts) is infinite in demerit. God is so holy that His nature demands eternal payment for sin.

What you never hear in other religions, my dear Reader, is the truth about who God really is and who man really is. In these false religions you will never learn why you are a sinner and why you need a Savior. The Bible says that God is a holy and righteous God, separate and distinct from His creation, and that we have sinned against His holiness. The Bible says that God is a God of wrath and justice and that no sin goes unpunished. God is so holy, perfect, and sinless that He would cease to be God if He did not eternally punish all sin. Now let's get back to why we are sinners and need a Savior.

Moses goes on to tell us in Genesis 3:6–7 what our first parents did concerning the one thing they were told not to do:

> So when the woman saw that the tree was good for food, and that it was pleasant to the eyes, and a tree desirable to make one wise, she took of its fruit and ate. She also gave to her husband with her and he ate. Then the eyes of both of them were opened, and they knew that they were naked; and they sewed fig leaves together, and made themselves coverings.

Adam and Eve directly went against God's will by asserting their own wills. Consequently, in that willful, rebellious act of eating the forbidden fruit, they died spiritually. They lost true spirituality, and the first thing they did was an act of self-righteousness. They tried to cover their own sin with fig leaves.

True Spirituality Versus False Spirituality

Man today is still trying to cover his sin with the fig leaves of religion—self-righteousness. If God had not done something on behalf of Adam and Eve, they would be burning in hell today. This is such a vital spiritual truth to learn, concerning what God did on their behalf. So don't miss this. We read in Genesis 3:21: "Also for Adam and his wife the LORD God made tunics of skin, and clothed them." In essence, what God was demonstrating by clothing our first parents in the skins of this innocent animal was to show them that their act of clothing themselves in fig leaves represented false spirituality, and His act of clothing them in innocent animal skins represented true spirituality. When God killed that innocent animal in the presence of Adam and Eve, He was teaching them eternal truths about the nature of Himself, the nature of sin, and His plan of salvation for them.

Five Spiritual Truths

There are five spiritual truths that God taught Adam and Eve by clothing them in the skins of that animal:

1. Sin demands payment. The Holy Judge of the universe cannot allow sin to go unpunished.

2. The payment for sin is death. That death is spiritual death—separation from God in hell for all eternity. An animal had to die in order to provide its skins for a covering for Adam and Eve.

3. However, the death God provided was a substitutionary death. In other words, that animal died in the place of Adam and Eve. God said they would die if they ate of the tree of knowledge of good and evil. They did die spiritually, but God brought them back into a spiritual union with Himself by killing an animal in their place. They should have paid for their own sin, but God in His grace and love provided a substitute for them.

4. The substitutionary death for them would be innocent. The animal that died had done nothing wrong. It was an innocent sacrifice.

5. God would clothe them in His own righteousness. By taking off Adam and Eve's fig leaves of self-righteousness, He was showing to them that there was nothing they could do to cover their sin. He was letting them know, by rejecting their system of self-

righteousness, that only His righteousness was the standard for having fellowship with Him.

Why Are We Sinners?

That entire act by God symbolically teaches God's plan of salvation. The first thing to understand in this plan is why we are sinners. The Bible tells us very clearly why: "Therefore, just as through one man sin entered the world, and death through sin, and thus death spread to all men, because all sinned" (Rom. 5:12). The text tells us that sin entered into the world through one man, and Adam was that one man. Adam was the federal head for the whole human race, and when he sinned he plunged the whole of humanity into sinfulness. Adam acted as the representative for every human being that would ever be born.

Therefore, the amazing truth of this verse is that the real ground of your condemnation before God has nothing to do with your personal sins. According to this verse you were condemned long before you ever committed any personal acts of sin. Adam's one act of disobedience was legally credited to you as if you had personally been there and ate of the forbidden tree.

Now because we are one of Adam's children we have inherited a sinful nature, and we sin from that evil nature. However, that nature is still not the legal ground for our condemnation as a race. Because we were condemned in Adam as a race before any of us had a sinful nature. Listen to what the Bible says about this in Romans 5:19: "For as by one man's [Adam] disobedience many were made sinners, so also by one Man's obedience [Jesus] many will be made righteous." There you have it, dear Reader, we are all sinners because of what Adam did. You may say, "I don't want to deal with this." You don't have to, it will deal with you! This is reality whether we want to believe it or not. Believing it does not make it true, and disbelieving it does not make it false. It is objective truth.

The Five Spiritual Truths Related to Jesus Christ

Now we have learned why we are sinners, and because we have sinned against God, we now can see that we need a Savior. Let's return to the five spiritual truths that God taught Adam and Eve after they sinned against Him. Romans 3:24–28 is a passage of Scripture that combines all five spiritual truths into one grand display of God's plan of salvation:

> Being justified freely by His grace through the redemption that is in Christ Jesus, whom God set forth as a propitiation by His blood, through faith, to demonstrate His righteousness, because in His forbearance God had passed over the sins that were previously committed, to demonstrate at the present time His righteousness that He might be just and the justifier of the one who has faith in Jesus. Where is boasting then? It is excluded. By what law? Of works? No, but by the law of faith. Therefore we conclude that a man is justified by faith apart from the deeds of the law.

The first two spiritual truths—that sin demands a payment and that payment is death—are found in the phrase "the redemption that is in Christ Jesus." The word *redemption* in this context means that a transaction or payment has taken place. The payment was to God the Father. The death of Jesus Christ was that payment. Can you imagine dear Reader, how great that is? God became Man so that He could die for you to pay your sin debt. God damned His own Son to set you free.

The third spiritual truth involves the idea of substitution: "whom God set forth as a propitiation by His blood." It was the blood of Jesus that was shed in our place. Jesus became our substitute, our sin-bearer. We should have paid for our own sins, but Jesus stepped in and said, "Step back out of the path of My Father's wrath, sinner. I will gladly take His wrath in your place."

The fourth truth stated that the substitute God would provide would be innocent; this passage says Christ Jesus was that substitute. Jesus was sinless; He did not die for His own sins. He was the innocent Lamb of God. He was the only sinless Person that ever lived on this planet after the spiritual fall of Adam. Look at 2 Corinthians 5:21, where Paul stated strongly, "For He made Him who knew no sin to be sin for us, that we might become the righteousness of God in Him."

The fifth spiritual truth is that God rejects our self-righteousness and freely gives us His righteousness. Look at the word *grace*. As an acronym it stands for God's Righteousness At Christ's Expense. This truth is clearly revealed in the phrase "to demonstrate at the present time His righteousness, that He might be just and the justifier of the one who has faith in Jesus" (Rom. 3:26).

God's Three Legal Transactions

Everything about God's plan of salvation is *legal*. The legal truths of Christianity set it apart from every religion in the world. In God's heavenly court of law there have been three legal transactions in His heavenly ledger.

1. Adam's Sin Credited to Our Account

Remember how we learned that the legal ground of our condemnation is that God legally credited Adam's sin to all of humanity? That was the first legal entry into God's heavenly ledger of debits and credits. God's first representative of all humanity was Adam, and Adam's sin was placed in God's ledger on the debit side for all of us.

2. Our Sins Credited to Jesus on the Cross

The second legal transaction took place in God's courtroom, when Jesus was legally credited with our sins on the cross. For three hours on the cross Jesus was treated as if He had committed every sin you will ever commit, even though He personally never committed any sins. Jesus on that cross was acting as our representative. This whole concept is called *representative truth.* You see, dear Reader, in God's mind there have been only two men that have represented humanity: the first Adam (Adam) and the last Adam (Jesus). Paul teaches this truth in 1 Corinthians 15:22, 45, 47: "For as in Adam all die, even so in Christ all shall be made alive. . . . And so it is written, 'The first man Adam became a living being.' The last Adam became a life-giving spirit. . . . The first man was of the earth, made of dust; the second Man is the Lord from heaven."

Therefore, the last Adam—your new representative, Jesus—legally paid your eternal debt to God. On that cross, almost two thousand years ago, God legally transferred your sin debt to Jesus' account. It is especially interesting to me that in John 19:30, when Jesus had finished suffering for our sins, He screamed out one word in the Greek language: *tetelestai. Tetelestai* means "paid in full," and in that one declaration Jesus called to His Father to cancel our sin debt in His heavenly ledger, because Jesus had just paid it in full! That transaction was the second legal act in God's heavenly courtroom.

3. God Credits His Righteousness to Believers in Christ

The third legal transaction takes place when a person trusts in Jesus as their Savior. God at that moment credits to the believer His perfect eternal righteousness in His heavenly ledger. The wonderful news about these three legal transactions is that God is the One doing everything. God decided the legal ground of your condemnation, which was Adam's sin. And this act was apart from us and outside of us. Then God decided that our sins would be legally transferred to Jesus on the cross, which was again outside of us. Furthermore, God legally credits His righteousness to us on the basis of what our representative did, which was outside of us and apart from any works we might do. Therefore, we conclude this is God's plan of salvation for His glory and for our good.

How Do You Get God's Righteousness?

Now, I hope it makes more sense to understand why God is just and the justifier of him who believes in Jesus. God is just in forgiving all your sins because Jesus paid the just price for your sins. Now God is legally free to lavish on the wickedest person in the world His own perfect righteousness through accepting Christ's legal payment for their sins. If you never learn anything else about God, this is one truth you *must* know. In order to live with God forever you must have the very same righteousness He has, or He will not have anything to do with you.

The main question is, How do we get His righteousness? Examine closely Romans 3:27–28: "Where is boasting then? It is excluded. By what law? Of works? No, but by the law of faith. Therefore we conclude that a man is justified by faith apart from the deeds of the law." No one can boast before God. No one can say, "God, I have kept the law, I have lived a good life. Look at all my good works, God! God, I am proud of what I have done, and surely, God, You will accept me into heaven on the basis of my good works." But what does God say in this verse? God says boasting is excluded. Why? Because what God demands is perfect righteousness, and we can't give Him what He demands. Praise God that what He demands, He provides for us in Christ Jesus as a free gift. Look at that phrase again: "Therefore we conclude that a man is justified by faith apart from the deeds of the law."

The word *justified* means "declared righteous." When God justifies you, He does much more than just forgive all your sins. At the same time He forgives all your sins, He also writes in His ledger that you now possess His righteousness forever. What do you think about that? He takes my sins, and I get His righteousness.

This debit and credit legal concept is brought home magnificently by the apostle Paul in Romans 4:6–8: "Just as David also describes the blessedness of the man to whom God imputes righteousness apart from works; Blessed are those whose lawless deeds are forgiven, And whose sins are covered. Blessed is the man to whom the Lord shall not impute sin." The word *impute* in these verses means "credit to an account." Therefore, in God's heavenly ledger, when you trust Jesus as your Savior, the debit side says "paid in full," and on the credit side it says "God's righteousness." What a wonderful plan of salvation!

What Do You Have to Do to Have All Your Sins Forgiven?

The big question is, What do you have to *do* to get all your sins forgiven and get God's righteousness? Here is the answer: NOTHING! That's right, there is nothing for you to do. You don't have to join a church, be baptized, stop sinning, promise God you will live a wonderful life from now on, or give up all your possessions. You might say, "Now, Jack, there must be something I have to do." And I would reply, "Absolutely not!" You see, dear Reader, *God saves sinners.* We do not save ourselves. God saves you without COST to you and without CAUSE in you. Salvation is a *free gift.* Salvation begins with a big "DONE" not with a big "DO." Jesus *did* all there was to do. Now, blessed Reader, you are to *believe* what Jesus *did* for you. Salvation isn't begging, but believing; it isn't asking, but receiving.

Paul summarizes this truth beautifully: "But to him who does not work but believes on Him who justifies the ungodly, his faith is accounted for righteousness" (Rom. 4:5).

It is no coincidence that you have read this book. God is calling you to Himself. He wants you to believe on His Son as your personal Savior. Please join me right now in this prayer, and let's get this issue of your salvation settled forever: "God, I believe Jesus is God in the flesh, and I believe He died on the cross for my sins and came out of the grave on the third day. God, I trust in Jesus right now to be my personal Savior. Thank You, Father, for saving my soul." Dear Reader, do you understand that God's plan of salvation is so simple that even that prayer does not save you? However, belief in the truth of that prayer does. You don't have to ask God for salvation—just believe in JESUS for salvation. If you believed the truth in that prayer you are eternally saved, and you can never lose your salvation, because God gave it to you as a FREE eternal gift.

Beginning Your Spiritual Walk with God

Dear child of God, the best way to build a deep, fulfilling relationship with God is to pray and read your Bible every day. When you pray, you talk to God, and when you read your Bible, God talks to you. You also must find a church that believes the truths you have learned in this chapter and join yourself to them. Finding a good church home that feeds you historical, biblical Christianity is indispensable to your growth in the Lord. I would also strongly suggest that you find a mature person in the Lord who would mentor you in the truth of God's Word. After I trusted Christ as my Savior, Bobby Cassell became my mentor in the Lord, and he has remained my best friend for thirty years. Thank you, Bobby, for sharing your wisdom in the Lord with me.

Dear Reader, this last secret, which is the spiritual truth about humans, is truly the secret of untapped potential, because the extraordinary God turns an ordinary person into an extraordinary performer for His glory and our good.

I would like to close with a prayer from God's Word found in Ephesians 3:14–21:

> For this reason I bow my knees to the Father of our Lord Jesus Christ, from whom the whole family in heaven and earth is named, that He would grant you, according to the riches of His glory, to be

strengthened with might through His Spirit in the inner man, that Christ may dwell in your hearts through faith; that you, being rooted and grounded in love, may be able to comprehend with all the saints what is the width and length and depth and height—to know the love of Christ, which passes knowledge; that you may be filled with all the fullness of God. Now to Him who is able to do exceedingly abundantly above all that we ask or think, according to the power that works in us, to Him be glory in the church by Christ Jesus to all generations, forever and ever. Amen.

Conclusion: The View from the Mountaintop

Y OU AND I HAVE JUST COMPLETED a fascinating and inspiring journey of discovery. We have climbed twelve mountain peaks, and at the top of each one has been a secret for unleashing untapped potential, both yours and others'. I know the climbing hasn't always been easy, but you've made it! We stand together at the top of the last mountain, and now, from the vantage point of the tallest and grandest mountain, the mountain of God's grace, love and mercy, you and I can look back over the entire mountain range we have traversed together.

Let me start, dear Reader, by giving you a humble and heartfelt "Thank you!" What an honor to have had your company on this trip! There were some who dropped off the trail along the way. Many people begin books and never finish. I am truly grateful to you for staying with me all the way to the end.

As we climbed each mountain to find each new truth, my desire was that you would say to yourself, "This is liberating! This is transformational! This is truth!" I wanted to move you from mountain peak to mountain peak, from truth to truth, until I brought you to the God of all truth, who resides at the top of this last, most majestic peak. I hope, by now, that you want to join me in rejoicing with King David in the glory of our God:

> Yours, O LORD, is the greatness,
> The power and the glory,
> The victory and the majesty;
> For all that is in heaven and in earth is
> Yours;
> Yours is the kingdom, O LORD,
> And You are exalted as head over all.
> Both riches and honor come from You,
> And You reign over all.
> In Your hand is power and might;
> In Your hand it is to make great
> And to give strength to all.
>
> Now therefore, our God,
> We thank You
> And praise Your glorious name. (1 Chron. 29:11–13)

As we stand together at this strategic vantage point, and gaze back over the entire range of truth we have walked through together, I want you to see that what I have tried to lay out for you throughout this entire book is *God's* truth. This isn't Jack Lannom's truth; it isn't Eastern truth; it isn't Western truth. This book is a survey and an exposition of God's truth about our personhood.

A Book for Our Children

When I first began serious discussions with Thomas Nelson publishers about creating this book, I seriously considered titling it, simply, *Legacy.* That is because I want this book to be a legacy for my three children and one that they will want to pass on to *their* children. I wanted this book to be a treasure chest of truth that would provide my children with life skills that will enable them to live life skillfully.

I have a huge library at my home, built up by more than twenty-five years of study and research. The shelves are filled with books on motivation, but what I found in them was that most of the writers were blind to God's truth. They were blind guides who could lead you and me into the ditch of destruction. I did find some nuggets of truth contained in these books. All truth is God's truth, and it cannot be ignored or denied. But while there were morsels of truth to be gleaned from the hundreds of books I read, it was truth taken out of context. It was like trying to find good food in the dumpster.

Dining Out at the Dumpster

Can't you just picture it? I arrive home from a hard day at the office and announce to my wife: "Honey, I want to take you out to the finest restaurant in town! Put on your best dress, and I'll get the kids ready. You're going to love the food at this place!"

We jump in the car, the kids giggling in anticipation of a "feast fit for a king," and drive to the city's finest five-star restaurant. But when we arrive, instead of leaving my car with the valet, I wheel into a cluttered parking lot in the rear of the restaurant. We all get out of the car, and I usher my increasingly confused wife and children over to the dumpster. "They've got really great food here, you'll love it," I assure my stupefied family.

My loving wife can stand it no longer. "This is a *dumpster!*" she explodes. "There's a bunch of *garbage* in here!"

"Oh, sure," I reply blandly. "But if we dig through all the garbage, we'll find some really good morsels of food in there."

That's what reading most of those books on motivation was like! What we need is a library of books that give us God's truth about human motivation. We don't need a library filled with half-truths and whole lies.

A Reflection of God's Glory

So many of the books you might pick up will tell you that you are engineered for greatness, which is perfectly true. But they miss the more important half of the truth, which is the Engineer. We were created and engineered for greatness *by God* to reflect His greatness!

The great light that we see coming from the moon at night is a reflection of the light that comes from the sun. When we see the moon "shining bright as day," this merely tells us that there is a great source of light out there, and the moon is acting as a reflector of that greatness. The purpose of the moon is to reflect the great light of the sun. If we were studying the universe, we wouldn't want to focus on the moon and believe that it is the source of power and energy that warms the earth. If you saw someone standing in awe of the moon, saying, "Wow, the moon is such a wonderful source of light!" you would likely stop and ask them, "Do you know the truth about where the moon's light comes from? There is something out there that is far greater and far brighter than the moon could ever hope to be!" Our thinking should not stop at the moon, but rather it should lead us to the source.

This truth applies even more importantly to mankind. We were made to be a reflection of the Creator. We have no life or light of our own. Jesus Christ is the Light of the world. "In Him was life, and the life was the light of men." He is "the true Light which gives light to every man coming into the world" (John 1:4, 9). Jesus is the light we want to be focused on! This is the real revelation concerning the profound truth of personhood.

In this book, dear Reader, I wanted to honor you, to love you, to respect you, and to hold up your human dignity and worth. In light of the fact that 180,000 people are killed *each year* throughout the world for their faith,[1] I think it is important to proclaim that human beings are made in the image of God. In a country that aborts more than a million unborn babies each *year,* I believe it is crucial to point out that each one of those precious children was formed *by God* (Ps. 139:13) in His image. In a world where such unthinkable slaughter takes place, we can see that human life is not defined as being made in the image of God. I wanted to write a book that would lift up the value of human worth. I hope you will take this message and shout it from the rooftops!

But I didn't proclaim the magnificence of mankind so that you would become prideful, or narcissistic, or egoistic. It is not for man to become God. This would be like the moon wanting to become the sun. Rather, it is my hope that you would discover a new sense of humility and that you would fall to your knees in praise and adoration of God. We *know* that we are made in God's image, and we thank Him and adore Him for giving us the gift of life made in God's image. I would seek to live life from that strategic vantage point.

The first twelve chapters of this book were written to honor both the Creator and the zenith of His creation, which is man. But I didn't want to stop there. I wanted you to really *know* Him. It isn't enough to be made in God's image. Although we are made in the image of God, because of the fall of man, we've become *fallen* greatness. Our greatness is rusted, tarnished. The image has become marred and distorted.

> The fool has said in his heart,
> "There is no God."
> They are corrupt,
> They have done abominable works,
> There is none who does good.
>
> The LORD looks down from heaven upon
> the children of men,

To see if there are any who understand,
who seek God.
They have all turned aside,
They have together become corrupt;
There is none who does good,
No, not one. (Ps. 14:1–3)

That's why the twelfth secret brings you out into the light! You can look up into the heavens and look into the face of the Lord of glory, the Light of all lights, and see the love that He has for you. There is forgiveness for all those "who have become corrupt" through faith in Jesus Christ. Then our lives can reflect the light of the Son.

And it shall come to pass
That whoever calls on the name of the
LORD
Shall be saved.
For in Mount Zion and in Jerusalem there
shall be deliverance. (Joel 2:32)

Dear Reader, we stand together at the top of Mount Zion. We hold in our hands this book, which I see as being an alternative book to all the blind guides that assure you that your greatness lies within. I hope *Untapped Potential* will be a beacon of light for future generations—for your children and grandchildren and mine. I wanted to write a book that was God-centered and man-related, not man-centered and God-related. I want future generations to have in their possession life skills that will make their lives worth modeling, and a knowledge of Jesus Christ that will make their lives worth living. This is a book of motivation that is based on the personal nature of God. If you live the truths of this book, God will get all the credit, and you will get all the benefit. Jesus assured us,

"What man is there among you, if his son asks for bread, will give him a stone? Or if he asks for a fish, will he give him a serpent? If you then, being evil, know how to give good gifts to your children, how much more will your Father who is in heaven give good things to those who ask Him!" (Matt. 7:9–11). I can tell you from my own personal experience, that the God of the universe *delights* in giving good gifts to those who ask Him!

The twelve truths about all humans—the secrets for unleashing our untapped potential—will cause you to stand upright and look into the eyes of our extraordinary God, the One who turns ordinary people into extraordinary performers! This approach to life will allow you to reach your untapped potential. Take the life skills I have described and apply them to *yourself* first, because you can't impart what you don't possess. But then I hope you will immediately begin to teach the twelve secrets to your family and begin to practice these precepts in your home. Then, just as the concentric circles on a target radiate outward, take the skills you are practicing in your personal life into the professional arena. Use the twelve truths to turn your company into a powerful, *purpose*-full, profitable concern!

Dear Reader, I love you. Thank you for finishing this learning journey with me. Perhaps I'll meet you someday, after a seminar, or talk to you on the telephone during a call-in radio show. I know that I'll be meeting a bright, shining model of excellence, a human being who reflects the radiant glory of God. May God bless you in your quest for personal and professional excellence.

Now to Him who is able to do exceedingly abundantly above all that we ask or think, according to the power that works in us, to Him be glory in the church by Christ Jesus to all generations, forever and ever. Amen. (Eph. 3:20–21)

Notes

Chapter One

1. Leon R. Kass, "Death by Ballot in Oregon," *Wall Street Journal,* 2 November 1994, Sec. A, p. 140. Mr. Kass cites *The Report of the Dutch Government's Committee to Investigate the Practice of Euthanasia.* Also, Cal Thomas, "Protect Right to Life: Don't Legalize Doctor-Assisted Suicide or Euthanasia," *Sun-Sentinel* (Fort Lauderdale), 31 October 1994, Sec. A, p. 11. Mr. Thomas cites Jane M. Orient's book, *Your Doctor Is Not In.*

2. R. C. Sproul, "Saving the Phenomena," *Table Talk* 14, (October 1990), 6. Published by Ligonier Ministries, Orlando, Fla.

3. Dr. Mark P. Cosgrove, *The Essence of Human Nature* (Grand Rapids, Mich.: Zondervan, 1977), 18.

4. Francis A. Schaeffer, *A Christian Manifesto,* (Westchester, Ill.: Crossway Books, 1981), 56.

5. David A. Noebel, *Understanding the Times* (Eugene, Ore.: Harvest House, 1994). Used by permission.

6. William J. Federer, *America's God and Country* (Dallas, Tex: FAME Publishing, Inc., 1994), 671.

7. Ibid., 661.

8. Ibid., 701–2.

9. Paul Johnson, *The World from the Twenties to the Nineties* (New York, N.Y.: HarperCollins, 1983), 656–7.

10. Excerpted from a 1989 interview conducted with Mother Teresa by Edward W. Desmond for *Time* magazine. The quote appeared in *The National Catholic Register,* and can be found on the Internet.

11. Helen Keller, *The Story of My Life* (Garden City, N.Y.: Doubleday, Page and Co., 1902), quoted in Frank Severin, ed., *Discovering Man in Psychology: A Humanistic Approach* (New York: McGraw-Hill, 1973), 142–43.

12. Quoted by John Bartlett, *Bartlett's Familiar Quotations,* 14th ed. (Boston, Mass.: Little, Brown, 1968), 608b.

13. William P. Hoar, "The Human Cost: Twentieth Century Human Sacrifice," *The New American* 11, no. 19, (18 September 1995): 36–38.

14. Paul Lee Tan, *The Encyclopedia of 7,700 Quotations: Signs of the Times* (Rockville, Md.: Assurance Publishers, 1979), p. 462, quote 1787.

Chapter Three

1. Catherine Owens Peare, *The Helen Keller Story* (New York: Thomas Y. Cromwell, 1959), 3–5.

2. *The Encyclopedia American, International Edition* (Danbury, Conn.: Grolier Inc., 1996), 349.

3. Keller, *My Life,* quoted in Severin, *Discovering Man in Psychology,* 142–43.

4. Doctor Mark P. Cosgrove, *The Amazing Body Human, God's Design For Personhood* (Ada, Mich.: Baker Book House, 1987), 17, 163–64.

Chapter Four

1. *Encyclopedia Americana,* 547d.

2. Quoted by Michael O'Brien in *Vince: A Personal Biography of Vince Lombardi* (New York: William, 1987), 16.

Chapter Five

1. Edward de Bono, *de Bono's Thinking Course* (New York: Facts on File Publications, 1982), 11–19 (PMI); 74–75 (CAF); 95–98 (OPV).

Chapter Six

References:

Linda Verlee Williams, *Teaching for the Two-Sided Mind,* A Touchstone Book published by Simon & Schuster, Inc., New York, N.Y., 1983.

Colin Rose, *Accelerated Learning,* published by Dell Publishing Co., Inc., New York, N.Y., 1985.

Faith Clark, Ph.D., and Cecil Clark, Ph.D., *Hassle-Free Homework,* published by Doubleday, a division of Bantam Doubleday Dell Publishing Group, Inc., New York, N.Y., 1989.

Dawna Markova, Ph.D., with Anne R. Powell, *How Your Child Is Smart,* published by Conari Press, Berkeley, Calif., 1992.

Chapter Seven

1. Dr. Mark P. Cosgrove, *The Amazing Body Human, God's Design for Personhood* (Grand Rapids, Mich.: Baker Book House, 1987), 20.

2. Ibid., 16.

3. Ibid., 17.

4. Dr. Patrick Quillin, *Healing Secrets from the Bible* (Tulsa, Okla.: Nutrition Times Press, Inc., 1996), 85.

5. Clara Hannaford, *Smart Moves, Why Learning Is Not All in Your Head* (Arlington, Va.: Great Ocean Publishers, 1995), 146.

6. Carol Hart, *Secrets of Serotonin* (New York: Lynn Sonberg Book Association, 1996), 221.

7. Dr. Jay Lombard and Carl Germano, *The Brain Wellness Plan* (New York: Kensington, 1997), 111–12.

8. Norman Cousins, *Anatomy of an Illness* (Norton, N.Y.: 1979).

9. Dr. Patrick Quillin, *Healing Secrets from the Bible* (Tulsa, Okla.: Nutrition Times Press, Inc., 1996).

10. Quillin, *Healing Secrets,* 36–47.

Chapter Eight

1. George Grant, *The Patriot's Handbook* (Elkton, Md.: Highland Books, 1996), 89. Used by permission.

2. William J. Federer, *America's God and Country* (Dallas, Tex.: FAME Publishing, 1996), 205. Used by permission.

3. Francis A. Schaeffer, *A Christian Manifesto* (Westchester, Ill. Crossway Books, 1981), 33.

Chapter Nine

1. Quoted directly from the sermon text, "David Livingstone, Texts That Have Changed Lives: (Secret of Commitment)." Used by permission.

2. Chuck Colson and Jack Eckerd, *Why America Doesn't Work* (Dallas, Tex.: Word, 1991), xi–xii. Used by permission.

3. Jack Lannom, *The Dynamics of Remembering Names and Faces* (Miami, Fla.: Grace Games Publishers, 1984), 4.

4. Viktor E. Frankl, *Man's Search for Meaning* (New York: Washington Square Press, 1984), 55–56.

5. Clarence B. Carson, *Basic American Government* (Wadley, Ala.: American Textbook Committee, 1993), 18.

Chapter Ten

1. John Robbins, *Reclaiming Our Health* (Tiburon, Calif.: H. J. Kramer Publishers, 1996), 279.

2. Tan, *7,700 Quotations,* 1095, quote 4797.

3. As published in *The Wall Street Journal* by United Technologies Corporation, Hartford, Conn., 1981.

4. Barry J. Farber, *Diamond in the Rough* (New York: Berkley Publishing Group, 1995), 53.

5. As published in *The Wall Street Journal* by United Technologies Corporation, Hartford, CT, 1981.

6. Tan, *Encyclopedia of 7,700 Illustrations: Signs of the Times,* 997, quote 4331.

7. Dave Dean, *Now Is Your Time to Win* (Wheaton, Ill.: Tyndale House, 1983), 40–41.

8. As published in *The Wall Street Journal* by United Technologies Corporation, Hartford, Conn., 1981.

9. Tan, *7,700 Quotations,* 1436, quote 6465.

10. Ibid., 1374, quote 6146.

11. Ibid., 1435, quote 6464.

12. Karen Pryor, *Don't Shoot the Dog: The New Art of Teaching and Training* (New York: Bantam Books, 1984), 16.

13. Viktor E. Frankl, *Man's Search for Meaning* (New York: Washington Square Press, New York, 1984), 41.

Chapter Eleven

1. Frank Minirth, M.D. and Paul Meier, M.D., *Happiness Is a Choice* (Grand Rapids, Mich.: Baker Books, 1994), 14.

2. Jack Lannom, *Transformational Coaching* (Miami, Fla.: Grace Games Publishing, 1996), 17.

3. Dr. James Dobson, *The New Dare to Discipline* (Wheaton, Ill.: Tyndale House Publishers, 1992), 59.

Chapter Twelve

1. David Bohm, *Unfolding Meaning: A Weekend of Dialogue with David Bohm* (London: Ark Paperbacks, 1987), 97.

2. Dr. Ron Jenson, *Make a Life, Not Just a Living* (Nashville, Tenn.: Thomas Nelson, 1995), 68.

3. Peter W. Stoner, *Science Speaks* (Chicago: Moody Press, 1963), cited by Josh McDowell, *Evidence That Demands a Verdict* (San Bernardino, Calif.: Here's Life Publishers, 1972), 167.

Conclusion

1. This figure was cited by Dr. D. James Kennedy during the broadcast of the nationally syndicated television show, 2 November 1997 *The Coral Ridge Hour.* The statistic was provided by The Voice of the Martyrs.

About the Author

JACK LANNOM is one of the most dynamic and inspirational leaders in America. He has been speaking and consulting for over twenty-seven years. Lannom's PBS television program, *Lannom's Memory Methods,* has been shown consistently since 1987, the first and longest running series of its kind, inspiring millions of people. You can reach Jack on the internet. www.JACKLANNOM.com